Glamour, Gidgets, and the Girl Next Door

ALSO BY HERBIE J PILATO

Glamour, Gidgets, and the Girl Next Door

Television's Iconic Women from the 50s, 60s, and 70s

HERBIE J PILATO

TAYLOR TRADE PUBLISHING
Lanham • New York • Boulder • Toronto • Plymouth, UK

Published by Taylor Trade Publishing
An imprint of Rowman & Littlefield
4501 Forbes Boulevard, Suite 200, Lanham, Maryland 20706
www.rowman.com

10 Thornbury Road, Plymouth PL6 7PP, United Kingdom

Distributed by NATIONAL BOOK NETWORK

British Library Cataloguing in Publication Information Available

Library of Congress Cataloging-in-Publication Data

Pilato, Herbie J.
  Glamour, Gidgets, and the girl next door : television's iconic women from the 50s, 60s,
and 70s / Herbie J Pilato.
      pages cm
  Includes bibliographical references.
  ISBN 978-1-58979-969-1 (cloth : alk. paper) — ISBN 978-1-58979-970-7 (electronic)
1. Television series—United States—Interviews. 2. Television actors and actresses—
United States—Interviews. I. Title.
  PN1992.8.S4P55 2014
  791.4502'8092273—dc23
                                                          2014011288

∞™ The paper used in this publication meets the minimum requirements of American
National Standard for Information Sciences—Permanence of Paper for Printed Library
Materials, ANSI/NISO Z39.48-1992.

Printed in the United States of America

Dedicated to the silent *inner* beauty named Peace

True beauty or true glamour . . . it is that essence that shines from an inner light—a spirit so seductive that people turn to bathe in its warmth. The glamour comes not from artificial dangles but from a sparkling within that shines forth from where a beautiful soul lives.

—Kathy Garver, Cissy, on *Family Affair*

Beauty and glamour are from within a person, not an evening gown, jewels or fur coat, but how one see's situations, reacts to others, being positive, a happy outlook, giving of one's self!

—Donna Douglas, Elly May, on *The Beverly Hillbillies*

What people think is beautiful changes though the ages.

—Barbara Bain, Cinnamon Carter, on *Mission: Impossible*

Contents

CONTENTS

Introduction

Glamour, Gidgets, and the Girl Next Door: Television's Iconic Women from the 50s, 60s, and 70s explores the feminine mystique of three decades of popular female stars of the small screen.

The terms "glamour" and "girl next door" speak for themselves, while the word "Gidgets" is the plural form reference to the *Gidget* franchise that has graced the big and small screens over the last five decades. The property originated with Frederick Kohner's 1957 novel about the adventures of a teen named Francine Elizabeth Lawrence and her surfing friends on Malibu Beach. Francine (a.k.a. "Francie"), a young female, otherwise known as a "girl," is small in stature, thus referencing the once-thought-affectionate (albeit now politically incorrect) term "midget." Subsequently, she was affectionately known to her family and friends as the mixed moniker of "Gidget."

The character became a cultural icon in the late 1950s and 60s due to three feature films starring Sandra Dee and the television series introducing future Oscar-winner Sally Field. Karen Valentine also portrayed the role in the TV-movie *Gidget Grows Up*, which aired in 1969, the same year she began playing novice teacher Alice Johnson in TV's first dramedy, *Room 222*. Monie Ellis took over the Gidget guise in a second TV-movie, 1972's *Gidget Gets Married*; and the character's last formal onscreen appearance was in the 1980s syndicated sitcom *The New Gidget* (featuring Caryn Richman, who bears a striking resemblance to Field), which began in 1985 with a TV-movie titled *Gidget's Summer Reunion*. Other than that, Francine Gidget Francie Lawrence appeared and/or was addressed in the 1980 short film *Gidget Meets Hondo* and in the 2010 feature documentary *Accidental Icon: The Real Gidget Story*.

Those profiled in the following pages have each made their unique and mainstream mark on television because their trademark characters were similar to and went beyond Gidget. In addition to Field and Valentine, other darling doll-faced actresses who presented at the very least Gidget-types include Gale Storm, who was a sitcom staple with shows like *My Little Margie* and *Oh, Susanna* (a.k.a. *The Gale Storm Show*), and Patty Duke, who delivered a daffy, daring, and darling double performance as the free-spirited tomboy Patty Lane—and her refined foreign twin-cousin Cathy—on *The Patty Duke Show*.

Also acknowledged is the pristine, discerning performance of Elinor Donahue as Betty "Princess" Anderson, the ideal, 1950s sweet-but-direct daughter from TV's classic *Father Knows Best*; the good and bad girl "duel" dichotomy displayed by Dawn Wells as downhome farm girl Mary Ann Summers and Tina Louise as glittery movie star Ginger Grant, both surreally marooned in the 1960s on *Gilligan's Island*; the delightful Donna Douglas, who with both gusto and grace played the hot and hollering Elly May Clampett, the diamond in the nouveau-riche rough on *The Beverly Hillbillies*; the barrier-and-race-breaking Emmy-nominated performance of the distinguished Diahann Carroll on *Julia*, the first African American–led sitcom in TV history; the smart, sassy, and sly delivery designed by Barbara Eden and her TV magic carpet ride via *I Dream of Jeannie*; the svelte, slinky, and very feminine swagger of Julie Newmar as the vixen Catwoman on the original *Batman* series; the dynamic duo of Lindsay Wagner as *The Bionic Woman* and Lynda Carter as *Wonder Woman*; the charismatic troika of Farrah Fawcett, Kate Jackson, and Jaclyn Smith, each of whom returned sophistication and style to television as *Charlie's Angels*; the Happy Hotpoint legs of Mary Tyler Moore, who in the 1950s danced in TV commercials and darted her hands around *Richard Diamond, Private Eye*, mere peeks into the poise she'd bring to the 1960s with her unshrinking-violet performance as Laura Petrie— the ideal Capri-pant-donning home engineer on *The Dick Van Dyke Show*—and into the 1970s with *The Mary Tyler Moore Show*, on which she played the revolutionary Mary Richards—the single working girl with a mind of her own.

Other legendary romantic TV female leads are chronicled in this book, each of whom are known for specific characters they portrayed; particular physical or personality traits; their beauty or intelligence; elegance or clowning; wit or wisdom; as groundbreaking lovers, sisters, cousins, coworkers, or friends. They are television's most memorable and formidable females of a particular age-group, style, heritage, and culture; actresses, singers, dancers, performers of every ilk; each shaped, formed, polled, and pulled from TV's earliest generations and most specific genres. The list is eclectic to say the least.

With each profile, and collectively, every effort was made to chronicle the appropriate female TV icon selection with dignity and respect. The criteria for each was and remains as follows: (1) She had to be or at least become a young woman while filming or taping her particular series; she could be a mom, but not a traditional mother and never an aunt figure or curmudgeonly older neighbor type. (2) She had to appear in a lead television role from any program of any genre specifically from the 1950s, 60s or 70s. (3) She had to make her mark as a relatively romantic figure or a mature but not matronly woman, with a vibrant personality and/or a portrayal of a particularly beloved character.

A few of the female television legends profiled are no longer living, but of those who are, a select group granted exclusive interviews for this book, including the aforementioned Elinor Donahue, Donna Douglas, as well as Adrienne Barbeau (*Maude*), Kathy Garver (*Family Affair*), Barbara Hale (*Perry Mason*), Mary McDonough (*The Waltons*), and Nichelle Nichols (*Star Trek*), among others.

Certain commentary from those like Diahann Carroll, as well as Barbara Eden, Julie Newmar, and Lindsay Wagner, was provided by David Laurell, editor in chief of *Life After 50 Magazine*, which profiled each of these actresses in recent years.

Additional exposition with regard to Melissa Gilbert (*Little House on the Prairie*), Valerie Harper (*The Mary Tyler Moore Show*, *Rhoda*), Kristy McNichol (*Family*), and others was culled from various insightful books that were written in and about the 70s by entertainment journalist Peggy Herz.

Information about those female icons who have passed away, or who were otherwise unavailable for an interview, was gathered from previous interviews, articles, or profiles that appeared in various other books, publications, online resources, magazines, newspapers, websites, or TV talk shows, specials, documentaries, or DVD extras.

Supplementary and key commentary that appears in this book was provided by those who knew or performed with particular female icons profiled, including Peter Ackerman (son of Elinor Donahue and famed TV executive and producer Harry Ackerman), actors Billy Gray (*Father Knows Best*), Tony Dow (*Leave It To Beaver*), and Mary Owen (daughter of Donna Reed and producer Tony Owen), the latter two offering specific commentary on Shelley Fabares (the former teenage female lead on *The Donna Reed Show*).

Into this mix, exclusive commentary was provided about several female leads by legendary writers of classic television, such as Sam Bobrick, Larry Brody, Ron Clark, Fred Freeman, Arnie Kogen, Bill Persky, and more.

INTRODUCTION

Core and supportive observations and insight are provided by an A-list of classic TV and film historians and authors, including Rob Ray and Steve Randisi, as well as writer/producers Dan Holm and Dan Weaver. Particularly insightful perceptions are delivered by the distinguished, respected, and veteran entertainment journalist, writer/producer, and TV host Margaret Wendt, who knew or worked with a good portion of the female icons profiled.

The chapters are divided into six sections, grouping the actresses into the categories with which their characters or personas are most associated.

The first section, "The Jills of All Trades," stands out from the rest as it profiles female stars who, although known specifically as television icons, also found fame and success via other entertainment venues; were gifted with multiple talents; became equally known for their charitable gifts and organizations; or became associated with more than one specific TV character (including and beyond the core 50s, 60s, and 70s decades). By the same token, certain actresses who were known for more than one TV show are presented in other sections.

Coordinated chapters for each actress are chronologically placed within every section matching the year or era during which the given performer was introduced to the audience. The chapter listings and numbers should not be perceived as "rankings" of any sort, as this book does not seek to signify or ignite a popularity contest of any kind. Some chapters focus more on the lives of those profiled, while other sections concentrate on careers. Some chapters are lengthier than others; some are shorter, depending on the general or specific impact of the given actress, available data, or the overall available space for the book. Each chapter closes with core abbreviated data, facts, and figures for each actress, with regard to birthday, personal life, career highlights, and so on. With certain chapters, some of this information is already stated in the narrative portion of the profile but was worth repeating in summary form to more fully and fittingly transmit conclusive thoughts.

Due to editorial demands and restrictions, allotted space, or general inaccessibility to certain female stars, living or deceased, not every young distinguished actress who was ever featured in a hit TV series or as a leading presence in some capacity is profiled within these pages. Since this book focuses on prime-time television programming, those also not explored in depth include daytime female superstars and news anchors and journalists. Other legendary TV women are not completely chronicled in this book because they found fame beyond TV's prime time.

The book does include a special appendix called "The Other Girls with Something Extra" (a title that references *Gidget* star Sally Field's third TV series) that simply lists as honorable mentions those not fully profiled.

In total, *Glamour, Gidgets, and the Girl Next Door* chronicles an equally elevated gathering of remarkable women who made a particularly unique and enchanting impression by way of television. It presents and prods, chronicles and charts, profiles and proves, in words and pictures, the elegant, fascinating, and captivating qualities that made some of TV's most iconic women stand out, tick, twitch, blink, think, holler, mug, pose, love, protect, defend, befriend, dance, sing, and so very much more. While it earnestly presents figures of a particular female type from a certain triangular era (the 50s, 60s, and 70s), and focuses on their specific appeal (however that may be defined), it's important to remember that beauty, as defined by both Shakespeare and Rod Serling (in an episode of *The Twilight Zone* starring Donna Douglas), is in the "Eye of the Beholder."

Enjoy!

PART I

THE JILLS OF ALL TRADES

Sally Field

(Gidget / The Flying Nun)

> I have never been beautiful in cliché terms.
>
> —Sally Field

It was Sally Field's spot-on interpretation of and effervescent performance as California surfer-girl Gidget that brought home the role in the classic 1960s sitcom of the same name. The actress auditioned for the part while attending Birmingham High School in Van Nuys, California. She was only 15 years old when the show first aired (on ABC, 1965–1966), and even at this early stage in Field's career, her broad range, natural talent, and sheer energy simply jumped off the screen. As she told Peggy Herz in 1973, "I had never done anything professionally before. . . . It seems so long ago. I was out of high school, but it seems like I was about 12 years old."

"I had to learn to surf for *Gidget*," she went on to say. "I don't surf anymore, though" [because it wasn't her type of sport]. "I'm really not adventurous. Surfing is . . . dangerous . . . and I'm afraid of dangerous things." Apparently, she was very apprehensive about filming the surfing scenes for *Gidget*, which she had to learn to do in just three months. "It was very frightening and [the water was] very cold," she

said. "It was in the middle of winter [when the series was filmed]. It was rainy and there were difficult waves. They chose a beach that was easy to film, but difficult to surf."

Gidget also starred Don Porter (*The Ann Sothern Show*) as Field's father and Peter Deuel (later of ABC's 1971–1973 comedy western *Alias Smith and Jones*, in which Sally was also featured) as her brother-in-law. Although low ratings forced its cancellation after its one and only season, the show became a hit in summer reruns. As such, ABC reconsidered its position and tried to regroup Sally with the series.

When that strategy failed, the network and executive producer Harry Ackerman (who later produced *The New Gidget*) cast her as Sister Bertrille in a subsequent ABC sitcom titled *The Flying Nun* (which was based on the novel *The Thirteenth Pelican* by Tere Rios). *Nun*, which ran for three seasons (and at one point interspersed *Gidget* footage in a flashback sequence to Sister Bertrille's alleged teen-surfing years), became a marginal hit for ABC and worked on several levels. Not only did it coincide with Ackerman's sturdy stable of family shows (which dated back to *Bachelor Father*), but it was in tune with the increasingly popular fantasy-type series that was filling the airwaves (including Ackerman's *Bewitched*).

After *The Flying Nun* was grounded, Field returned to the small screen (opposite John Davidson) in a *Bewitched*-like series called *The Girl with Something Extra*, which debuted on NBC in the fall of 1973. Instead of magic, Field's character possessed the power to read minds, a.k.a. ESP (extrasensory perception). But the show only lasted one season.

From there, Field gradually worked her way into more dramatic roles, for both the big screen and small, including her Emmy-nominated performance in *Sybil*, the 1976 TV miniseries based on the book by Flora Rheta Schreiber about a young woman with 13 different personalities. She also went on to star in a series of successful feature films she made with Burt Reynolds, with whom she became romantically involved. The two had met and fell in love on the set of the very successful *Smokey and the Bandit* motion picture, released in 1977, and they'd costar again in the 1980 *Smokey* sequel.

In 1979 Field delivered her career-changing big-screen performance in the critically acclaimed box-office hit *Norma Rae*, for which she received her first Oscar.

In subsequent years she delivered stirring performances in stellar motion pictures such as *Absence of Malice* (1981, with Paul Newman), *Places in the Heart* (1984, which garnered her second Oscar), *Murphy's Romance* (1985, with James Garner), *Steel Magnolias* (1989), and *The Amazing Spider-Man* (2011).

Additional performances for the big screen included her first, *The Way West* (1967, with Kirk Douglas), and groundbreaking TV-movies and miniseries like *Maybe I'll Come Home in the Spring* and *Marriage: Year One* (both airing on ABC in 1971); *A Woman of Independent Means* (1995) and *David Copperfield* (2000); a dozen episodes of *ER* (NBC, 2000–2006); and her Emmy-winning role as matriarch Nora Walker in *Brothers & Sisters* (ABC, 2006–2011), among others.

As Margaret Wendt observes:

Everyone loved Sally Field as Gidget. *Gidget* made you happy, and Sally was fabulous in the role. And then when you heard the backstory . . . that she had not received any formal theatrical training . . . and that she had parents who were in the business who lived in LA . . . that was pretty interesting. And then she did *The Flying Nun*. And I liked her in that, too, because she went from being in bikinis—or two-piece bathing suits, which is what we called bikinis in those days . . . to flying around as a nun. Well, I don't think many people can make that transition. But she did—and the audience believed her. And as Catholic school girls, my friends and I wanted her to do everything naughty to the nuns that she possibly could. We could hardly wait to see what she was going to do next.

What proved additionally intriguing is that representatives from the Catholic Church served as advisors on *The Flying Nun*, which was also the first regular network prime-time scripted series to feature Catholic or Christian images— if only in the form of statues of the Blessed Mother and Jesus—placed in the background. "That's really why we loved that show so much," Wendt emphasizes. "Sally as Sister Bertrille gave those of us attending Catholic schools something to identify with in very real ways. People, in general, always thought that Catholic school girls behaved themselves . . . or they said that when the nuns weren't looking the girls would grab the boys . . . that was not true . . . at least not while in school. Most of the jokes we played were geared toward the nuns, and so Sally Field was our hero," so much so that Wendt and her then-classmates periodically made the attempt at trying to pull off the same kind of shenanigans as Sister Bertrille. "Of course we knew it was a high-concept show," Wendt clarifies, "but we loved it. And actually, too, the nuns in our school loved it. They felt that they were at least . . . you know . . . being recognized."

Wendt also enjoyed watching Field in her more serious roles like *Norma Rae* or when she played mother to Julia Roberts in *Steel Magnolias* (1989). "She transitions very well into every role she plays," and that's not always easy:

When Sally was just starting out, television people didn't deal with movie people, and vice versa . . . and certainly no one from Broadway talked to TV or the movie industries. Now, everyone in feature films is working in television. But when a television actress wins an Oscar as Sally had done not once but twice . . . that was a big deal. And then she returned to television in

Brothers and Sisters [ABC, 2006–2011], and she was wonderful in it. She's always believable in anything she ever does. She wasn't like Suzanne Pleshette, who you wanted to copy her hair style . . . or like Loretta Young, who you wanted to buy her cosmetics. Sally Field was just someone that you wanted to watch . . . because she's so talented.

In an exclusive interview, Peter Ackerman, son of *Gidget/Flying Nun* executive producer Harry Ackerman, shares his memories and insights of Field:

One of my earliest memories is a huge evening party that was taking place at my parents' house and for whatever reason we boys were allowed to be present. There were Rams football players, an African explorer, actors, and actresses, and the like. I remember that night being lifted up by my dad so that I could say goodnight to Sally Field, who then was filming *The Flying Nun*. I was pretty quiet and shy and he held me and referring to Sally, he asked: "Peter, do you know who this is?" I nodded, and he asked "who?" and I replied "Sister Bertrille" (her character's name) which earned me a hearty laugh from all who were gathered around us, and I tried to nurture my ability to make people laugh since.

I have heard good things about Ms. Field commenting positively about my dad in some documentary/interviews, but I do not think he was ever alive to hear those, which is a shame. After she had been discovered (I believe she was a college cheerleader), tested and cast as Gidget, everyone was ready to go on the first day of filming, and Sally was understandably petrified. She came to my dad in tears and said she could not do this, and explained how frightened she was. Dad told her that the rough part was already over, that she *is* Gidget and all she had to do to play the part was get in front of the camera and recite her lines. He and the others had total faith in her; otherwise she would not be there. That gave her the support she needed to get out and do the part.

Some years later when *The Flying Nun* was being developed and cast, my dad could only settle on one actress who could carry off what the part of the flying sister needed . . . Sally . . . while my mother, Elinor Donahue, played Sally's sister in a few episodes of the show!

TV writing legend Larry Brody offers this conclusion on Sally Field's landmark contribution to entertainment industry by way of *Gidget*:

As a kid watching her on TV I thought Sally Field was the perfect woman. She was my age and her TV personality was what I thought every woman should be . . . bright, eager, idealistic, pretty—sexy in a sweet kind of way—able to stand up and fight for herself and what she believed in.

ICONIC FACTS

Birth Data: Born Sally Margaret Field on November 6, 1946, in Pasadena, California.

Education: Attended Birmingham High School in Van Nuys, California.

Family: Parents, Margaret Field and salesman Richard Dryden Field. While her parents also gave birth to Sally's brother Richard, their marriage unfortunately ended in divorce in 1950. Shortly thereafter, her mother wed stuntman Jock Mahoney, a union that produced yet another sibling for Sally, this time a sister named Princess O'Mahoney. Meanwhile, Sally later married Steve Craig (1968–1975), and they had two sons (Peter Craig and Eli Craig), and Alan Greisman (1984–1993), with whom she had one son (Sam Greisman).

Most Memorable TV Roles: Frances Gidget Lawrence on *Gidget* (ABC, 1965–1966) and Sister Bertrille on *The Flying Nun* (ABC, 1967–1970).

Benchmarks: Won an Emmy Award for playing the lead in the 1976 TV miniseries *Sybil*, based on the novel of the same name about an abused girl who develops multiple personalities; continued on to have a distinguished career in feature films, garnering several awards and nominations, namely, three Oscar nominations and winning two (*Norma Rae*, 1979; and *Places in the Heart*, 1984); played Nurse Abby Lockhart's bipolar mother, Maggie Wyczenski, in NBC's *ER*; Tom Hanks's mother in *Forrest Gump* (1994); Nora Walker in the TV series *Brothers and Sisters* (ABC, 2006–2011); Mary Todd Lincoln in *Lincoln* (2012) and Aunt May in the *Amazing Spider-Man* films (2012–2014); and was awarded a 2012 Human Rights Campaign Ally for Equality award for her advocacy for gay rights issues. The award was presented by her youngest son, Sam Greisman, who is openly gay.

Prime Quotes: "My country is still so repressed. Our idea of what is sexual is blonde hair, long legs, 22 years old. It has nothing to do with humor, intelligence, warmth, everything to do with teeth and cleavage." * "There are not a lot of places for an actor to explore what it's like to be a woman in her 60s. There aren't any films about it and there are very few TV series about it." * "If the mothers ruled the world, there would be no . . . wars in the first place." * "I couldn't give up acting. Every aspect of the work is so rewarding." * Best catchphrase from Field's *Gidget*? "Toodles!"

A Living Legend.

Marlo Thomas
(That Girl)

> I realize now that I was a feminist, and the minute I heard the word I
> certainly knew it meant me, but at that time I don't think we had the
> label yet. But there's no doubt about it that I was born a feminist.
>
> —Marlo Thomas

"THAT Girl!"

Such is the key phrase that was voiced by the one-shot guest character at
the opening of every episode of the same-named ABC sitcom that featured then-
aspiring actress Marlo Thomas (daughter of TV legend Danny Thomas) as aspiring
actress Ann Marie.

Airing on ABC from 1966 to 1970, *That Girl* showcased the mega-
melodramatic life of Marlo's Marie on and off the stage. Ann had left the old-
school security of hometown Brewster, New York, where she was born and reared
by her moderately conservative upstate parents Lou and Helen Marie (Lew Parker
and Rosemary DeCamp). While Mom remained confident and carefree that their
daughter would make it on her own, "Daddy," as Ann would affectionately refer to

him, was more intensively protective of his little girl, making frequent trips to New York to check on her weekly adventures.

Lou also had his issues with Ann's boyfriend, "Donald!" . . . Hollinger, as played by the equally likable Ted Bessell. You couldn't help fall in love with both that girl and that boy, because he became as much a part of her as any of her color-coded outfits. So Lou needn't have worried. Hollinger, as he called him, was always there to save the day, or to at least protect Ann through the microcosm of the periodic mayhem that her theatrical life induced. Marlo's independent take on Ann allowed the character to shrug off her father's overprotective nature and convince both him and the audience that she could make it on her own, no matter how trying the situation.

For example, there was the time her foot got stuck in the bowling ball before she was to accept an important award for a friend ("This Little Piggy Had a Ball," 3-23-67); or the time she became involved with the Latin racial politics of a theatrical play ("That Senorita," 12-11-70, which featured Alejandro Rey, who performed with fellow female TV icon Sally Field in her second hit sitcom, *The Flying Nun*).

Through it all, Ann came out smelling like a rose . . . or better yet—a daisy, which was the favorite flower of both the character/actress and the real-life actress off the screen. Daisies were used as decoration throughout Ann Marie's apartment and sprinkled over a few pieces of wardrobe worn by Marlo. The clothes and the pad were top-notch, of course, as each was nicely fashioned and decorated, hardly the mark of a struggling young actress.

In October 1967, the beginning of *That Girl's* second season, entertainment journalist Florine McCaine profiled its star in *TV Radio Magazine*: "Marlo Thomas is a star—and she looks it. Everything about her spells glamour, from her dark mane of hair, to the round brown eyes framed by thick black lashes, to the slim lithe figure. You can guess that stardom came easily to this bright, bubbly young woman who has everything going for her—talent, drive and beauty."

Marlo as Ann delivered one of the most likable television performances in history, becoming the girl every guy wanted to date and every girl wanted to be (or at least dress like). She presented an identifiable effervescence as Ann, coupled with her real-life headstrong sensibility that proved to be the driving force of *That Girl*. A hit from the second it aired, *That Girl* became TV's first presentation of an independent working woman of the modern era. While Gale Storm and Ann Sothern before and Mary Richards afterward pervaded the small screen with a confident air, it was Marlo's Ann who drove the women's liberation movement forward. Moore has gone on record as saying that Thomas on *That Girl* "opened the door that I walked through" on *The Mary Tyler Moore Show*.

TV viewers were attracted not only to the exquisite style presented by both Marlo and Ann, but also to their support for the underdog and their boundless enthusiasm. Or as McCaine sized it up in 1967, Thomas was a "very determined young lady, and once she makes up her mind what she wants, she usually gets it." Apparently, too, Marlo's coworkers may have agreed, as McCaine said the actress was referred to "in awed tones as the *velvet steamroller*."

According to Bill Persky, *That Girl* cocreator and writer, the show is "very special," and that's mostly due to Thomas. In describing Marlo's performance as Ann Marie, Persky says she "was aggressive with a certain innocence in her aggressiveness. . . . She was never [solely] aggressive . . . she was just like a kitten that wanted to get ahead and get at things. That was part of her charm . . . that she was just unstoppable. She was a ball of energy." In transferring the character to the actress, Persky adds, "And she's still like that today. She's an amazing person."

Fellow TV writing legend Treva Silverman wrote for several classic shows, including *That Girl*, during which time she befriended Thomas, with whom she remains friends today. As she sees it, Thomas is "so quick, so outgoing, so in love with life. Marlo's mind is brilliantly sharp and insightful, and it's almost redundant to talk about her natural humor. Women love her, too. She doesn't give off an all-inclusiveness. That's Marlo as Ann Marie . . . that's Marlo as Marlo. . . . She's one of the few people on Earth I can say I've learned from. She is wise. She is authentic. She tells it how it is—a role model on how to be honest without being hurtful."

Indeed. On her blog post for October 25, 2013, at the *Huffington Post*, Thomas wrote, "Nothing is more inspiring to me than a young girl who has found her strength and confidence, and has a healthy self-image."

She was referring to how proud she was of New York City for its launching of the new NYC Girls Project, a public awareness campaign designed to remind girls, ages 7 to 12, that self-esteem isn't built by slipping into a pair of designer jeans or cool shoes, but by celebrating who they are inside. "Not since we at the Ms. Foundation launched Take Our Daughters to Work in 1993 has there been such an exuberant celebration of what it is to be a girl," Thomas wrote.

She went on to explain how the $330,000 campaign is not just a "feel-good" experiment, but that it will help to confront a social infrastructure that is becoming significantly destructive for young girls. As Thomas continued to point out, according to the *American Journal of Maternal/Child Nursing*, more than 80 percent of 10-year-old girls have a declining self-image with regard to their weight, and that worsens by the time they reach 12 and up until they are approximately 20 years old—and beyond. Such negative self-worth, says Thomas, may result in several detrimental behaviors (i.e., substance abuse, eating disorders, bullying, sexual promiscuity, and more). She talked about the assault of overt fashion print ads and television shows that misrepresent young girls. However, she said, her campaign "beautifully answers the negative effects of the media by featuring real girls in the posters who are the daughters of city workers or friends of friends. And none are professional models."

Ann Marie would be proud.

ICONIC FACTS

Birth Data: Born Margaret Julia Thomas on November 21, 1937, in Detroit, Michigan. Her parents called her Margo as a child, but she became known as Marlo, she told the *New York Times*, because that's how she pronounced it.

Education: Marymount High School in Los Angeles; graduated from the University of Southern California with a teaching degree; attended the Actors Studio, where she studied with Lee Strasberg; studied drama at HB Studio in Greenwich Village in New York City.

Family: Parents, comedian Danny Thomas and Rose Marie Cassaniti; a sister, Terry; brother, Tony Thomas (TV and film producer). In 1980, she married talk show host Phil Donahue, with whom she has five stepchildren (from his previous marriage).

Most Memorable TV Role: Ann Marie on *That Girl* (ABC, 1966–1971), for which she created the concept about a young woman who leaves home, moves to New York City, and aspires to be an actress.

Benchmarks: Marlo was raised in Hollywood, surrounded by showbiz legends like Jack Benny and Milton Berle. One of her earliest roles was the live stage lead in "Gigi," performed at the renowned Pasadena Playhouse, where, upon viewing her performance, her famous father, who originally objected to Marlo's thespian aspirations, was charmed by her talent. "I won't bother you anymore," he said. "You belong in the theater." Later she appeared in a

London production of the Broadway hit "Barefoot in the Park," directed by Mike Nichols (today married to Diane Sawyer). Early TV roles before *That Girl* included *My Favorite Martian* and *Bonanza*. In 1970, she was cast in the feature film lead for *Jenny*. She made several groundbreaking TV-movies, including *Consenting Adult* (1985) and *Nobody's Child* (1986), for which she won an Emmy, among others. Her most famous small-screen film, however, remains 1977's *It Happened One Christmas*, a gender-changed remake of the 1946 holiday feature film classic *It's a Wonderful Life*. She remains the national outreach director for St. Jude Children's Research Hospital in Memphis, Tennessee, which was established by her father. She launched wowOwow (http://www.wowowow.com), where women can converse about topics such as family, relationships, children, careers, marriage, and reinvention after age 40. She released a Grammy-winning CD titled "Thanks and Giving," and is the author of six best-selling books: *Free To Be . . . You and Me, Free To Be a Family, The Right Words at the Right Time, The Right Words at the Right Time*, volume 2: *Your Turn, Thanks & Giving All Year Long, Growing Up Laughing*, and *It Ain't Over . . . Till It's Over: Reinventing Your Life—and Realizing Your Dreams—Anytime, at Any Age*. Thomas won an Emmy as producer for the groundbreaking 1974 TV special "Free To Be You and Me."

Prime Quotes: "My father said there were two kinds of people in the world: givers and takers. The takers may eat better, but the givers sleep better." * "A man has to be Joe McCarthy to be called ruthless. All a woman has to do is put you on hold." * "Never face facts; if you do you'll never get up in the morning." * "Fame lost its appeal for me when I went into a public restroom and an autograph seeker handed me a pen and paper under the stall door." * Regarding *The Golden Girls*, a show coproduced by her brother Tony Thomas: "[It] certainly proved that there was a large audience for a show about older women." * When she was 17 years old, father Danny Thomas told her: "I raised you to be a thoroughbred. When thoroughbreds run, they wear blinders to keep their eyes focused straight ahead with no distractions, no other horses. They hear the crowd, but they don't listen. They just run their own race. That's what you have to do. Don't listen to anyone comparing you to me or to anyone else. You just run your own race."

A Living Legend.

3

Diahann Carroll

(Julia)

> I like to think I opened doors for other women, although that wasn't
> my original intention. . . . All I ever wanted to do was sing. What
> happened was more.
>
> —Diahann Carroll

Diahann Carroll is a Tony award winning and Oscar and Emmy nominated actress/
singer. Carroll's appeal as an artist and a human being on so many levels combines
to form the complete package of a woman who was destined from day one to
bring, be, and do something special in the world. Each of her artistic gifts and
humanitarian traits became icing on the creative cake that was baked to delicious
profundity when she was first introduced as Carol Diahann Johnson on July 17,
1935, in the Bronx, New York, by way of subway conductor John Johnson and his
wife Mabel Faulk Johnson.

Some 33 years later she made her legendary television debut as nurse Julia
Baker on *Julia,* which, when on NBC from 1968 to 1971, became the first series to
feature a female African American lead. Editor in chief David Laurell interviewed

Carroll in 2011 for *Life After 50 Magazine*. When Laurell wondered if there were any similarities between herself and Julia Baker, Carroll replied:

> When people ask me how I came up with the characterization for Julia, I tell them that I simply watched my family. My mother was a nurse, and I have cousins who were doctors. The adjustment for me was finding out that there were an awful lot of people who didn't know about that part of the black community. In every community there is a ghetto, there is a middle class, and there is an upper class, so why would the black community be any different? Julia was very real and alive—all over the country—all over the world. I have had Chinese, Japanese, Hawaiian, Peruvians all tell me that they loved that show. They tell me they grew up on the show and that I reminded them of their mother or sister.

According to reports by WebPro News and UPI.com, Carroll was pleased to be joined on stage at the Emmys in 2013 by contemporary female TV star Kerry Washington, of ABC's hit *Scandal*. They were copresenting the award for Outstanding Supporting Actor in a Drama Series to *Boardwalk Empire*'s Bobby Cannavale. Both African American women have been associated with Emmy-nominated TV series. While next to Washington at the podium, Carroll said:

> It's been such a long time since I've been standing in this place, I don't know what to do. But the men are much more beautiful than when I was doing television. I don't know where you came from, but I'm very happy to see you. After all, my leading man [on *Julia*] was [the much older] Lloyd Nolan, and those of you who know what that means—don't repeat to anyone . . . I feel we're a little behind. We need to catch up. We're all very grateful to the Emmys because

they've been on our side. At the same time, we'd like it to be a little more with what's going on in the world.

That same year, she performed in the feature film *Peeples*, which marked her first big-screen appearance since portraying Elzora in 1997's *Eve's Bayou*.

Through it all, she has embraced and continues to enjoy her craft, while generously donating time, money, and support to various civic and humanitarian causes.

On May 13, 2013, Carroll appeared on the esteemed PBS talkfest *The Tavis Smiley Show*. As she told Smiley, "I am very happy to be busy." For her, acting is a "full-time job." "I love it," she said. With a varied career that has spanned decades before and after *Julia*, on television, in feature films, and on the stage, Carroll has always displayed her elegance, intelligence, multitalents, and generous spirit on several levels, defining her iconic status and allure in the process. She's nothing but grateful for selecting a vocation that has afforded her many luxuries, and, as she continued to tell Smiley, "I don't feel I have missed out on anything in life. . . . I can't say that I prefer one part of my life or another."

Decades earlier, for the January 1969 edition of *Movie Life Magazine*, Diahann spoke with Hollywood luminary reporter Army Archerd about her most famous character from *Julia*, who was allowed to date but never to marry. As show producer Hal Kantor had recalled to Archerd, the reasoning behind that strategy was simple: Diahann was the star and it was a challenge to find an actor of equal stature to play her husband—from an aesthetic as well as economic viewpoint.

Kantor called Carroll, "One of God's great creations—bright and sweet."

DIAHANN CARROLL (*JULIA*)

ICONIC FACTS

Birth Data: Born Carol Diahann Johnson on July 17, 1935, in the Bronx, New York.

Education: Attended Music & Art High School and New York University, where she majored in sociology.

Family: Parents, John and Mabel Johnson; married record producer Monte Kay (1956–1963), with whom she had one daughter—Suzanne Kay Bamford; boutique owner Fredde Glusman (1973); Robert DeLeon, managing editor of *Jet* magazine (1975 to 1977, until his death); actor/singer Vic Damone (1987 to 1996).

Most Memorable TV Role: The title role in *Julia* (NBC, 1968–1971), making her the first African American actress to star in a TV series in which she did not play a domestic worker. She won the Golden Globe Award for *Julia* in 1968, and was nominated for an Emmy Award in 1969, becoming the first African American to earn such an honor.

Benchmarks: Her first love was music and singing, both of which she started doing at age six—with her Harlem church choir. She later took voice and piano lessons, considered a career in opera (after receiving a Metropolitan Opera scholarship at New York's High School of Music and Art), and, as a teen, modeled for *Ebony Magazine* and Macy's in New York. At 16, she changed her name to Diahann Carroll, appeared on *Arthur Godfrey's Talent Scouts* radio show, won, and performed there for three weeks. In 1962, Carroll garnered her Tony for "No Strings," in which she played fashion model Barbara Woodruff—a role that was created especially for her (by Samuel A. Taylor and Richard Rogers)—and delivered a groundbreaking performance of a character who was defined by neither culture nor color (although she was the first African American woman to be so honored). In the 1960s she was engaged to

Sidney Poitier and dated British TV host and producer David Frost. In 1974, she received her Academy Award nomination for the lead in *Claudine*. From 1984 to 1987, she played Dominique Deveraux on ABC's *Dynasty*, making her, as she said, the "first black bitch" on TV. She had also portrayed Marion Gilbert on NBC's *A Different World*, a role for which she earned a third Emmy nomination. In 2006, she received another Emmy nod for portraying Jane Burke on ABC's *Grey's Anatomy*. In 2010, she filmed her stage show "The Lady. The Music, The Legend" for PBS-TV. In 2009, she began playing June on USA-TV's *White Collar* series. Some of her finest work has been in TV-movies, notably as the century-old Sadie Delany in *Having Our Say: The Delany Sisters' First 100 Years* (1999) and as Natalie Cole's mother in *Livin' for Love: The Natalie Cole Story* (2000). Other stellar performances include her live stage take on the silent screen diva Norma Desmond in the musical version of *Sunset Boulevard*, and her American tour performing Broadway standards in the concert show "Almost Like Being in Love: The Lerner and Loewe Songbook." Through it all, she is a breast cancer survivor and activist. She's also written two books: *Diahann: An Autobiography* (Little Brown & Co, 1986) and *The Legs Are the Last to Go: Aging, Acting, Marrying and Other Things I Learned the Hard Way* (Amistad Books, 2008).

Prime Quotes: "I like to think I opened doors for other women, although that wasn't my original intention." * "I learned quickly that almost any time a third world face became prominent on TV, we became responsible for the whole minority community." * "All I ever wanted to do was sing. What happened was more." * "I'm always getting involved in the wrong relationship. I do that very well." * "I considered Nat King Cole to be a friend and, in many ways, a mentor. He always had words of profound advice." * "You have to keep your sanity as well as know how to distance yourself from it while still holding onto the reins tightly. That is a very difficult thing to do, but I'm learning." * "In the beginning, I found myself dealing with a show business dictated by male white supremacists and chauvinists. As a black female, I had to learn how to tap dance around the situation. I had to . . . find a way to present my point of view without being pushy or aggressive. In the old days, the only women I saw in this business were in makeup, hairdressing, and wardrobe departments. Now I'm surrounded by women executives, writers, directors, producers, and even women stagehands."

A Living Legend.

4

Goldie Hawn
(Laugh-In)

Ditzy dumb blonde? I can be ditzy. I can be.

—Goldie Hawn

Everything about Goldie Hawn is the stuff of legends: her trademark blond locks, her iconic laugh and smile, her genius comedic talent, her business savvy. All of it began in the 60s on TV's *Rowan & Martin's Laugh-In*.

Starring comedy team Dan Rowan and Dick Martin, and produced by George Schlatter, *Laugh-In* originally aired on NBC from 1968 to 1973 (though it was briefly reprised in 1979—with an all-new cast). According to actress, writer, and television historian Tamara Ann Fowler, it was Goldie Hawn's giggle that got her the original *Laugh-In* gig, for which she ultimately won an Emmy Award. "She couldn't stop laughing during her audition," Fowler says, "which the producers found endearing, so they cast her."

The season before *Laugh-In* premiered, Goldie (named after her mother's aunt) made her television debut on a sitcom titled *Good Morning, World*, which aired on CBS and was produced by Carl Reiner and Sheldon Leonard (the year after their

Dick Van Dyke Show ended its successful five-year run). *World* featured Joby Baker and Ronnie Shell as an early-morning radio disc jockey team called Lewis and Clarke. Schell's Larry Clarke was single; Baker's Dave Lewis was newlywed to Linda, played by Julie Parrish. At home, the Lewises lived next door to the flighty-but-lovable single-female-neighbor Sandy Kramer, portrayed by Hawn.

Legendary writer Sam Bobrick wrote an episode of *World* called "The Wedding Present," which featured Hawn's Kramer character: "Everyone knew she was going to be a big star. Then she went on to do *Laugh-In* and became just that. She had that something special . . . that spark. The camera either falls in love with you or it doesn't. And it fell in love with Goldie Hawn—as did the audience."

With a remarkable energy that commenced on the small screen and graduated to the big screen, Hawn expanded her reach with a line of feature films that began with *The One and Only Genuine Original Family Band*, released in 1968—and in which she was billed and known as none other than the "Giggly Dancer Girl." In 1969, she costarred with Walter Matthau in the critical and box-office hit *Cactus Flower*, for which she garnered an Academy Award, and which became a game changer for her.

Other notable feature films followed, such as Steven Spielberg's *The Sugarland Express* (1974), *Shampoo* (1975), *Foul Play* (1978, with Chevy Chase), and *Private Benjamin* (1980), which became a significant benchmark for the multifaceted artist. On *Benjamin* she served as a coproducer and became one of the most successful, independent feature female producers of all time.

A *Benjamin* TV series spin-off later aired on CBS, casting Lorna Patterson in the role first played by Hawn, who served as one of the project's producers there.

Hawn kept working in motion pictures like *Overboard* (1987, costarring her real-life love, Kurt Russell), *The First Wives Club* (1996), *The Banger Sisters* (2002), and more. Ever a charitable force in Hollywood, in October 2013 she lent her star power, along with supermodel Linda Evangelista and designer Kenneth Cole, for AIDS research and prevention at a $2,500-per-plate black-tie gala organized in Rio de Janeiro by the international nonprofit organization amfAR.

According to the Associated Press and the Canadian Press, Hawn praised Rio, naming its residents "so kind and wonderful," and encouraged those who attended to donate generously. "It's great to help, and it's great to have fun."

While "fun" certainly seems to be the operative word when it comes to pinpointing Hawn's allure, actor Ronnie Schell and her *Good Morning, World* costar shared his thoughts about working with the actress for a 2005 documentary produced by S'More Entertainment for the show's DVD release. Schell believed from the beginning that Hawn was going to reach stardom and beyond, based on her physical appeal, astounding talent, and bright personality. Yet he opted not to pursue her romantically. "You know, people often ask me if I ever had romantic leanings toward Goldie, and I was trying to think back because one of the reasons I got into this business was to make a little money and meet pretty ladies, which I'm proud to say that I met a lot of beautiful ones, the best, of course, being my wife. But, uh, that is one of the reasons I didn't— can we say politely?—hit on Goldie?"

When he first met Hawn and began working on *World* he had just fallen in love with his future wife, to whom he is still wed (Janet Rodeberg). Hawn wasn't interested in Schell because she was dating a man she later married (all prior to her relationship with Kurt Russell).

Schell remembers his *World* rehearsals with Hawn in his apartment in Toluca Lake, California. He preferred to rehearse as much as possible, whereas Hawn preferred not to overdo it, for fear that doing so would detract from their actual filmed performance onscreen. Schell joked that she should have listened to him, despite the fact that, two years later, she won an Oscar for her performance in *Cactus Flower*, which he found out about while he was "working *a toilet* [a less then elegant live theater] in Omaha."

ICONIC FACTS

Birth Data: Born Goldie Jeanne Hawn on November 21, 1945, in Washington, D.C.

Education: Attended Montgomery Blair High School in Silver Spring, Maryland, and American University in Washington, D.C., where she majored in drama. She was awarded an honorary degree from Loyola Marymount University after delivering the 2004 commencement address.

Family: Parents, Edward Rutledge and Laura Hawn; married Gus Trikonis (1969–1976); Bill Hudson (1976–1980), with whom she had two children: Oliver Hudson and Kate Hudson (both actors). Since 1983, her partner has been Kurt Russell, with whom she has one son: Wyatt Russell.

Most Memorable TV Role: As a regular on *Rowan & Martin's Laugh-In* (NBC, 1968–1973).

Benchmarks: At age 3, she began ballet and tap dance lessons. At age 10, she danced in the chorus of the Ballet Russe de Monte Carlo production of "The Nutcracker." At 19, she ran and instructed at a ballet school, having dropped out of college. She made her professional stage debut in 1961, playing Juliet in a Virginia Shakespeare Festival production of "Romeo and Juliet." She also ran and taught in a ballet school in New York City, later becoming a go-go dancer. At the age of 39, she posed for the cover of *Playboy*'s January 1985 issue. In 2002, she founded the Hawn Foundation, which provides educational programs for young people; she also supports other charitable causes, including the fight against cancer. Through her father, she is a direct descendant of Edward Rutledge, the youngest signatory of the Declaration of Independence.

Prime Quotes: "The only thing that will make you happy is being happy with who you are, and not who people think you are." * "We have to embrace obstacles to reach the next stage of joy." * "So curiosity, I think, is a really important aspect of staying young or youthful." * "All I ever wanted to be was happy." * "I'm a woman who was raised to believe that you are not complete unless you have a man. Well, in some ways it's true. I am a feminist to a point. But I'm not going to deny the fact that I love to be with men."

A Living Legend.

5

Mary Tyler Moore

(The Dick Van Dyke Show / The Mary Tyler Moore Show)

> I'm not an actress who can create a character. I play me.
>
> —Mary Tyler Moore

From before playing Laura Petrie in the 60s to after portraying Mary Richards in the 70s, and more in between, Mary Tyler Moore has been turning the world on with her smile.

As the sexy home engineer on *The Dick Van Dyke Show* (CBS, 1961–1966), the single-minded Richards on *The Mary Tyler Moore Show* (CBS, 1970–1971), or any of the countless characters she has portrayed on stage, film, or television, Moore has brought to each role an appeal that combined her A-type personality with her A-list talent. In front or behind the cameras, with creative differences at work or personal struggles at home, she has never backed away from a challenge. Conflicts surfaced and she always dealt with them head-on. Whether confronting diabetes, alcoholism, the accidental death of her only child, her admitted obsession with plastic surgery, or her recent brain surgery—nothing was considered an obstacle but only par for the course of life. For Moore it's never been about the destination, but the journey, a path on which she's remained steady.

The Dick Van Dyke Show and *The Mary Tyler Moore Show* remain more popular than ever. They air frequently on networks like TV Land, the Hallmark Channel, Antenna TV, and ME-TV. With Moore at their core, the appeal for both programs is timeless and is further solidified by consistently strong DVD sales.

Donna Reed never wore Capri pants on the family sitcom that bore her name. Barbara Billingsley's June Cleaver vacuumed in pearls on *Leave It To Beaver*. And Elizabeth Montgomery bewitched us all as Samantha Stephens with her magical wriggling nose. But Moore's Mrs. Petrie was the closest thing 1960s television had to a realistic wife. As author Ronald L. Smith deciphered in his excellent book *Sweethearts of '60s TV* (S.P.I. Books, 1993), "Despite the constraints of situation comedy reality, Laura was legitimate: sitcom silly but emotional, sitcom conservative but impish. She was a happy housewife and mom but she could purr, *I'm a woman*, as she sauntered into the bedroom (which she did in the show's pilot episode)." As Smith concluded, Moore's Laura left little doubt that she and Van Dyke's Rob were having fun in the sack, even if they had to push those long-distance twin beds together to make it happen for five hit seasons.

A few years after the *Van Dyke Show* ended, CBS reunited the sitcom's double leads for the 1969 TV special *Dick Van Dyke and the Other Woman*. Viewers loved it, and were left with wanting Moore, along with a little additional Van Dyke. The audience cried to have their favorite fictional couple back on television where they belonged. Within two years, the viewers' demands were met. The *Other Woman* special gave birth to separate shows for Van Dyke and Moore. *The New Dick Van Dyke Show* debuted on CBS in fall of 1971, one year after *The Mary Tyler Moore Show* arrived, and both were instant contemporary hits for their classic TV leads.

Continuing where Marlo Thomas's *That Girl* left off, the *Moore Show* (technically titled *Mary Tyler Moore*) was about a single career woman in the guise of the gullible and lovable Mary Richards, who became Moore's second most popular sitcom persona. Valerie Harper, Moore's costar from that series, told Peggy Herz in 1975, "Mary's incredible in comedy. She's a comedienne, but she's not a clown. She's chic—and she fills a real need on TV."

According to scribe Arnie Kogen, who wrote for Moore's show, "Mary Tyler Moore was America's sweetheart; probably Canada's sweetheart and Bulgaria's sweetheart, too. The character of Mary Richards was loved worldwide. She was strong, independent, vulnerable and funny."

Kogen admits that Moore was "not quite as successful in her subsequent TV projects" after her groundbreaking sitcom ended.

> I was involved in one of them. I was head writer for the *Mary* [variety] show in 1978. It was . . . with a cast that included Dick Shawn, Swoosie Kurtz, Jim Hampton, Judy Kahan and two up and coming comedy actors: Michael Keaton and David Letterman. This was an edgier Mary. Some very funny sketches and material but this was an edgier Mary. She sang songs like "Dead Skunk in the Middle of the Road" and once introduced the Ed Asner Dancers, six chubby Lou Grant look-alikes in shirts and ties disco dancing around the stage. America (and Canada and Bulgaria) did not like this "new" Mary. They wanted Mary Richards. Mary Tyler Moore was not thrilled with the series either. Neither was CBS. The show was cancelled after three episodes.

Bill Persky, another TV writing legend, cocreated *That Girl* with Sam Denoff, and directed over 100 episodes of *Kate & Allie* (CBS, 1984–1989). He also wrote countless classic episodes of *The Dick Van Dyke Show* featuring Moore, including "Coast to Coast Big Mouth," in which Laura Petrie inadvertently reveals on national television that her husband's boss (Carl Reiner as Alan Brady) is bald. Persky discusses Moore's appeal in relation to her portrayal of Laura.

> The *Van Dyke Show* was the first show that presented a husband and wife as peers. She didn't work. But he was as worried about making her angry, as she was about making him angry. In all [television] shows previous to that, it was the wife who was always so concerned about what's he going to say. But [the *Van Dyke Show*] featured two people who were equals . . . who respected one another.
>
> And Mary [as Laura] just had a way of doing things. You were always on her side . . . you just always loved even the way she squirmed . . . even down to the way

she cried. But Mary really didn't cry . . . she tried *not* to cry . . . and that's how she cried. And the reason she did that is because, one day she said to Carl [Reiner, who was also the show's creator], "I don't know how to cry." And he said, "Well, then don't cry." And that's when she went on to develop that stuttering-about-to-cry style—which we used to call the sups-sups—[which] carried her through every comedic scene she did on the show. In no comedy moment has Mary ever full-out cried. As to the Laura character, she remained a contemporary American woman who was exploring new opportunities.

With regard to Moore's appeal as Mary Richards on *The Mary Tyler Moore Show*, Persky, with a little help from his spouse, explains how that rested with the TV icon's innate ability to connect with the audience:

Like my wife always said, if Mary [Richards] didn't have a date on Saturday night, it was okay that I didn't because she was so adorable and so attractive. So her character was living the experience of a lot of the women viewers. At the same time, viewers always loved Mary—the actress . . . she was just a delightful person and performer. She was sexy as hell, but she was vulnerable. She did ballsy things . . . but never in a ballsy way. She was always a lady at all times.

Treva Silverman, who was executive story editor and wrote 16 episodes of *The Mary Tyler Moore Show*, for one of which she won an Emmy, adds her perspective on Moore's appeal as one of America's favorite female TV characters:

When Mary was playing Mary Richards, [her] genuine niceness always shone through. You got an impression of *what you see is what you get*—a beautiful woman who's a combination of confidence and shyness. Enough confidence to leave a small Midwestern town and move to Minneapolis. That is gutsy. But on the other hand, an innate reluctance to reveal too much about herself . . . a polite façade. What was so gorgeously set up by [James L. Brooks and Allan Burns, the show's producers] was taking who Mary was in real life, and using it. Mary had been brought up Catholic, did the whole schooling thing with the nuns stuff, and had parents who were anything but *touchy-feely*. So, at that time, there was a built-in [sense of] holding back.

That has always been the case with Mary Tyler Moore, onscreen as a professional actress and offscreen as a caring and compassionate human being. She's retained a youthfully aggressive and courageous spirit, confronting head-on a myriad of challenges. An Emmy-winning actress who, despite several personal traumas and professional struggles (several TV comebacks failed), always fought the good fight, and prevailed. She continued smiling, through the tears, the not-so-easy moments, and the toughest times. Always in forward motion, she kept working and never stopped. To this day, she lives life to the fullest and remains tirelessly dedicated to her craft as well as to various social and political causes, particularly around the issues of animal rights and diabetes.

ICONIC FACTS

Birth Data: Born Mary Tyler Moore on December 29, 1936, in Flatbush, Brooklyn, New York.

Education: Attended Immaculate Heart High School in Los Feliz, California.

Family: Parents, Marjorie and George Tyler Moore. At 18, she married Richard Carleton Meeker (1955–1961), whom she once described as "the boy next store." Within six weeks of their nuptials, she was pregnant with Richie, Jr., who was born July 3, 1956 (and died October 15, 1980). In 1962, she wed CBS executive Grant Tinker, who was later chairman of NBC. In 1970, she and Tinker formed

MTM Enterprises; they divorced in 1981. In 1983, she married Dr. Robert Levine (at the Pierre Hotel in New York City), whom she met when he treated her mother on a weekend house call (following Moore's trip with her mother to the Vatican and a personal audience with Pope John Paul II).

Most Memorable TV Role: Laura Petrie, *The Dick Van Dyke Show* (CBS, 1961–1966), for which she received two Emmys; Mary Richards, *The Mary Tyler Moore Show* (CBS, 1970–1977), for which she received three Emmys.

Benchmarks: In 1955, Moore had her first break—as a dancing kitchen appliance named Happy Hotpoint, the Hotpoint Appliance elf, in TV commercials (broadcast during *The Adventures of Ozzie & Harriett*). She played "Sam," the sultry answering service girl, on *Richard Diamond, Private Detective*, during which her face was never shown, only her legs (usually dangling a pump on her toe). In 1961, she was cast as Laura on *The Dick Van Dyke Show*. In 1970, she began her long run as Mary Richards on *The Mary Tyler Moore Show*. Shortly thereafter she was diagnosed with Type 1 diabetes. In the late 70s, she attempted to revive the music-variety format two times, but failed. First with a show called *Mary* (1978), which was then retooled as *The Mary Tyler Moore Hour* (1979). Around this time, she made an acclaimed TV-movie for CBS titled *First You Cry*, which was the story of journalist Betty Rollins. Her 24-year-old son Richie ironically shared the same name of her TV son from the *Van Dyke* show. He accidently shot himself to death with a sawed-off shotgun in 1980—the same year she received an Oscar nomination for her chilling, career-changing performance in *Ordinary People* (directed by Robert Redford, her childhood crush), in which she played the emotionless Beth Jarrett, whose onscreen son Conrad (played by the Oscar-winning Timothy Hutton) attempted suicide. She returned to the small screen with several notable TV-movies, including the *Lincoln* miniseries (in which she played Mary Todd Lincoln). She then attempted three more series, all for CBS:

Mary (1986, a short-lived sitcom she ended because she was displeased with its creative direction), *Annie McGuire* (1988, a one-camera filmed half hour), and *New York News* (1995, a one-hour dramedy, for which she dyed her hair bright red). She then went on to make more TV-movies and various guest-star appearances on shows like *Ellen* and *That '70s Show*. In 2000, she reunited with Valerie Harper for *Mary & Rhoda*, a TV-movie pilot (which never sold). In 2003, she reunited with Dick Van Dyke on PBS for *The Gin Game*. The year before, a bronze statue capturing Richards's signature hat toss went on display at the Minneapolis intersection where the scene was originally filmed for *The Mary Tyler Moore Show*. She'd reunite with Van Dyke two more times: in 2005, for TV Land's *The Dick Van Dyke Show Revisited*, and in May 2011—on *The Rachael Ray Show*, shortly after which she underwent elective brain surgery to remove a benign meningioma. In 2013, she reunited with her *Mary Tyler Moore* female costars for an episode of TV Land's *Hot in Cleveland*. She is the International Chairman of JDRF (formerly the Juvenile Diabetes Research Foundation), and has authored two memoirs: *After All* (Putnam, 1995) and *Growing Up Again: Life, Loves and Oh, Yeah—Diabetes* (St. Martin's Griffin, 2010).

Prime Quotes: Explaining her famous hat toss, which takes place in the opening credit sequence of *The Mary Tyler Moore Show*: "It was a hat that my aunt had given me for Christmas, and I brought it with me because they said: 'Be sure and dress warm. It's going to be freezing in Minneapolis.' So—I forget which writer it was—but we were all outside, and he said: 'You know what would be good? If you take that hat, the beret, and throw it in the air.'" * "There is a dark side. I tend not to be as optimistic as Mary Richards. I have an anger in me that I carry from my childhood experiences—I expect a lot of myself and I'm not too kind to myself."

A Living Legend.

6

Cher
(The Sonny & Cher Comedy Hour)

I'm not a role model, nor have I ever tried to be a role model. The only thing about me as a role model is I've managed to stay here and be working and survive . . . for 40 (and counting) years.

—Cher

"Gypsies, Tramps and Thieves!" That's the song most identified with music and acting sensation Cher when she was partnered with her then-husband, producer, and co-vocalist Sonny Bono on their hit CBS TV show, *The Sonny & Cher Comedy Hour*. Following in the footsteps of actress/comedienne Carol Burnett, the Bonos became the stars of the "eye" network's second major hit variety series of the 60s and 70s. As a result, other musical-teams-turned-TV-stars hosted variety shows of their own, including *Tony Orlando & Dawn* and *The Captain & Tennille*. But neither of those programs came close to the pristine wit, slapstick, and sophistication that Cher created with Sonny. He was savvy enough to remain in the background, allowing Cher to shine and sparkle like no other with personality, musical talent, and spitfire comedic timing (mostly directed toward him in their

show's weekly opening segment). Of course, it didn't hurt that she also happened to be extremely sensual, attractive, and in top physical condition. Every week, her slim and trim form was decked out from head to toe in beaded, shiny, shape-forming gowns and garbs designed especially for her by Bob Mackie (who also dressed Carol Burnett).

Cher knew how to "work it." Unfortunately, she and Sonny couldn't seem to work it out offscreen. They separated, and eventually divorced, which led to the cancellation of their hit variety show.

They tried their separate hands at singular-hosted comedy-variety shows of their own. But *The Sonny Bono Comedy Hour* on ABC and *The Cher Show* on CBS failed; viewers missed seeing the dynamic duo duel—for fun. With remarkable stamina and resilience, the couple, now divorced, recombined their talents for a new edition of their old series, which they called *The Sonny & Cher Show*. This, too, was swiftly rejected by the home audience. The new show wasn't the same. The once dynamic twosome had moved on with new spouses (he with model Susie Coelho; she with rock star Gregg Allman), and it was now time to move on with their careers.

Sonny made periodic TV guest-star roles (on shows like *The Six Million Dollar Man*), opened a restaurant, and eventually turned to politics (becoming the mayor of Palm Springs); Cher had bigger fish to fry—as a solo singing sensation, and ideally as an actress on the big screen. After dazzling TV viewers in the 60s and 70s, through her own variety shows or with guest appearances on programs like *Shindig!, The Ed Sullivan Show,* and *The Man from U.N.C.L.E.*, Cher found a new artistic outlet in the 80s: theatrical motion pictures.

The tide turned toward the big screen in 1983, when she played Dolli Pelliker, a lesbian in love with Meryl Streep's lead character in *Silkwood*—a performance that earned her first Oscar nomination. Other film roles followed with *Mask* (1985), *Suspect,* and *Moonstruck*, both released in 1987—for the latter of which she finally won the coveted Academy Award for her portrayal of the frustrated dreamer Loretta Castorini (opposite Nicholas Cage).

Other films followed, such as *Mermaids* (1990), *Tea with Mussolini* (1999), and *Burlesque* (2010), and many more.

In 1996, tragedy struck: Sonny Bono was killed in a freak skiing accident. Cher gave the eulogy at a church in Palm Springs, which was one of the first public celebrity eulogies to be televised—and a new Cher was born. Without any makeup, and dressed simply and unspectacularly in dowdy black, she sobbed with sincerity at the podium, minus any bright or Hollywood professional lighting. It was a raw moment that proved to be an indirect game changer for the icon. It was if she was set free from what may have been Bono's special hold over and bond with her.

Only twice did they reunite in public after their failed postdivorce attempt with a variety show. In the spring of 1979, they appeared on *The Mike Douglas Show*, singing a medley of "United We Stand" and "Without You," and then November 13, 1987, on *Late Night with David Letterman,* where they performed their signature hit single, "I Got You Babe."

The two had remained close friends over the years, mostly due to their daughter Chastity, who, after sexual reconstructive surgery in 2011, transformed into Chaz, their son (all of which was chronicled that year in the heralded documentary *Becoming Chaz*). But once Sonny died, Cher seemed destined to become an even bigger star. Following her ill-advised involvement with an infomercial campaign that briefly derailed her acting career, she returned to music with the hit "Do You Believe in Love after Love?"

It was the first of many new chapters for Cher . . . a new energy and her status as an icon was forming in the stone that would eventually be set throughout the entirety of her career.

In 2013, she released *Closer to the Truth*, her first album since *Living Proof* (in 2002). As Mark Bego explained in his profile of Cher for *Boulevard Magazine* in December 2013, the superstar has never been satisfied to rest upon her "significant laurels." Instead, she decided to return to the recording studio. "I keep coming back," she told Bego, "because I have no place else to go. What else would I do? I love to sing."

ICONIC FACTS

Birth Data: Born Cherilyn Sarkisian on May 20, 1946, in El Centro, California.

Education: Attended Fresno High School but dropped out at the age of 16 in search of her acting dream.

Family: Parents John Sarkisian and Georgia Holt. Married Sonny Bono (1964–1975) and Gregg Allman (1975–1979, divorced). Children: Chaz Bono and Elijah Blue Allman.

Most Memorable TV Role: *The Sonny & Cher Comedy Hour* (CBS, 1971–1974), which she hosted with her then-husband Sonny Bono. The show was originally supposed to be a summer replacement series, but high ratings commanded a permanent spot on the schedule. Before they became TV stars, they were originally billed as Caesar & Cleo, a music duo that later rose to fame as Sonny & Cher with their first hit single, in 1965, "I Got You Babe."

Benchmarks: All of Cher's Emmy nominations have been for variety series or music programs with her name in the title. Pursued acting full force in the

1980s with films like *Silkwood*, for which she received a Best Supporting Actress Oscar nomination; and *Moonstruck*, for which she won the Academy Award for Best Actress. In 2010, she played Tess in the feature film release *Burlesque*. In November 2013, she appeared as a guest performer and judge on the seventeenth season of *Dancing with the Stars*. Her 40-city tour, *Dressed to Kill*, began in March 2014. The only female performer in music history to have had a certified U.S. number one single in the 1960s, 1970s, 1980s, and 1990s, Cher's only fear is flying.

Prime Quotes: "Husbands are like fires—they go out when they're left unattended." * "If you really want something you can figure out how to make it happen." * "I've always taken risks and never worried what the world might really think of me." * "I haven't a clue why I've lasted so long. There's no reason. There are many people more talented than me. I think it's luck." * "The trouble with some women, they get all excited about nothing—and then they marry him."

A Living Legend.

Marie Osmond

(The Donny & Marie Show)

MARIE OSMOND (*THE DONNY & MARIE SHOW*)

> You don't work 30 something years in this business without knowing
> how to push yourself.
>
> —Marie Osmond

Marie Osmond is talented, kindhearted, and generous, and that is no exaggeration. She displays the embodiment of everything good that someone in the public eye should display, thus confirming her status as a glamorous young female icon of television.

Marie is a member of the legendary and multifaceted performing Osmond family, who got their start on *The Andy Williams Show* in 1962. At the time, she was not yet a part of the act or the family. However, once she did come along, and became a teenager, she was interested in being a secretary, her mother's profession.

But stardom was her destiny.

Marie is the only female sibling in the brood, which includes her brothers Virl, Tommy, Alan, Wayne, Merrill, Jay, Donny, and Jimmy, the children of George and Olive Osmond. Only Virl and Tommy, due to hearing impairments, were not part of the musical acts through the decades, and consequently worked in other areas. Yet it was with her brother Donny, in the fall of 1975, that Marie's star truly began to shine: *The Donny & Marie Show* became a mainstay hit on ABC Friday nights.

Produced by Sid and Marty Krofft, *Donny & Marie* originally aired from September 1976 to 1979, and featured a galaxy of guest stars, such as Farrah Fawcett, Lee Majors, Milton Berle, and Lucille Ball, the latter embracing their family-oriented style of performing. Marie was "a little bit country" to Donny's "little bit rock and roll," and the show contributed to massive hit records for Marie in particular, including "Paper Roses," "In My Own Little Corner of the World," "Who's Sorry Now?" and her number one hit with Dan Seals, "Meet Me

GLAMOUR, GIDGETS, AND THE GIRL NEXT DOOR

in Montana." She also recorded songs with Donny such as "I'm Leaving It All Up to You," "Make the World Go Away," and "Morning Side of the Mountain."

Writer Arnie Kogen worked on the *Donny & Marie* show, and as he assesses today, "Marie, like her brother, had a great smile and a good voice and was perky, apple-pie, all American and was clean cut. And it didn't hurt that she had a few hit songs. When all that's packaged together with a strong variety show format you sometimes have a hit TV series."

As to the "country" connection, Marie once said, "You know, it's funny. When I started singing, no matter what I sang it had a country flavor to it. When I went to Nashville, they said, 'Try some country music.' I sing more country pop. I just enjoy it—and nobody else in the family sang that way."

Along with her family, Marie is a member of the Mormon Church, and she and her brother Donny continue to perform together. For example, their bright stars illuminated Hollywood's famous Pantages Theatre from December 4 to December 23, 2012, with "The Donny & Marie Christmas Show," which was also billed as "Christmas in Los Angeles with Donny & Marie." Thousands of Osmond fans sold out the theater night after night, many experiencing their favorite performers live for the first time. There was a sense of whimsy and the surreal about seeing Marie and Donny live after enjoying them for years on television. Near mythical figures, their talent, humor, and humanity became legendary. The Pantages performances proved their spectacular capabilities all these years after their TV show. Their individual and combined sense of song, style, dance, and comic timing—mixed with their pure intentions—made for a breathtaking show, one for which their half century of hard work, raw talent, and graceful likability had fittingly prepared them.

Marie returned to television in January 2013—with a new, if short-lived, talk show on the Hallmark Channel. She and Donny had made their mark in a syndicated talk show that aired from 1998 to 2000. But now Marie was on her own; with a warm and welcoming tradition of yesteryear's Mike Douglas and Dinah Shore talk/variety shows, her new daily hour brought a certain class and distinction to contemporary television that has been sorely missed for far too long.

A showbiz veteran of over five decades, with a seemingly immortal, youthful glow and energy, Marie went against the grain of the mean-spirited, edgy, nonstop sarcastic banter that is so prevalent on other talk shows today. She employed her wit and media savvy with a pervading grace that actually allowed her guests to talk, and she made every attempt not to interrupt them. She was a cordial host, and she made the audience feel "at home," whether she was chatting with a celebrity or a member of the studio audience. Unlike many public personalities who are only "nice" when the cameras roll, Marie treated everyone the same: with respect. On or off camera, she asked real questions about real life ("How's your mom?"), and played no favorites, only because she made everyone feel like they were her favorite.

As a result, the viewers at home were brought to the party as if by special invitation—and just plain didn't want to leave or have that party end. A multientertaining icon, Marie's truest talents rest with her God-given ability to communicate, her sense of humor (which is direct but never hurtful or insulting), and her ability to see everyone as equal. Any medium, although especially television, is brightened by her spirit, combined with enormous talents and generosity. Her Children's Miracle Network Charities, which she cofounded with actor John Schneider (*Dukes of Hazzard*, *Smallville*), has raised countless millions.

Linda Burton, a close friend of Osmond's, says: "Marie is a real person with a real sense of humor, and a very confident demeanor without leading anyone to believe that she is better than other people. She loves her fans like family. And because [all of] the Osmonds are so nice to their fans, the fans have been loyal to them for over 50 years. People travel around the world to see them in Las Vegas and to see their Christmas shows all over the world."

Virginia Reeser, a communications professional who lives in Los Angeles and embraces lifelong learning, has attended many of Marie's performances over the years, including the live stage Christmas show at the Pantages Theatre in December 2012. Reeser offers these conclusive thoughts with regard to Marie's core appeal:

Entertainers who are the complete package are true gems, and Marie is one of these sparkling jewels. She brings light and joy to all her work and that heartfelt sparkle is what stays with audiences young and old after they see her perform.

I first saw Marie perform with her brother Donny in the 1970s at the Wisconsin State Fair. I immediately admired her talent and of course couldn't believe my favorite singer and actor was live and in person. She was funny, had great vocal range, and lifted my spirits.

Fast-forward 30 years to the Pantages Theatre in Hollywood, where I found myself having the same joyful reaction as I was swept up in her energy and love during her performance with Donny at their Christmas show.

My admiration for her took on a new dimension as I was struck by the amazing new facets artfully added to her talent jewels. Singing, dancing, acting—everything she did seemed to have more energy and depth than ever.

I found myself admiring her with a new perspective, not only for that unstoppable energy, but also for how she had pushed herself to expand her voice into opera and her acting into impromptu audience participation. All age-groups were in attendance, those who have loved her for many, many years and others discovering her for the first time.

At a time in life when others might be content to stick with "what has worked" I loved her message—perhaps even unintended—keep growing . . . and never stop challenging yourself to learn new things.

Marie has staying power and true talent. I look forward to seeing how much she continues to sparkle in years to come as she inspires a whole new generation.

ICONIC FACTS

Birth Data: Born Olive Marie Osmond on October 13, 1959, in Ogden, Utah.

Education: The American School, a nonprofit distance education institution.

Family: Parents, Olive May and George Virl Osmond; has eight brothers: Virl, Tom, Alan, Wayne, Merrill, Jay, Donny, and Jimmy Osmond. Married Steve Craig (1982–1985), Brian Blosil (1986–2007), and remarried Craig in 2011. Children: Stephen Blosil (a.k.a. Stephen James Craig), Jessica Marie Blosil, Rachael Lauren Blosil, Michael Brian Blosil (committed suicide in 2010), Brandon Warren Blosil, Brianna Patricia Blosil, Matthew Richard Blosil, and Abigail Olive May Blosil. Five of Marie's children are adopted.

Most Memorable TV Role: From 1976 to 1979, she and her brother Donny hosted the TV variety show *Donny & Marie*.

Benchmarks: In 1983, along with actor John Schneider, Marie cofounded the nonprofit organization Children's Miracle Network in 1983. In 1991, she premiered a successful line of dolls via QVC. Her last charting single came in 1995 with "What Kind of Man (Walks on a Woman)." In 1998, she reteamed with Donny on TV for a talk show. In October 1999, disclosed that she was treated for a severe bout of postpartum depression following the birth of her seventh child, Matthew. In 2007, she was positioned in third place on the fifth season of *Dancing with the Stars*. On April 29, 2009, revealed that her second oldest daughter, Jessica, is a lesbian, and that she loves all of her children unconditionally. As she said on *Entertainment*

Tonight, "Love is love." From 2012 to 2013, she hosted the talk show *Marie!* on the Hallmark Channel. She performs regularly at the Flamingo Hotel in Las Vegas with brother Donny; is the respected author of several best-selling books and the reigning spokesperson for Nutrisystem. A multitalented performer in every field of the entertainment industry, she sings many different styles of music (including opera!), and has starred in revivals of two legendary Broadway musicals: "The Sound of Music" and "The King and I."

Prime Quotes: "When you have a baby, love is automatic, when you get married, love is earned." * "I found for me that my safe place was work. I could control my environment. I became very fastidious and detailed, and wanted things a certain way." * "If you're going to be able to look back on something and laugh about it, you might as well laugh about it now." * "I wish my parents could have raised every man out there." * "I never had a sister growing up. Donny was the closest thing."

A Living Legend.

PART II

THE TEEN ANGELS

Elinor Donahue

(Father Knows Best)

> I had gone from playing Daddy's little girl [on *Father Knows Best*], into
> immediately playing a woman [on *The Andy Griffith Show*] who had not only
> gone to college, but to graduate school, lived on her own and could run a
> business. So, it was a big jump, emotionally, on a week-to-week basis in a series.
>
> —Elinor Donahue

Elinor Donahue is imbued with a particular sweetness suited for a medium as intimate as *the television set*—the innovative device itself, in combination with the actual individuals or groups of individuals who have for decades planted themselves in front of the TV since and before Donahue's image was first displayed there in the 1950s.

Donahue is best known to TV viewers as Betty "Princess" Anderson on *Father Knows Best* (FKB), which originally aired on CBS, NBC, and ABC from 1954 to 1960. With a show business career that began when she was a mere two years old, Donahue continues to this day utilizing her theatrical gifts and charms in the craft she so dearly loves.

She made her debut as a radio singer and vaudeville dancer while just a toddler, and was contracted by Universal Studios at five years old. Soon cast in movies like *Mister Big* (1943), Donahue later switched to MGM in films such as *The Unfinished Dance* (1947, with Margaret O'Brien) and *Love Is Better Than Ever* (1952, with Elizabeth Taylor). In 1954 she found teen fame as the sweet-natured Princess on FKB, which, based on the 1949 radio show, starred former movie idol Robert Young and fellow female TV icon Jane Wyatt as her parents James and Margaret Anderson. Her younger siblings were portrayed by Billy Gray (James, Jr., a.k.a. Bud) and Lauren Chapin (Kathy, a.k.a. Kitten).

After *Father* folded, Donahue played Ellie Walker, an early steady love interest to Sheriff Andy Taylor on the first season of *The Andy Griffith Show*.

ELINOR DONAHUE (*FATHER KNOWS BEST*)

By the early 1970s, Donahue returned to acting with a recurring role as Miriam Welby, girlfriend to Tony Randall's Felix Unger on the hit ABC series *The Odd Couple* (based on the Neil Simon play and feature film). The Welby name was a nod to Robert Young's post-*Father* ABC hit, *Marcus Welby, M.D.*, and, as Donahue muses today, it was Randall's idea to pay tribute to Young's TV doctor: "Tony thought that was funny."

Following *The Odd Couple*, Donahue was featured in a new family show on NBC called *Mulligan's Stew*, which began as a movie-of-the-week. The film was well received in the ratings then became a series, if only lasting one season. According to Donahue, the show was "rushed into production before it was ready." But it was a valiant attempt to return family programming to the small screen. She portrayed Jane Mulligan, opposite Lawrence Pressman as her husband Michael, both of whom oversaw a brood that featured a then teen Suzanne Crough (the youngest from *The Partridge Family*). The show was a modern-day version of *The Waltons*, in which Donahue played a grown-up version of her FKB Princess persona with a family of her own. In actuality, she would play in two holiday *Father* TV-movie sequels in late 1977: *The Father Knows Best Reunion* and *Home for the Holidays*.

Donahue later appeared in countless other television shows, including guest shots on *Barnaby Jones*, *Newhart*, *The Golden Girls*, and *Friends* and had regular roles on the 1990s sitcom *Get a Life* and the CBS western drama *Dr. Quinn, Medicine Woman* (as Rebecca Quinn, older sister to Jane Seymour). She's also enjoyed regular roles on the daytime serials *Santa Barbara* and *Days of Our Lives*, on which she played Nurse Hunnicut.

With her pleasant personality, Donahue portrayed mostly affable parts in both sitcoms and drama shows, delivering a calming presence that shined by way of just her voice, which was also utilized for various commercials and animated series.

As to her days as Betty on *Father Knows Best*, Donahue assesses:

I was a teenager playing a teenager. How hard could it be? You know, really, truly. I did, however, before filming began attend Beverly Hills High for about five weeks, as I'd never experienced a lot of things that normal young people do. I'd never been in a large classroom experience. I'd never run to classes or had a locker. I never took a gym class, never went to a football game or a sock hop. I got to do all those things and I'm sure it helped. I used a nickname when I was at Beverly Hills High. It seemed like all the girls had cute monikers. And mine was Mimi. So that's where Betty Anderson kind of came from.

While fellow female teen angels like Shelley Fabares were showcased in Hollywood magazines and publicity spreads of the day, Donahue was not. It was something Eugene B. Rodney, FKB's producer, would not allow. As she explains, "He wanted us to be thought of as family as far as the show went and every now and then I would get some publicity or I would be invited to a something and he would kind of allow me to go to a beach party or something with Natalie Wood or whatever . . . but very, very, very, very seldom."

Town & Country Magazine wanted to feature Elinor in a fashion spread, but, in Rodney's eyes, the periodical was ultimately not considered appropriate for Betty Anderson, so the feature was scrubbed. She does, however, recall one particular article and photo essay that was acceptable in Rodney's view. It was with a then young Jack Jones, who later became famous in the classic TV world for performing the opening theme song for TV's *The Love Boat*. "We were seeing one another at some point," Donahue explains, "and we were, you know, sipping a soda together and going bowling together—I don't bowl. You know, it was a setup. And he kind of allowed that because I was at an age where that was an okay thing to do."

Apparently, FKB star and coproducer Robert Young believed in the same press restrictions for Donahue and her young costars Billy Gray and Lauren Chapin. As she recalls,

> It's possible. To us, he was just one of the guys. So, I don't know? On the weekends, maybe they sat down and worked out production stuff, but I don't think so. I think he just did what he did and Mr. Rodney took care of what he did. Even though he was a coproducer on the show, he stayed totally away from any one of us thinking he had anything to do with the work except playing his part. And if he wanted to change a line, he had to go to the telephone on the set and call Mr. Rodney in the office and work it out with him. We couldn't change an "if," "and," or "but" once we got those scripts. No ad-libbing, whatsoever. Robert Young called Mr. Rodney the benevolent despot!

Although her FKB days may not have been filled with many magazine features, there were other monumental moments that helped to fill in the gap, before and after the series was in production. Years after the show stopped filming, a Catholic girls school in the area of South Pasadena, California, hosted Betty Anderson Day. As Donahue recalls, the day's festivities centered around a school luncheon at which she was the guest of honor. "It was just so cute and very sweet."

As to how it feels all these years later to be considered a television icon, Donahue replies, "It's flattering that anyone would consider me an icon, but I don't."

That isn't to say she hasn't enjoyed the experience of being recognized by fans on the street. She recalls two humorous instances in particular, during which she happened to be accompanied by her husband, prolific television producer Harry Ackerman:

> We were in a store and checking out of a little gift shop. The cashier pointed her finger at me and said, "I know you. You used to be on—on, uh—on, uh—gosh, what was it?" And I said, "*Father Knows Best*." And she said, "No, no." She said, "It starred that man—what was his name?" And I said, "Robert Young." And she said, "No, no . . ." And this went on until Harry and I looked at each other and I said, "Gee, I just don't know."

> My most memorable encounter with a fan was in New York for the Daytime Emmys in the mid-80s. Harry was nominated for an afternoon special and it won. I don't remember what it was called. And I was at that time appearing on *Days of Our Lives*. I'd been on for about a year and a half, two years, and I did ultimately close to three seasons. So, we came in the back way of the Waldorf Astoria to miss the crowds and the red carpet—all that *foofaraw* because both he and I were shy and what we didn't know was that the entrance that we came in had another crowd of diehard fans of *Days of Our Lives*. And we came through the door and then we paused to look at this printout we had to try and find the ballroom. And I heard this thundering like *b-rum b-rum b-rum*—footsteps behind me like a herd. And people yelling, "Nurse Hunnicut! Nurse Hunnicut!" And I turned around and this group of people swooped down—it must have been twenty people, which seemed like a lot when they were all, you know, rushing at you. And that was very funny. I thought Harry was very pleased. And I enjoyed it.

Peter Ackerman, one of Elinor's three sons with Harry Ackerman, offers this assessment about his famous mom:

I know she enjoys meeting her fans, and I always liked those encounters growing up. I remember very well grocery shopping with my mother when, to me, a grown man would walk up to her and begin stammering while he worked to get out that he was in love with Betty Anderson, when he was growing up, and thus had a crush on her. Even today I meet people like him or women (and sometimes men) who say "I wanted to be just like her." I consider it a privilege that I got to see grace in action as my mother acknowledged these people when they approached her. I think rather than an idol or an icon, these examples show that she was a part, on *Father Knows Best*, of a show that illustrated what the American family could be like; she emulated the standard to which people could try to attain. This reminds me of my dad's shows, as well; they showed us who we could try to be if we lived out our better natures. Instead, today, in television there is so much that presents humor as dumbed down.

ICONIC FACTS

Birth Data: Born Mary Eleanor Donahue on April 19, 1937, in Tacoma, Washington.

Education: A radio singer and vaudeville dancer as a toddler, under contract to Universal Studios at the age of five.

Family: Parents, Doris and Thomas Donahue. Married Richard Smith (1955–1961; divorced), Harry Ackerman (1962–1991; until his death), Lou Genevrino (1992–present). Children: Brian Ackerman, Peter Ackerman, James Ackerman, and Chris Ackerman, and two stepchildren: Susan Peterson and Stephen Ackerman.

Most Memorable TV Role: The eldest daughter, Betty "Princess" Anderson, in *Father Knows Best* (CBS, ABC, NBC, 1954–1960), for which she was Emmy nominated in 1959.

Benchmarks: Played Ellie Walker, girlfriend to Sheriff Andy Taylor in the first season of *The Andy Griffith Show* (1961); Miriam Welby, girlfriend to Felix Unger (Tony Randall) on *The Odd Couple* (1972–1975); played Rebecca in the CBS TV series from the 1990s *Dr. Quinn, Medicine Woman*. Guest-starred: *Cold Case* (2009); Judge Anderson (her character's surname from *Father Knows Best*) on *The Young and the Restless* (two episodes; 2011, 2012). In 2004 she, along with the rest of the cast of *The Andy Griffith Show*, won a TV Land Legend Award.

Prime Quotes: On winning the role of Ellie on *The Andy Griffith Show*: "I was called into a meeting with the producers and was told what the show was about. It hadn't been on yet. It was brand new and [they] asked if I would be interested and [I] said yes, and by the time I got home, the call had been made to my agent and the deal was in the works." * On working on the show in general: "It was a darling part . . . really cute. I loved working with Ron Howard. I think it was fabulous. The best child actor I had ever worked with . . . just extraordinary." And "*The Andy Griffith Show* hit a chord in people's hearts . . . the small town . . . the warmth of the people relating to one another on an everyday basis."

A Living Legend.

Shelley Fabares

(The Donna Reed Show)

GLAMOUR, GIDGETS, AND THE GIRL NEXT DOOR

We need to appreciate how precious life is.

—Shelley Fabares

If you were a young male teen sprouting up in the 1950s, and you had a thing for Patty Duke or Elinor Donahue, you most likely were also in love with Shelley Fabares, who for five years on *The Donna Reed Show* portrayed Mary Stone, the dainty, darling, and beyond-perfect ideal daughter of the small screen.

Although she may have frequently bickered, if lovingly so, with her TV brother, Jeff Stone (played by the eclectic Paul Peterson), she never dared to speak a cross word to her mother and father (portrayed by Donna Reed and Carl Betz).

Adorable and loyal, petite and pretty, Fabares's Mary Stone was nothing less than angelic throughout her entire run of the series. She proved so popular that Fabares parlayed her sweet all-American appeal into a lengthy career beyond the *Reed* series, leaving the show after the fifth of its eight seasons (when Mary was said to have attended college), appearing in only two episodes afterward.

While playing Mary on the *Reed* show, Fabares kept to herself in real life. As she told Peggy Herz in 1973, in junior high she was "a loner." She had a happy home life but spent most of her childhood in her bedroom with the door closed. "I wasn't unhappy, I was just reading and writing." She enjoyed school and did well. She and her sister, Nanette (named for their aunt Nanette Fabray), both attended Catholic schools. "We were serious students," she said, even though her sister was more outgoing that she was.

As to her stint on *Donna Reed*, Fabares started on the show in 1958, when she was 14 and she had been acting since she was 3 years old. "Both my sister and I enjoyed working," she said. "It sounds like we had one of those stage mothers who pushed us and made us work, but that wasn't the case. We could stop at any time for any reason. We did it because we enjoyed it." Before Fabares began *The Donna*

Reed Show, she surmised that it would be a good experience. "It turned out to be a thousand times better than that," she said.

Decades later, on August 18, 1994, Fabares appeared on ABC's *Good Morning, America* to promote *Coach*, her then-new show on the network. Here, she played girlfriend-turned-wife Christine Armstrong to series lead Craig T. Nelson from 1989 to 1997. More than anything, *Morning* host Charlie Gibson wanted to know about her stint on *Reed*. "It was hard for me to realize we were doing a television show," she replied. "We were a family. For years after the show was over, we would get together once a month and have lunch. We would talk to each other in between times, but we had a standing date, just so we could keep that connection. We really did become a family."

When Gibson further prodded her on what she recalled the most from the show, Fabares said:

> The sense of family. It really was my "growing-up" years . . . that's what they were . . . and that's what I hold very dear. It's hard for me to realize that we were doing a television show . . . I mean without being naïve about it. [Of course] we were doing a television show. But really, it was a very family-oriented experience.

And did she ever watch the reruns?

> Yes . . . when I can . . . I mean, life tends to get really busy, and that's sort of hard. But I do. And it's really an extraordinary experience. I mean, sometimes you go, "Oh, I can't believe this!" or "That's so embarrassing" . . . that everybody is watching this right along with you. But it's a very touching show also.

Fabares went on to chat with Gibson about her success as a recording star, which began during her *Reed* reign with the Billboard number one hit single

"Johnny Angel." Music also contributed to her performances in a list of feature films, including three consecutive musicals with Elvis Presley: *Girl Happy* (1965), *Spinout* (1966), and *Clambake* (1967). Before those films, she appeared in *Never Say Good-bye* (1956, as Rock Hudson's daughter), and played kid sister roles in the also-music-themed film *Rock, Pretty Baby* (1956) and its sequel *Summer Love* (1958), both with John Saxon.

By the time she appeared with Elvis (they were only "good friends," and "nothing romantic"), Fabares had matured into a sultry young woman who looked nothing less than stellar in a big-screen bikini and who, by today's standards, would have most likely been described as sizzling "hot"! After she made additional motion pictures like *Ride the Wild Surf* (1964), and *Hold On!* (1966), she returned to television in the 70s with a string of hit TV-movies and shows.

More than any other character, it is still Shelley's appearance as Mary Stone on *The Donna Reed Show* that remains her trademark performance. The character was named for Reed's real-life daughter Mary. Although Mary (Owen) was just a toddler when the *Reed* series was in production, her recollection of Shelley and company, including Paul Peterson, her TV brother, is clear:

> I have nothing but super-warm memories and feelings toward Shelley and Paul. They would come over for some holidays and Easter, and so forth. But I think it's interesting that my father—well, I'm just going to attribute it to my father—managed to pick someone so perfectly to play the daughter. And I can't tell you how many men who tell me, "I had such a huge crush on Shelley Fabares when I was little." And then Paul, the same thing, he was a huge heartthrob for all the girls—and plenty of gay guys, too. My gay guy friends are like, "Oh, my God—I really loved Paul!" I think it's interesting that my dad managed to cast the perfect actor and actress who ended up becoming so popular with teenagers.

SHELLEY FABARES (*THE DONNA REED SHOW*)

Classic TV actor Tony Dow, who played older brother Wally on *Leave It To Beaver* (CBS/ABC, 1957–1963), went on to enjoy a second career as a TV director, including guiding episodes of *Coach* with Shelley. He compares working with her on that series and their friendship during the *Beaver/Reed* era:

> *Coach* was an interesting show because it was basically a typical sitcom, three-camera audience type show . . . so it was done much differently than *Leave It To Beaver* or *Donna Reed*. And the working experience was different. The hierarchy of the show was the writing/producing group and then there were the actors . . . who, on practically every episode I directed didn't think the jokes were funny . . . and the writers thought the actors couldn't deliver the jokes. But Shelley with her wonderful, polite, sweet personality just did her job . . . and she did it perfectly. She never complained about anything. She needed very little direction. She understood her character. She was a real pro . . . like many former child actors who were brought up with such discipline. I didn't work with her on *Donna Reed*, but I always remembered her as so sweet and attractive.

On Fabares's appeal in general, Dow decides:

> When you're on a series, you tend to rely on your instincts . . . a lot more than if you're doing a guest-starring one-shot role when you're actually creating a character for one episode . . . and so on *The Donna Reed Show*, Shelley's lovely personality just shined through.

Entertainment historian Rob Ray concludes, "I'm glad Shelley Fabares is as nice as she seems. As her aunt, Nanette Fabray, told me at a Collectors' Show years ago when we were on a variant of this very topic, 'The camera doesn't lie.'"

ICONIC FACTS

Birth Data: Born Michele Ann Marie Fabares on January 19, 1944, in Santa Monica, California.

Education: Began tap dancing at the age of three and acting in television by the time she was ten; attended Immaculate Heart High School.

Family: Parents, James and Elsa Fabares; niece to actress Nanette Fabray; married Lou Adler (1964–1980); Mike Farrell (1984–present); became stepmother to Farrell's two children from a prior marriage.

Most Memorable TV Role: Mary Stone on *The Donna Reed Show* (ABC, 1958–1966).

Benchmarks: Recorded number one Billboard hit song in 1962, "Johnny Angel"; appeared in three movies with Elvis Presley from 1965 to 1967. Her post-*Reed* TV appearances include *The Brian Keith Show* (NBC, 1974–1975) and *The Practice* (starring Danny Thomas, NBC, 1976–1977), among others. She also appeared as a semiregular on Norman Lear's groundbreaking sitcom *One Day at a Time*, playing against type as Francine Webster, business rival to Bonnie Franklin's Ann Romano. *Time* was a family reunion of sorts as it also featured Shelley's aunt, Nanette Fabray (with an alternate spelling), who periodically played Franklin's mother. In 1972, Fabares delivered a moving performance as Joy Piccolo, in the Emmy-winning 1972 TV-movie *Brian's Song*, which was based on the true and tragic story of football star Brian Piccolo (played by a then-unknown James Caan, who was just about to become a movie star via *The Godfather*, released that same year).

From 1981 to 1984, she played Francine Webster, Bonnie Franklin's boss on *One Day at a Time* (CBS, 1975–1984); in 1989 she starred as Christine Armstrong Fox, girlfriend-turned-wife opposite Craig T. Nelson's lead character in the sitcom *Coach* (ABC, 1989–1997). In more recent years, she provided the voice for Martha Kent on the acclaimed *Superman* animated series. She received a liver transplant in October 2000 when her liver failed due to an autoimmune disorder. She continues to work with the Donna Reed Festival of the Performing Arts (still held annually in Donna Reed's hometown), where students who want to pursue a career in the performing arts are awarded scholarships in Donna's memory.

Prime Quotes: On playing Joy Piccolo in *Brian's Song*: "For me as an actress, it was the most important thing I'd done. For me as a person, it enriched and fulfilled my life to a degree that I couldn't believe. The story became part of us—the lives we portrayed became a part of us. It's still difficult to talk about it. When you feel deeply, words aren't enough. It was an experience I shall cherish forever."

A Living Legend.

10

Patty Duke

(The Patty Duke Show)

PATTY DUKE (*THE PATTY DUKE SHOW*)

> I subscribe to the theory that says you're a product of all your experiences. And I am finally, most of the time, happy with the product. I now think it is okay to be Patty Duke.
>
> —Patty Duke

She was tiny, but talented; precocious but attractive; devious but delightful; distant but downright adorable.

So describes the double identity, onscreen and off, of the multitalented and multi-award-winning actress Patty Duke. For three seasons on *The Patty Duke Show* (ABC, 1963–1966), she brought a unique and diametric energy to the dual role of Patty Lane and her British, more refined look-alike cousin Cathy.

As with Sally Field on *Gidget* (which also aired on ABC in the 60s), Duke as the Lane twins combined an exuberance and natural theatrical talent that was well beyond her years. She would perform both tender and comical scenes with an ability that seemed to stem from pure instinct.

Behind the camera, however, she was the tortured young performer with monumental personal struggles, all of which she courageously overcame with astounding rebound.

Hailing from Elmhurst, New York, Patty was introduced to acting by her brother's managers, John and Ethel Ross, and began acting in commercials, which led to several noteworthy stage, film, and television roles. Her big break arrived in 1961, when she was cast as Helen Keller on the Broadway version of "The Miracle Worker."

In 1963, at age 16, she won the Academy Award for her portrayal of Keller in the feature film adaptation of "Miracle," and became the youngest Oscar recipient at the time. As her success continued, she fell prey to substance abuse and depression, which she apparently inherited from her alcoholic father and bipolar mother.

With *The Patty Duke Show* she earned her first Emmy nomination and, in 1965, she headlined the heralded TV-movie *Billie*, which became the first small-screen film ever sold to a television network. From then on she was known as the "Queen of TV-Movies" (a crown later worn by fellow female icons Elizabeth Montgomery and Valerie Bertinelli, among others). Duke went on to star in the cult classic *Valley of The Dolls* in 1967 and, in 1969, appeared in an independent film called *Me, Natalie*. Although the latter production was a box-office failure, it garnered Duke her second Golden Globe Award.

In 1976, she won her second Emmy for the highly successful miniseries *Captains and the Kings*, and continued working in TV-movies, such as the 1979 remake of *The Miracle Worker* in which she now portrayed Annie Sullivan, a role that won her a third Emmy.

In 1984, she was elected president of the Screen Actors Guild.

Although it was her classic TV sitcom that sealed her status as a female icon of television, working on the show was not always a pleasant experience for her, particularly because of the nature of playing two roles. As she explained in her book *Call Me Anna*, her abusive managers, John and Ethel Ross, never allowed her to watch the show, sending her to her room whenever it aired. Into this mix, she felt uneasy about playing the teenage Patty, because Duke never went to a high school dance in real life or did anything that a regular teen girl would do, mostly because of the unpleasant demands placed upon her by the Rosses. Duke was equally frustrated with playing Cathy, Patty's foreign twin cousin on the show, especially because the character was not given a clear-cut heritage. "Cathy should be from someplace," Duke wrote. "That's one of the reasons I tend to think of my work [on *The Patty Duke Show*] the same way I do the split screens we used, as part of the trick as opposed to genuine performance."

Duke made it clear that she enjoyed playing Cathy more than Patty because the former was "more sedate, seemed older and was less silly." Cathy was somewhat boring, Duke said, "but at least she wasn't called upon to do the things that I felt were demeaning and scatterbrained."

The actress felt the same way about the wardrobe of both characters. She preferred Cathy's clothes because they were more conservative in color and style. "Others might think they were boring," she relayed, "but that was less offensive than skirts that were too short and too wide, things that were in general stiff and unreal." As far as Duke was concerned, "they were trick clothes," an extension of the trick photography and her trick accent as Cathy.

Fortunately, the experience of *The Patty Duke Show* for the viewers at home was only a positive experience. As writer and Duke fan Dan Holm explains:

The Patty Duke Show ranks among my very first "must-see" series. It was appointment television in our house. Her ability to pull off two contrasting roles consistently week after week is a testament to Patty Duke's formidable talent. Patty was cute, fun, and ready to take on life. Cathy was studious, conservative, and wanted to understand life before approaching carefully. She exemplified the yin and yang of growing up and the tumults of teenagerdom. Patty and Cathy were relatable and accessible. In *The Patty Duke Show*, she captured that time of life when you can't decide which side of the brain is in control. The great part about watching Patty and Cathy is that we didn't have to. She/they proved both hemispheres can work it out, especially when you put them together. Ironically, in her dual roles as Patty and Cathy, Patty Duke gave us a hint of the personal conflicts that would plague her for years to come.

ICONIC FACTS

Birth Data: Born Anna Marie Duke on December 14, 1946, in Elmhurst, Queens, New York.

Education: Received honorary doctorates from both the University of North Florida and the University of Maryland Eastern Shore.

Family: Parents, Frances and John Duke; married Harry Falk (1965–1969), Michael Tell (1970–1970), John Astin (1972–1985), and Michael Pearce (1986–present). Children: Sean Astin with Michael Tell (later adopted by John Astin), Mackenzie Astin, and Kevin Pearce.

Most Memorable TV Role: Identical cousins Patty and Cathy Lane on *The Patty Duke Show* (ABC, 1963–1966).

Benchmarks: Portrayed Helen Keller in the Broadway and feature film adaptation of *The Miracle Worker* (1962), the latter for which she won the Oscar—classifying her as the youngest to ever do so in a competitive category. In 1967, she played Neely O'Hara in the movie *Valley of the Dolls*; has appeared in various roles on stage; made guest appearances on TV shows like the latest edition of *Hawaii 5-0*. She played Jan in the TV show *Glee*, as part of a lesbian couple with Meredith Baxter (fellow female TV icon). Her father was an alcoholic who left the family when Patty was six. Her mother was prone to violence and when Patty was eight put her in the care of John and Ethel Ross, who managed her acting career. At the age of 12, she won $32,000 when she appeared on the quiz show *The $64,000 Question*. In 1982, she was diagnosed with bipolar disorder, after which she devoted her time advocating and educating the public on mental health issues. Her 1987 autobiography, *Call Me Anna*, was made into a TV movie in 1990. Her second book, *A Brilliant Madness: Living with Manic Depression Illness*, was published in 1992.

Prime Quotes: More about the clothes she wore on *The Patty Duke Show*: "Not only did I hate those clothes, but they put my name on some and successfully merchandised them, so a lot of other poor girls were walking around with the same ugly clothes I had to wear." * About acting in general: "Actors take risks all the time. We put ourselves on the line. It is creative to be able to interpret someone's words and breathe life into them."

A Living Legend.

11

The Lennon Sisters

(The Lawrence Welk Show)

THE LENNON SISTERS (*THE LAWRENCE WELK SHOW*)

> *The Lawrence Welk Show* conjures up an innocent time spent with
> parents and grandparents.
>
> —Janet Lennon

Harmony . . . in voice . . . in appearance . . . in performance . . . in life . . . such is the case with The Lennon Sisters, who were introduced to the world of television by way of musical variety shows hosted by Lawrence Welk and Jimmy Durante. The Lennons debuted on the Christmas Eve 1955 episode of *The Lawrence Welk Show* on ABC, which later paired them with Durante for a program titled *Jimmy Durante Presents The Lennon Sisters*, which aired for only one season (September 26, 1969, to July 4, 1970).

Of the original foursome Dianne (a.k.a. Dee Dee) is the eldest, followed by Peggy, Cathy, and Janet. Youngest sister Mimi replaced Peggy when she retired in 1999. Dianne retired shortly thereafter. Today, each of the songbird siblings continues to lead a full life, while three of the youngest are still harmonizing for paying audiences.

The Lennons originally presented themselves to the mainstream TV audience as close-knit sisters from a solid Catholic family background of five boys and six girls who were raised in a small home in Venice, California. The key to their spin-off musical-group appeal was and remains as unique as their individual personalities; they each exuded dynamite talent . . . but together they became explosive.

Dianne projects a sincerity and warmth that's mature yet enchanting. Her visual appeal is not unlike that of Julie Andrews.

Peggy has a slight cast to her eyes that, rather than mars her beauty, somehow adds to it. She has a sweetness all her own that's most alluring.

Cathy is the most vivacious and conventionally attractive of the sisters, and as such, may have been the most overlooked over the years.

Janet has always been perceived as everyone's favorite kid sister. She's the one we watched grow up and took to our hearts. Talent aside (for they were all equally talented), she was to the Lennon Sisters what Donny Osmond was to The Osmond Brothers and Michael Jackson was to The Jackson Five. It was she who may have been granted the most solos mostly because she was so darling.

On January 4, 2013, KCET, a PBS station in Los Angeles, screened a rerun of *The Lawrence Welk Show* from 1967 with the Lennon siblings. After the broadcast, Dianne sat down for a revealing on-air interview with former *Welk* regular Mary Lou Metzger. "We were all little girls when we started on the show," she said. "I had just turned 16 and was a junior in high school." She mentioned how at times being on the show was "a little embarrassing," because the producers always tried to "keep us young," with certain wardrobe selections; how for an Easter segment, they found themselves singing the children's song, "Here Comes Peter Cottontail."

Dianne also revealed how she was the only sister in the group who did not meet her husband on *Welk*. When she did marry, more than a thousand guests were invited to the wedding, which had to be scheduled for a Sunday because *Welk* taped on Saturdays. Because they were strict Catholics, Dianne and her husband had to receive special permission from the Catholic Church to have the ceremony on a Sunday.

Dianne "loved" being on *The Lawrence Welk Show*.

Matthew Worley, a Los Angeles–based journalist (who hosts *By The Book*, a syndicated weekly author-themed talk radio series) is writing an in-depth biography of Welk, and, as he sees it, the Lennons never intended to be performers—at least not in the traditional sense. "They began singing simply to earn extra money playing little service clubs," such as the Lions Club, which was close to their home in Venice. "As a family singing group, the girls could make ten or fifteen dollars for a performance. But it was never intended to be anything beyond that [but] just a way to earn extra money."

As Worley goes on to explain, while growing up, the Lennon ladies had shared one bedroom, while their brothers shared another, and their parents slept in the living room on a convertible sofa. "So those were close quarters," he says. "And the initial impetus for the girls singing was to earn enough extra money that their father might be able to build an additional room on the house. Those were the beginnings, at least. It was rooted very simply in the practical need to earn a few extra bucks."

The girls' "big break" arrived at the hands of Welk's teenage son Larry, who happened to attend the same high school as Dee Dee. "After hearing the Lennon Sisters sing," Worley explains, the younger Welk pressed his father to consider them for his ABC show, which had recently debuted.

"When the Lennons finally sang for Welk," Worley reveals, "the maestro was home in bed with a cold—a captive audience, if you will. And he was impressed enough to contact George Cates—his producer at Coral Records, and a man who was, in many ways, the musical brains of the Welk organization. Ironically, Cates had recently been hospitalized following a heart attack, but Welk telephoned him, and the girls sang over the wire. So, in the end, both men heard the Lennons while lying in bed—and both were favorably impressed."

Worley calls *Jimmy Durante Presents The Lennon Sisters* "an interesting milestone," explaining how it arrived swiftly on the heels of their opening and closing break with the *Welk* show, whose host had somewhat infamously stated the following about their departure: "The Lennon Sisters are digging their own funeral."

Worley believes the Lennons maintained a considerable fan base through the change, but their "pairing with Durante was bizarre at best." The variety show format was "a fading genre by that time, so the program never really caught on in its Friday timeslot." In hopes of saving the series, ABC moved the Durante/Lennon series to Saturday, with the Welk show as its lead-in. "But the audience just wasn't there."

Worley believes the key to the Lennons' appeal was their "purity of youth," as with most of Welk's musical family. "There was a well-scrubbed innocence that played perfectly against the backdrop of America's social turmoil—particularly in the Heartland. It was a unique convergence of the right kind of talent at just the right time, and Welk would spend the rest of his career trying to duplicate it. He tried several other brother and sister acts in the years that followed, but there was no way to recreate the magic."

Not one member of Welk's troupe ever eclipsed his popularity, but the Lennon Sisters, "at least for a time, came close," says Worley. The lady bandoliers were one of the few Welk performers to receive attention in television fan magazines like *Modern Screen* and *TV Radio Mirror*, "and certainly they were the only performers to land their own network variety series."

Welk was "a notoriously frugal impresario who paid the sisters group scale, meaning they received only one paycheck, instead of four. As their popularity increased, this became a real sticking point for Bill Lennon, the girls' father. And while they did eventually receive individual paychecks, their pay was never really commensurate with their popularity."

Fellow entertainment historian Rob Ray offers this conclusion:

Of all the many singers that Lawrence Welk introduced to America on his long-running show, The Lennon Sisters were the ones that could truly be called "a sensation." They were the epitome of the wholesome younger generation of singers that he showcased. They had by far the most successful careers. He knew they would appeal to his older core audience and hoped that their young, fresh personas would attract new generations to his old-fashioned, clean-cut entertainment. To the extent that so many of us today remain fans would indicate that he succeeded. They were perhaps the only ones whose popularity was so large that they were able to voluntarily leave *The Lawrence Welk Show* for bigger success on their own.

ICONIC FACTS

Birth Data: Born Dianne Barbara (Dee Dee) on December 1, 1939; Margaret Anne (Peggy) on April 8, 1941; Kathleen Mary (Kathy) on August 2, 1943; and Janet Elizabeth Lennon (Janet) on June 15, 1946; all in Los Angeles, California.

Education: Attended Catholic schools.

Family: Parents, William and Isabel Lennon. Married: Dianne/Dee Dee—Dick Gass (1960–present), three children; Peggy—Dick Cathcart (1924–1993), six children, and Robert Felt (1995–present); Kathy—Marlon Clark (1923–1979), Jim Daris (1982–present); Janet—Lee Bernhardi (May 7, 1966, to unknown), three children, and John Bahler (1976–present), two children.

Most Memorable TV Role: Debuted on *The Lawrence Welk Show*, Christmas Eve, 1955. Dee Dee was 16; Peggy was 14; Kathy was 12; Janet was 9; performed a cappella version of "He." The audience loved them and they became show regulars for the next 13 years.

Benchmarks: Dianne and Peggy have retired, but the group appears as a trio, with Janet and Kathy and younger sister Mimi performing in Branson, Missouri, at the Lawrence Welk Champagne Theatre. In 1960, their father was murdered in a golf course parking lot by a deranged fan who thought he was married to Peggy. After Dianne was married, she and her sister Peggy found themselves pregnant, simultaneously. By this time, the Welk series was now being filmed in color at the Hollywood Palace Theatre, which only had dressing rooms on the second floor. The stairs proved a challenge for both Dianne and Peggy, so the show's producers had constructed a special dressing room on the first floor just for them; it was amusingly called the Stork Club. The Lennons sang for seven U.S. presidents—Eisenhower, Kennedy, Johnson, Nixon, Ford, Carter, and Reagan; they also sang at the funeral of Paul Lynde. The Lennon family includes a total of 11 siblings.

Prime Quotes: Both from Peggy: "In 50 some years of sitting in dressing rooms together, day after day after day, we never talked about singing, only if we really had to. We never, ever considered being The Lennon Sisters as important in our lives. It was a job; we did the best we could do. And yet . . . if we hadn't had the Lennon sisters—we hadn't had to 'be' The Lennon Sisters in order to raise our families—we wouldn't have had 50 years of sharing sisterhood like we did, just day in and day out. Because being a mom, being part of a family, respecting the others' privacy and respecting the others' personal life was more important than being a Lennon Sister." * "The Lawrence Welk Orchestra played wonderful music and, for some viewers, the only entertainment they got was dancing in their living room to *Lawrence Welk* on Saturday night. So that generation, and the generation after, stayed with Welk because it was part of the family dynamic. Their parents still watched it, and they may have been teenagers, saying, 'I don't want to watch it.' But then the Lennon Sisters came on, and we were their age. So they would see us in the movie magazines, you know. I think it was just a part of the

American experience . . . and it was a touchstone to a simpler time." * What Dianne learned from Lawrence Welk: "To always do what you're supposed to do—when you're supposed to do it . . . and to be ready for whatever happens." * More of what Dianne told Mary Lou: "Someday, I'd like to open a little book shop, with a baker on top."

Living Legends.

12

Kathy Garver

(Family Affair)

KATHY GARVER (*FAMILY AFFAIR*)

I've been in the entertainment business my entire life, and I've been
able to endure and persevere because of my family and my education.

—Kathy Garver

Buffy, Jody, and Cissy.

Those are the three names most associated with the classic TV show *Family
Affair*, which first aired on CBS from 1966 to 1971, starring Brian Keith and
Sebastian Cabot as uncle and houseman, respectively. Jody, Buffy, and Cissy were
the young siblings Keith's Uncle Bill adopted, played by Johnny Whitaker, Anissa
Jones, and Kathy Garver. The vibrantly attractive and personable Garver was the
eldest, a teen who attained idol status during the show's run. Fortunately she did
not succumb to the usual pitfalls and challenges that have, at least statistically,
haunted former child stars, including her own *Family Affair* costars Anissa Jones,
who committed suicide at the tender age of 18, and Whitaker, who battled his own
demons with substance abuse.

Instead, Garver, with her Gidget-like girl appeal, carefree personality, and
significant intelligence, has remained consistently happy and healthy before and
after performing on *Family Affair*. She credits her mother and father. "I had good,
hardworking parents, and I come from a well-educated family," which includes two
siblings, including a sister who graduated from UCLA at only age 19. "They are all
wonderful. . . . And they didn't take my money. My father worked as an architect,
and my mother, a registered nurse, [and they] saved every single penny that I
[made on *Family Affair*]. If she loaned me [money], she would write it down and
she would take it back, and I would repay her. So, they were very grounded people.
We all went to Catholic school until the sixth grade. Then my mother put us all
into public school for, as she said, a 'dose of reality.' We got a firm foundation in
our morals and in what's right and wrong."

Garver began her professional career at age eight in the role of a slave in Cecil B. DeMille's epic 1956 film *The Ten Commandments*. "Not the silent version," she muses. "I wasn't a contract child actor, going to school on the set every day. I was just a freelance actor. But my mom encouraged me not to make a big hoopla about that. When I was absent from my regular school, she just said, 'Oh, don't tell people where you [work].' And that worked for me in a couple of ways. First of all, I was not going around telling everyone, 'Oh, look at me—I'm a star' and getting all of that attention! And secondly, it really helped me to develop humility. It took me a while before I was able to trumpet and blow my own horn in many ways."

Garver can't stress enough the importance of everyone getting an education, specifically actors. Not doing so, she says, "makes it very difficult for them to do anything else besides acting. If they are only using their emotions, then they are not using their brains so much. I personally think that the best acting is using both sides of your brain, the analytic part and the more emotional part. You have a broader base."

It's a philosophy she's passed down to her own son, Reid, who is in college and studying business. She tells him, "If you want to be a business entrepreneur, you're going to have to talk to people. You now have to know where Cambodia is. You have to know who a president was. You have to know what our culture is."

Garver is of an independent spirit, which has added to her allure and appeal as an actress, all of which she addresses in her book *Surviving Cissy: My Family Affair of Life in Hollywood* (BearManor Media, 2010). Garver invested her money, primarily in real estate. "I bought a house in Sherman Oaks [California] when I was 23 or 24. My neighbors said: 'Chicken Wednesday (one day), feathers the next.' They didn't like this 23-year-old actor moving in next door to them. But I said, 'Tough!' So I bought a house anyway. And then I purchased some real estate in Burbank."

Garver has remained diverse in her performing. "If I'm not on camera doing a film, then I'm doing an audio book. If I'm not doing an audio book, I'm going to do a stage play. If I'm not doing a stage play, I'm going to write a book. If I'm not writing a book, I'll do [voiceover work on] an animated series. I have found many ways to put myself out there—and not to rely so much on other people. Not even on my husband or, you know, an agent, or whatever. But to make it my own way, which I really think you have to do. You make your own life."

She prides herself on keeping busy. A friend recently joked and said, "Kathy, on your tomb, it's going to say 'Kathy isn't here; she's out on another interview.'"

As to *Family Affair*, Garver assesses, "So many people still watch the show, and remember it as very touching. Even guys cry when they watch the episodes. It was the first dysfunctional family. No, we didn't have a mom and a dad; here was an uncle taking on three kids. And there was a structure to the series, from a creative standpoint. It really followed a classic format, one that was used on everything from *I Love Lucy* to *Laverne & Shirley*. Each episode starts out with a problem, which becomes more complicated, then reaches a climax, and then finally ends with the denouement. The audience always knew what to expect so they weren't startled. They could get into the emotions of the people and what was happening with those particular characters and not wonder, 'Well, why are we back on the street? That problem was solved. So, why are they doing this?'"

"One thing about *Family Affair*," she adds, "is that the unique pace with which it was filmed . . . it was very slow, but lingering, with great big close-ups. Every episode was almost like a movie. And you got to know those characters. One of our producers, Edmond Hartmann, had done so many things, including working with Abbott & Costello, as well as Bob Hope and Walter Matthau. And he would say, 'Acting is all through the eyes; you act through your eyes. The soul is the window through the eyes!' That was part of the great, big close-ups on our show, which allowed the audience to get to know our characters."

Such an elegantly filmed format also allowed the *Family Affair* audience to appreciate the many appealing characteristics of Kathy Garver.

ICONIC FACTS

Birth Data: Born Kathleen Marie Garver on December 13, 1945, in Long Beach, California.

Education: Graduated from Pacific High School in 1966, and from UCLA with a bachelor's degree in speech and a minor degree in psychology; went on to earn a master's degree in theater arts; also attended the Royal Academy of Dramatic Art in London.

Family: Parents, Hayes Gilbert, an architect, and Rosemary Garver, a registered nurse; married David Travis (1981–present); they have one son, Reid Garver Travis.

Most Memorable TV Role: Cissy Davis, the teenage niece of Brian Keith's Uncle Bill Davis on *Family Affair* (NBC, 1966–1971).

Benchmarks: First major role was as a slave in *The Ten Commandments*. As she explains, "It was a great entrée into the movie world. My agent was Hazel McMillan—who was the mother of Gloria McMillan, who was in *Our Miss Brooks*, the radio show and then the TV show," the latter in which Garver appeared; also appeared in *Night of the Hunter* and many episodic series like *Sheriff of Cochise*; has provided voiceover work for several animated series and films, including *Apollo 13* and *Ransom*; won an Audie Award for Excellence in audio recording for her narration of *The World's Shortest Stories* and for directing author Amy Tan in the reading of her book *The Opposite of Fate*. Garver has recorded more than 60 audio books. She is president of the Family Affair Foundation, which provides reading companions to the elderly and at-risk youth.

Prime Quotes: "The hardest thing is being accepted as someone who has depth. Fortunately, my parents stressed education and normalcy all through my childhood and during my *Family Affair* days. In learning to think and work independently, I [now] firmly believe in hoisting one's own sails."

A Living Legend.

13

Maureen McCormick

(The Brady Bunch)

MAUREEN MCCORMICK (*THE BRADY BUNCH*)

> Playing Marcia was a double-edged sword . . . it always will be
> whenever you play a character like that. . . . You will be known as that
> character forever.
>
> —Maureen McCormick

Maureen McCormick played Marcia Brady on ABC's *The Brady Bunch*, which
aired from 1969 to 1974. Like *Star Trek*, *The Brady Bunch* took on a life of its own,
becoming a super hit in syndicated reruns, and then in various sequels.

With her near-hypnotic breathy voice, Maureen's Marcia became every teen
boy's dream girl, and every teen girl's idol. McCormick's Marcia was hot, before
the word "hot" was used to describe hot. She was svelte, sexy, and worked her
hip-hugging bell-bottom jeans like no other of her generation; and she bared her
midriff decades before Britney Spears made a billion dollars for doing so. *Brady
Bunch* enthusiast, or "Bunchie," Pat McFadden explains why McCormick stands as
the optimum Brady girl:

> I don't mean to shortchange Jan [played by Eve Plumb] and Cindy [Susan
> Olsen], it's just that they didn't blossom quite as dynamically as Maureen
> McCormick's Marcia did, either physically or aesthetically—not their fault, they
> were younger, and had the series continued a few more seasons, Marcia might
> have moved out to college and given her sisters more of a chance, but it wasn't
> to be. Marcia was always leading the pack, and truly was the most important
> woman of the show. It's hard to believe now, but the now antiquated episode
> in which she is caught on the TV news approving of "Women's Lib" was, at the
> time, actually considered too controversial to be repeated in some markets.
>
> Marcia was the sole character of the show that the writers, whether
> they realized it or not, could fashion as the representative of the new women
> of the liberated generation. And Carol [the Brady mom, played by Florence
> Henderson], unapologetically settled in her role as housewife and mom, was

clearing the path for her eldest daughter to step into Mary Tyler Moore's shoes and make it after all. Maureen McCormick had it and knew how to use it. Who cares that she lost the attic [room] battle and didn't win the better driver contest? We all knew that she was the bigger person for letting Greg [Barry Williams] have the room first, and that even though she flatfooted that pedal and broke that stupid egg, she was smarter than Greg could hope to be.

McFadden goes on to explain how McCormick and Henderson have been and remain the most sought-after interviews of all the show's performers. "People are still fascinated by them," he says. "We are still devoted to the other performers in a *Where-are-they-now?* curiosity. But we want to actually reunite with Florence and Maureen as though they are actual relatives."

According to McFadden, there is an iconic moment in the original *Brady* series that exemplifies why. In the segment "The Show Must Go On," which originally aired on November 3, 1972, Marcia and Greg recruit their parents to perform with them in Westdale High's Family Frolic Night. Greg and Mike have to improvise and come up with an awkwardly funny way to revive a stale Longfellow poem forced upon them, but McFadden says Carol and Marcia have "zero trouble" performing "Together (Wherever We Go)" from the Broadway play, "Gypsy."

"Totally believable as mother and daughter, they also showcase the charisma of the actresses playing them."

ICONIC FACTS

Birth Data: Born Maureen Denise McCormick on August 5, 1956, in Encino, California.

Education: William Howard Taft High school in Woodland Hills, California.

Family: Parents, Richard and Irene McCormick; has three brothers: Michael, Dennis, and Kevin. Married Michael Cummings (1985–present); they have one daughter, Natalie Michelle Cummings.

Most Memorable TV Role: Marcia Brady on *The Brady Bunch* (ABC, 1969–1974).

Benchmarks: At age six, Maureen won the Baby Miss San Fernando Valley beauty pageant. At age seven, she performed in her first live stage production and, within a year, she was the go-to girl for TV commercials and sitcoms. In addition to ads for Barbie and Kool-Aid, she appeared on shows like *Bewitched* and *My Three Sons*. She also did voiceover recordings for a dozen Mattel talking dolls. Maureen provided the voice for Mattel's newly designed Chatty Cathy doll in 1970. When The Brady Kids became a singing group on the side (along with having their own Saturday morning cartoon), producers noticed her special talent for singing and encouraged her to record a number of solo tracks, some of which turned up later on the LP *Chris Knight and Maureen McCormick*. Years later, she attempted to revive her singing career with the 1995 Country CD *When You Get A Little Lonely*. Immediate post-*Brady* TV appearances included *Happy Days*, *Harry O*, and *The Streets of San Francisco*. Years later she was featured in the reality series *Outsider's Inn* on Country Music Television. In 2009, she released her autobiography *Here's the Story: Surviving Marcia Brady and Finding My True Voice* (Harper Collins), which stayed on the New York Times Best Seller list for three weeks. In the book, she admitted that for many years, starting in her teens, she suffered from bulimia.

Prime Quotes: "I'll always be struck by how much a part of people's lives Marcia is and always will be. But now, I'm not bothered by the connection. It took most of my life, countless mistakes, and decades of pain and suffering to reach this point of equanimity and acceptance."

A Living Legend.

14

Mary McDonough

(The Waltons)

True beauty is the ability to connect to one's life purpose and then share that passion with others from the inside out.

—Mary McDonough

Three actresses played the sisters on *The Waltons*, one of television's most realistic family shows, which originally aired on CBS in the 1970s. Judy Norton Taylor was Mary Ellen Walton, the oldest and tomboy toughest of the trio. You didn't want to fool with Mary Ellen. She was sensitive and later became a physician, but in her teens, she could wrestle to the ground even the strongest boy in the county. Kami Cotler played Elizabeth Walton, the youngest and most nurturing and optimistic of the three; all she ever wanted was the family to stay together forever.

Then there was Erin Walton, the middle sister as portrayed by Mary McDonough.

For many teenage fanboys of the series, Erin was the hottest and most kissable sister in the money-poor/love-rich family on the show, which was set in the timberland of southern Virginia, during the mid to late 1930s depression era. Her sense of romance and fancy was frequently entangled, and she fell in love at the drop of a dime. But she was no less endearing. As compellingly played by McDonough, Erin had her share of boyfriends on the show, but she didn't suffer fools gladly. She may have had a different romantic interest on what appeared to be a weekly basis, but that didn't mean she'd tolerate any guff from anyone, beau or otherwise.

At various points in the series, Richard Thomas as John-Boy, the eldest Walton son (and the show's aspiring writer and narrative voice, literally) left Walton's Mountain for the green-less but more professional literary pastures of New York; Mary Ellen married (twice), and their mother, Olivia Walton (lovingly played by the Emmy-winning Miss Michael Learned), took temporary leave due to an illness. In each case, Erin stepped up to the plate and became a far cry from the airheaded brainless beauty persona that was one-too-many times displayed by the TV teen set through the years.

McDonough's Erin blossomed from an adorable young girl into a beautiful young woman, and she contributed to running the Walton household in a leadership role. She was one of the first Walton children to find work outside the home, as a telephone operator for Fanny Tantum (who was played by Sheila Allen, widow to producer Irwin Allen, of TV's *Time Tunnel* and the 1972 feature film *The Poseidon Adventure*). As McDonough explains, Tantum was "a little busy body and listened in sometimes [on the phone conversations of others]. But she was sweet and supportive of Erin and her job."

In short, Erin had it together—and she was put together by the talented and intelligent McDonough, who had her own vision and definition of the character. As the actress explains today:

> Erin knew that there were other things more important than winning a beauty contest; it's who she was on the inside that mattered most. . . . And I know she always lost all the beauty contests . . . but I do love hearing that succinct list of how she grew beyond her looks. She worked outside the home . . . she took over the [military's defense plan] . . . and in the end, she even [raised her voice against various injustices when she had to]. She really did have more of a spine than I thought she had when playing her.

As to her inclusion as a female icon for this book, McDonough was surprised, shocked, and somewhat amused. She herself now has a teenage daughter, who has said, "Mom, it's really creepy. Whenever I tell one of my teachers or the parents of one of my friends who you are, the dad will say, 'Oh—I had *a big crush* on her.'"

However, McDonough struggled with her self-image as Erin, and wrote brilliantly about those struggles in her best-selling book *Lessons from the Mountain:*

MARY MCDONOUGH (*THE WALTONS*)

What I Learned from Erin Walton (Kensington Books, 2011). As she continues to assess:

> What I hear from people now is, "I always loved you," and I see it on my Facebook fan page all the time. People are always saying "I had a crush on you" or "You were my ideal girl." But it's not me . . . it was Erin . . . and yes . . . there wasn't a lot of makeup. I never thought I was pretty or described myself as a classic beauty, but I think people could relate to her because I'm a very All-American girl. I'm not Sophia Loren. I'm not Audrey Hepburn. I have freckles, and I think my look is very accessible because of that. I always hear, "Oh, you look like my sister!" "You look like my cousin!" "You look like my college roommate!" I call myself very middle-of-the-road looking. And I think part of the appeal is that I never thought of myself as beautiful.

One of McDonough's favorite episodes in the series had to do with how Erin cared for one of John-Boy's friends who returned from the army in a wheelchair. McDonough received letters from Vietnam veterans who said, "I wish there were girls like you in my town who would go on a date with a guy who has no legs." McDonough viewed that as a huge display of compassion from all those concerned . . . from Erin toward the disabled soldier . . . from the TV viewers toward Erin . . . and from the more applicable viewers toward Mary McDonough. The actress also received a significant amount of letters about Erin being so virtuous. "I think in our country, at that time, during the hippie movement . . . Erin represented a certain type of ideal of a girl who waited . . . and I think that that was very appealing to people as well."

It's as if people believe they already know Mary . . . or at least think they know her by way of watching her play Erin on *The Waltons*. McDonough:

That's true. . . . People *do* feel like they know me, and I am very accessible.
When I look at myself in pictures with people on my Facebook fan page, it's like
. . . I'm all over people. They just *climb right in*, right? And sometimes I look at
that, and say, "I shouldn't be like that. I should be more reserved and a little bit
more circumspect." But when I see pictures of me literally with my arms around
people, holding them or they have their arms around me, and it's like we've
known each other for years.

Mary also enjoys her interactions with fans at her various book signings. "I
look at other [authors] who took book signings . . . and they don't touch people.
One hand is on the book, and the other hand is holding the pen . . . and they're
leaning toward the person."

But the actress does more. When she is approached by fans at one of the
book signings, or one of the autograph shows that have become popular in recent
years, she makes every attempt to listen to as many single personal stories or
experiences that fans have of *The Waltons*; even as her own husband advises her
otherwise. "You can't be all things to all people," he tells her. "You've got to
reserve a little bit."

In the fall of 2012, a special *Waltons* 40th Anniversary event was held in Los
Angeles, and anyone who had anything to do with the show, as a star, guest star, or
producer in any way, was in attendance. "That night," McDonough recalls, "I never
sat down. I never had a bite to eat. There were so many people coming up to me
and taking pictures and getting autographs. I mean, after midnight, my husband
finally said to my daughter, 'Go get your mom, because we're going to have to take
her home.'"

However, one fan put a stop to that, saying, "She's not going anywhere! I don't
have her autograph yet."

Like Erin Walton, Mary McDonough knows her own mind. When she gets tired, she gets "quiet. When I'm dealing with my life, I don't check my e-mails as much. And I *do* need to scale back a little bit more to recharge." But then she hears once more, "Are you tired?" to which she replies:

> Here's the thing . . . sometimes there are hundreds of people telling me that they enjoyed my book, or that it made a difference in their life and they want to tell me something nice. Who gets to have that in life?! Not very many people. So I appreciate it and enjoy it all!

McDonough feels "incredibly blessed and fortunate" to have been on *The Waltons*. She loves it when "people tell their stories or when somebody tells me something special about Erin or even about my book. I mean, that's why we're all here, right? It's why I wrote the book? To help people . . . to touch people. The inscription in my book says, 'To anyone who has ever felt they weren't enough.' I know we are in this together and my lesson was to learn I was enough. Whenever I get a message or a post, I am reminded of the lesson and the journey to actually feeling that I am enough. We all are."

The world is clearly a better place because of Erin Walton—and Mary McDonough.

ICONIC FACTS

Birth Data: Born Mary Elizabeth McDonough on May 4, 1961, in Van Nuys, California.

Education: Graduated from Chaminade College Preparatory School in West Hills, California; attended UCLA.

Family: Parents, Elizabeth Murray and Lawrence McDonough; married Rob Wickstrom (1988–1996), with whom she has one daughter, Sydnee Wickstrom; Don Couch (2011–present).

Most Memorable TV Role: Erin Walton on *The Waltons* (1971–1997).

Benchmarks: Mary has made a number of notable guest-star and semiregular appearances on many renowned television shows since *The Waltons*, including *The New Adventures of Old Christine*, *Boston Legal*, *Will & Grace*, *The West Wing*, and *Ally McBeal*, among others. Her numerous TV-movies include *Christmas at Cadillac Jack's* (2007) and *Lake Effect* (2012). Multitalented, Mary is also a TV producer and director, as well as a public speaker and workshop leader. In her seminars, she addresses topics like personal change and growth.

Prime Quotes: "We were about three years before *Little House [on the Prairie]*. At the time there were no family shows like it. *The Waltons* kind of paved the way for others to come on the air. We were a large family living in the depression and *Little House* was a small family living on a prairie. There are some similarities. They both have morals and lessons that they teach in their storylines. Having three generations living under the same roof is a little bit different. Their storekeeper had a kooky wife and so did ours. We both have similar fan bases also."

A Living Legend.

15

Melissa Gilbert

(Little House on the Prairie)

> There's a part of me that's always going to be Laura [Ingalls].
>
> I think every girl has a Laura in them.
>
> —Melissa Gilbert

Melissa Gilbert was one of 500 young girls who auditioned for the role of Laura Ingalls Wilder in the classic NBC TV series *Little House on the Prairie* (1974–1983), and she was the only one whose screen test was sent to be considered by the networks.

That says volumes about Gilbert's star appeal. Like fellow former child star (and female icon of television) Kristy McNichol, Gilbert never had a lesson in acting, a profession she began at the tiny age of three, when she did TV commercials for infant clothing. As she told Peggy Herz in 1979, "I love acting. I never get tired of it."

As McNichol found it challenging to cry as a child actress, Gilbert discovered it was relatively easy on *Little House*, which was creatively supervised by its male lead: Michael Landon (Little Joe on *Bonanza*, NBC, 1959–1973). "You just think of something sad," she explained to Herz. "Then you cry." For Melissa, laughing was the more difficult emotional activity to fabricate as an actress. "Sometimes you can't think of anything funny," she said. "It's hard to laugh and not sound like you're forcing it. It's especially hard to laugh when you have to do a scene over and over."

As to how she made herself laugh on cue, she said, "I imagine everybody in their underwear," a technique that just so happened to be utilized by another former female child star and TV icon, Maureen McCormick (if in character as Marcia Brady on *The Brady Bunch*, when Marcia was nervous about taking her driving test).

It was Michael Landon's daughter Leslie Landon who told Melissa that she had won the role of Laura on *Little House* when the two of them were standing in line at their school cafeteria. All of that seems appropriate, too, as the father Landon played Melissa's dad, Charles Ingalls, on the show. "He was very much like a 'second father' to me," the actress told Herz in 1972. "My own father passed away when I was 11, so, without really officially announcing it, Michael really stepped in."

Regarding offscreen life and emotions with *Prairie* in general, Gilbert once offered two conclusive thoughts:

Not a day goes by that I don't think about it and burst into tears. It's like stepping through a looking glass. There's a part of me that's always going to be Laura. I think every girl has a Laura in them.

It reminds people of what we as humans and Americans are capable of if we do it together. We tend to live in bubbles. . . . There is very little real sense of community anymore. This show reminds people of that.

ICONIC FACTS

Birth Data: Born Melissa Ellen Gilbert on May 8, 1964, in Los Angeles, California.

Education: The Buckley School, Sherman Oaks, California.

Family: Parents, David Darlington and Kathy Wood; Melissa was put up for adoption and adopted by Paul Gilbert (actor and comedian) and Barbara Crane (dancer/actress). Her younger sister is actress-turned-talk-show-host Sara Gilbert (*Roseanne*, *The Talk*). Melissa married Bo Brinkman (1988–1994); actor Bruce Boxleitner (1995–2011); actor Timothy Busfield (April 2013 to present). She has two biological children: Dakota Paul Brinkman and Michael Garrett Boxleitner.

Most Memorable TV Role: Laura Ingalls Wilder on *Little House on the Prairie*
(NBC, 1974–1984), for which she appeared in 191 of the 205 episodes (more
than any other actor on the series).

Benchmarks: Michael Landon, Jr., had escorted Melissa to her senior prom in
1981. In 1998, Melissa was inducted (as a cast member of *Prairie*) into the
Hall of Great Western Performers of the National Cowboy and Western
Heritage Museum. She has appeared in several highly rated TV-movies;
is also known for providing the original voice of Batgirl in *Batman: The
Animated Series*; and served two terms as president of the Screen Actors
Guild (2001–2005). In 2009, she authored the memoir *Prairie Tale*, in which
she discussed her struggles with alcoholism and drug abuse. While playing
the role of Caroline "Ma" Ingalls in the touring musical "Little House on
the Prairie," a visit to the doctor revealed that she had been working with
a broken back for months. On July 22, 2010, Gilbert underwent surgery
to replace a disc as well as fuse a vertebra in her lower spine. The surgery
was described as a complete success. In 2011, she played Vera Parks in the
TV-movie *The Christmas Pageant*. In March 2012, she joined the cast of
season 14 of *Dancing with the Stars*. During week four, while dancing the
paso doble, she fell and hit her head and suffered a mild concussion and was
taken to a hospital.

Prime Quotes: "The mother/daughter relationship is one of mankind's great
mysteries, and for womankind, it can be hellaciously complicated. My
mother and I are quintessential examples of the rewards and frustrations,
and the joys and infuriations it can yield." * From her book: "I saw an
opportunity at a time in my career when, like many female actors my age,
opportunities are drying up left and right. So for me to have a chance to
do something new and create a new facet to my career at 45 is a blessing

I just couldn't ignore." * "My mother, whom I love dearly, has continually revised my life story within the context of a complicated family history that includes more than the usual share of divorce, stepchildren, dysfunction, and obfuscation. I've spent most of my adult life attempting to deconstruct that history and separate fact from fiction." * "I made my share of mistakes, which I think of as the stones I stepped on to get to where I am today, and through luck, hard work, serious reflection, and a desire to face the truth about myself, I ended up at a place where I now enjoy the peace that comes from allowing myself not to be perfect."

A Living Legend.

Valerie Bertinelli

(One Day at a Time)

VALERIE BERTINELLI (*ONE DAY AT A TIME*)

If you say you're fat, all of a sudden people like you!

—Valerie Bertinelli

No teenage star, female or male, ever delivered a line quite like Valerie Bertinelli as Barbara Cooper on the groundbreaking sitcom *One Day at a Time*, which aired on CBS from 1975 to 1984. "Precocious" couldn't begin to describe Barbara, and "young genius" couldn't begin to define Bertinelli and her performance as the character. The wordplay is endless when it comes to the actress and her multitalents, as "pro" and "old soul" might seem to be the most succinct ways to pinpoint her abilities; that, and "hot," as in *Hot in Cleveland*. The latter is the sitcom in which she went on to star decades later (alongside Jane Leeves, Wendy Malick, and Betty White).

On *Time*, Bertinelli's Barbara was younger sister to Mackenzie Phillips. In reality, Bertinelli and Phillips are approximately the same age. As Valerie revealed to author Peggy Herz in *TV's Fabulous Faces* (Scholastic, 1977), she was only five months younger than Mackenzie. "When the show started, I was supposed to be 14. But after we'd been on the air 13 weeks they made me 15 and a half! My [onscreen] sister [Phillips] is supposed to be 17."

Barbara was born in Wilmington, Delaware, and while working on *One Day at a Time*, she lived in Northridge, California, with her family, which included three brothers, one older and two younger. "We left Delaware when I was eight," she told Herz. For her at the time, it was "kind of scary to move" at such a young age. Her father worked for General Motors, and she was forced to leave all her friends to commence a new beginning in Michigan, to which she had never traveled. "Once we got there," Valerie said, "I liked it. We lived near a ski resort. My dad taught me to ski. We moved as my dad got promoted to better jobs. We also moved to Los Angeles, then to Oklahoma, and finally back here to California."

Valerie was shy as a child and never thought of becoming an actress until her family moved to LA. As she went on to tell Herz, the family noticed an ad in the newspaper for an acting school, and she enrolled in classes mostly because her father wanted her to become more outgoing. However, at first, she was somewhat apprehensive about the theatrical lessons. "I was scared to death. My first audition was for a deodorant commercial. My mother took me to the audition. I was so scared. All the girls who were there looked about three years older. I was 12 then."

She didn't get a part in the commercial, but she kept trying. "You have to keep trying. You may go on 100 interviews and not get anything. I [would] always tell myself, 'Well, better luck next time.' A lot of it is luck. There are so many talented people around."

Valerie was very close to her family. "They . . . really kept me going. They gave me confidence to keep trying."

When she wasn't working, Valerie was a junior at Granada Hills High School. She liked math and English, and she loved to play football. "I play[ed] touch, tackle, flag—everything," she said. "I play[ed] it in P.E. [physical education], and sometimes people from the studio and I [would] go out on Saturdays and play. My brothers taught me how to play. I [was] pretty good!"

Today, she excels in her multitude of talents, not the least of which is being one of Hollywood's most likable actresses and personalities.

ICONIC FACTS

Birth Data: Born Valerie Anne Bertinelli on April 23, 1960, in Wilmington, Delaware.

VALERIE BERTINELLI (*ONE DAY AT A TIME*)

Education: Clarkston Middle School, Clarkston, Michigan; attended Granada
Hills High School and studied acting at the Tami Lynn School of Artists, Los
Angeles, California.

Family: Parents, Nancy and Andy Bertinelli, a General Motors executive. Married
rock guitarist Eddie Van Halen in 1981; they separated in 2001 and divorced in
2007, although not before having one son, Wolfgang.

Most Memorable TV Role: Barbara Cooper Royer in *One Day at a Time* (CBS,
1975–1984).

Benchmarks: Plays Melanie Moretti in the TV Land sitcom *Hot in Cleveland* (2010
to present); appeared on *Hollywood Game Night* and was a judge on *Iron Chef
America*. Valerie's long and celebrated career has expanded to include roles as
an equally beloved TV personality, spokesperson, and best-selling author. For
a time, she was considered one of the Queens of TV-movies, beginning with
small-screen gems like *Shattered Vows* (1984), on into the miniseries *I'll Take
Manhattan* (1987) to *Personally Yours* (2000), among several more. Her other
regular series roles include *Café American* (NBC, 1993–1994), and a stint as a
rookie angel on the last few seasons of *Touched by an Angel* (CBS, 1994–2004).
She's ranked number 29 on VH1's list of 100 Greatest Kid Stars. She rejected
several feature film roles in the 80s because of gratuitous nudity.

Prime Quotes: "I don't think I was quite aware of what was really going on in my
life." * "Everybody complains that people are so flaky in LA. I'd rather be
flaky than mean." * "If you say you're fat, all of a sudden people like you!"
* "Happiness is a choice. You can choose to be happy. There's going to be
stress in life, but it's your choice whether to let it affect you or not."

A Living Legend.

Kristy McNichol

(Family)

KRISTY MCNICHOL (*FAMILY*)

I [wanted] to be a kid at 18 instead of being a young woman.

—Kristy McNichol

Former child star Kristy McNichol worked her craft magically and what appeared to be effortlessly when she played the budding young Leticia "Buddy" Lawrence on the 1970s ABC drama *Family*. But it was clear that she was a star from the minute she hit the screen in the spring of 1976, when the series commenced with a limited run of only six episodes.

Riding on the monumental success of ABC's two hit miniseries *Roots* and *Rich Man, Poor Man*, and doubling as a midseason replacement series, *Family* was an instant elegant hit. From producers Aaron Spelling and Leonard Goldberg, the show stood out from the pack of other programs that Spelling/Goldberg had brought to the small screen. Minus the violence of their police shows like *The Rookies*, and missing the camp of Spelling's *The Love Boat* (which he coproduced with Douglas S. Cramer), *Family* returned quality drama and talent to the small screen and, of the latter, McNichol became exhibit A.

With a stellar surrounding cast that included fellow female icon Meredith Baxter (a few years following her TV series debut with *Bridget Loves Bernie*), McNichol also got to work with costars like Gary Frank (who played her older brother), as well as distinguished acting vets James Broderick and Sadie Thompson (her parents on the show).

Around the same time, McNichol appeared in other TV shows, like the *ABC Afterschool Specials*, *The Pinballs*, and *Me & Dad's New Wife*. She was also one of the youngest cohosts that talk show titan Mike Douglas invited to share his stage. She rarely became nervous when on camera, but, as she told journalist Peggy Herz in 1978, she admitted to some anxiety when she appeared with Douglas, mostly because it was her first talk show appearance. "If you make a mistake on TV, you can always stop and start over. Even on live TV I wouldn't get nervous. Most of the people watching you like you. They're not going to hate you if you make a mistake."

But she didn't make any gaffes when doing *The Mike Douglas Show*, and certainly, she clearly got it right in playing Buddy on *Family*, as both the home viewers and her Hollywood peers completely embraced her in the role. During its original run, *Family* was a ratings winner for ABC, and McNichol earned two Emmys for playing Buddy: a role she never thought was difficult to play because, as she also told Herz, "I see a lot of myself in Buddy."

What she did find challenging at the time was crying on camera. "A director says to me, 'Walk in a room, act like you're real mad, and then start crying.' I just can't seem to do that, especially when I'm happy—and I'm happy most of the time. I can cry, but it just takes time to work up to it."

That was in 1978. For an additional profile of the actress one year later, Herz assessed that McNichol "was an actress with genuine, natural talent," who never once took an acting class. Years later, and following her other regular role on TV—on the sitcom *Empty Nest* (NBC, 1988–1995), McNichol battled bipolar disorder. As such, sadness became a prevalent emotion.

She beat her demons and has recently made rare appearances to meet and greet fans at the popular autograph shows that are increasing across the country.

In the summer of 2013, she appeared at the Hollywood Show in Los Angeles. At one point, she was asked by a fan how she knew instinctively what to do as an actress, how she performed theatrical techniques that performers twice her age sometimes never even attempt to visualize.

Her response: "I don't know."

Of course she didn't know.

Genius most usually never recognizes itself.

ICONIC FACTS

Birth Data: Born Christina Ann McNichol on September 11, 1962, in Los Angeles, California.

Education: Attended North Hollywood High School in North Hollywood, California.

Family: Parents, Carolyn McNichol Lucas, a business manager and actress, and James Vincent "Jim" McNichol, Sr., a carpenter; has one brother, Jimmy McNichol, also an actor. Her significant other is Martie Allen (1991–present).

Most Memorable TV Role: Letitia "Buddy" Lawrence on *Family* (ABC, 1976–1980), for which she earned two Emmy Awards as Best Supporting Actress in a Dramatic Series (in 1977 and 1979).

Benchmarks: In 1988, she was cast as Barbara Weston on the sitcom *Empty Nest,* a spin-off of *The Golden Girls*; made early TV guest appearances, including on *Starsky & Hutch* and *The Bionic Woman*. In 1992, she retired from acting after being diagnosed with bipolar disorder. On January 6, 2012, she publicly announced she is a lesbian and had been living with her partner, Martie Allen, for 20 years. She teaches at a private school in Los Angeles and devotes much of her time to charity work.

Prime Quotes: "A lot of people have wondered what I've been up to. I retired from my career after 24 years. My feeling was that it was time to play my biggest part—Myself! I must say that it has been the best thing that ever happened to me. So many fans are disappointed that I'm not currently acting; however, some may not realize that the process I'm in at this time is necessary and vital for my personal happiness and well-being." * "From the time I was very young, I was a professional, making money and assuming responsibilities. I didn't live the life of a child. I was living the life of a 30-year-old."

A Living Legend.

PART III

THE COUNTRY GIRLS

18

Donna Douglas
(The Beverly Hillbillies)

I was very fortunate with Elly May. She was a slice right out of my own life. I knew how to play her in a second.

—Donna Douglas

Donna Douglas is an honest-to-goodness Southern Belle who displayed a heartbreaking natural beauty in playing her most famous TV role as the hot, hollering, rope-wearing, whistle-happy, and critter-cuddling Elly May Clampett on the hit CBS TV classic *The Beverly Hillbillies*, a country comedy which originally aired from 1963 to 1971.

Margaret Wendt offers her insight on Douglas:

Donna Douglas as Elly May was just beautiful. You just loved her . . . and loved everything she said . . . whether it was to Jethro (Max Baer), Uncle Jed (Buddy Ebsen), or Granny (Irene Ryan). She didn't overplay the part. She played Elly May like she was indeed Elly May. Her body was gorgeous—and when she wore those clothes . . . she wore them realistically . . . and gave the impression as if she really

did come from the hills . . . but country livin'. She just looked natural in the role
. . . she looked innocent and sweet and you wanted to know her. And everyone
always remembers Elly May. And it's important to remember that anytime there
was a similar female look in a movie like *Smokey and the Bandit*—and even in a TV
show like *The Dukes of Hazzard*, they were all trying to copy Elly May . . . the Daisy
Dukes short-shorts, etc. Donna Douglas created a look with Elly May that many
tried to re-create over the years but were never able to do it.

Douglas as Elly May became one of the first female blond icons in TV history,
shortly after Ann Sothern on her same-named series (CBS, 1958–1961), and just
prior to Elizabeth Montgomery's first twitch on *Bewitched* (which debuted on ABC,
September 17, 1964) and Barbara Eden's initial blink on *I Dream of Jeannie* (NBC,
September 1965), and a decade or so before Farrah Fawcett on *Charlie's Angels* (ABC,
Fall 1976) and Suzanne Somers in *Three's Company* (ABC, January 1977).

Born and raised in Pride, Louisiana (today a Baton Rouge suburb, then
a timberland), and after graduating from the local high school (now known as
Redemption High), Donna went on to win, unsurprisingly, more than a few beauty
contests. She also pursued a cross-country acting career from New York to Los
Angeles, making several sexy TV guest appearances on shows like *Dr. Kildare*, *77
Sunset Strip*, *Route 66*, *Surfside 6*, *The Defenders*, and more.

A particularly memorable and non-*Hillbillies* stand-out performance was her
quite *visual* take as the conflicted Janet Tyler in "Eye of the Beholder," a fan-
favorite segment of Rod Serling's *The Twilight Zone* (CBS, 1959–1964).

In "Eye," which aired November 11, 1960, Donna's Tyler lived in some
future time—on some Earth-like planet where, when we meet her, she's already
undergone several experimental surgeries to alter her looks, enough so to fit in
with society. The story twist, a *Zone* benchmark, was that, to us—the viewer—her
appearance was more than acceptable. In fact, she was exceptional looking. But

not to her fellow citizens, whose faces were presented as pig-like (with makeup designed by John Chambers who, in 1968, won an Oscar for the similarly designed facial applications on display in *Planet of the Apes*, the script for which *Zone*'s Serling had adapted from the novel by Pierre Boulle).

Douglas brought a specific sincerity to every role, including the *Twilight* performance as Tyler. Although she did not speak a line of dialogue in the segment (Tyler's voice was provided by Maxine Stuart when the character's face was fully bandaged), once unmasked, Donna's eyes delivered varied forms of expression. It's an appearance that's garnered quite a following over the years. "People ask me about Janet all the time," she says. "Rod Serling was a dear man, and I enjoyed working on that show. It was really my first dramatic part, and it was rather easy." Ironically combining her real-life slang with Elly May's, Donna concludes of playing Janet Tyler, "She was just so disappointed in how she looked. She just wanted to be the same as everyone else—and we all feel that from time to time, I reckon."

"I'm amazed at the huge following with *The Twilight Zone*. People bring photos and masks to [sci-fi/classic TV] conventions. They dress up as the characters. After all these years, it's something else."

Soon after "Eye" aired, Douglas won the role of Elly May on *Hillbillies*, and her female TV icon status was born—years after her own birth—into a real life which, in more ways than one, mirrored Elly's fictional existence. Douglas explains:

> Elly just had a good sense of family, knew right from wrong; she had the same upbringing that I did; back then you had respect for your parents, elders, community. We had the same values, morals, and love of critters. They are like children, they can sense whether a person is sincere, they are a good judge of character!

DONNA DOUGLAS (*THE BEVERLY HILLBILLIES*)

We lived so far out in the country, back of a dirt road; my mom would place me and my brother on a horse and take us to our grandparents that way. Eventually we moved into town, Baton Rouge, where I graduated high school. I was the only girl in my family, an older brother and all male cousins, so I grew up a tomboy, swinging from vines, swimming and playing softball. I was getting ready for Jethro [as played by Max Baer on *Hillbillies*] long before we ever met!

As to being named an icon, she says:

That's a funny word to use on oneself. I never had any desire to be an actress, just a wife and perhaps a mother; those were my thoughts growing up. I only had a pinch of modeling back home prior to leaving for New York. Once there, I slowly built up my portfolio book with photos; got a job here, a job there . . . illustration modeling, products. I knew I didn't want to be a fashion model. However, I could hold up a tube of toothpaste and smile into the camera. I couldn't have spoken a word; that would come later [with *Twilight Zone*]. And in the meantime, one print job led to another. I just considered myself blessed to be working, to be able to send some money home on a regular basis to my parents who were looking after my little boy for me. Plus, it was a steady income. I now have third and fourth generations of fans. People tell me all the time, they wish television shows were made like that today. It makes me happy and proud to have been a part of that. Those were great years for me.

Years that were distinguished by Elly's whistle, which Douglas says, "was all mine, from childhood." As to the rope belt, the actress adds how the prop was placed in "a chance moment in the wardrobe department, and it ended up being a trademark for me!"

As she goes on to explain, over 500 women tested for the role of Elly, and it was narrowed down to six young women on the day of her interview. "They asked if I thought I could play Elly. I was so excited all I could do was nod my head up and down." She was then asked if she could milk a goat, tied up, and she thought, "Well—they were equipped just like those cows back home, so I went for it. When I had to say my lines, the director said, 'Cut! If you don't speak any faster than that, no one but you will be on the 30 min. show.' Back home in Baton Rouge, we tended to draw our speech out."

It was also back home in Baton Rouge where she met her first husband, while playing softball in high school. "I was 17 going on 12 when we got married. I was so unprepared. I had never been anywhere or done nothing. We got married and moved into my room at home with Momma and Daddy. And then my husband got a job out of town and went away."

Instead of going with him, Douglas told him, "I'll just stay here at home until you can come back." After a while he came back. But the marriage didn't work out. They separated while she was expecting their infant son, and they later divorced. "We didn't know how to make the marriage work. I tried to get my life together. I worked as a file clerk for the local police department . . . at a gift shop trying to find my way and raise my little son."

Douglas had also done what she calls "a pinch of modeling," which brought her to New York, and ultimately introduced her to acting. "I thought maybe I'd find something I'd be interested [in], and Momma and Daddy said they would look after my son and I knew what love I had as a child, so I thought things might work out for me."

"Work out" they did, certainly when she was later cast as Elly May, which ultimately solidified her timeless status as a female icon of television—and allowed her many opportunities, namely, to travel extensively and see the world.

During the *Hillbillies* heyday, Douglas was invited to Japan. "The Japanese people loved Elly and the show. It was such an exciting trip. They lined the streets to see me. They're such warm people. It was quite an experience for a little girl who had never been more than 75 miles from home. Now, I've been to Israel more than five times, with 16 cruises, all over the US and Canada. Playing Elly opened a lot of doors for me, and I'm grateful!"

ICONIC FACTS

Birth Data: Born Doris Smith on September 26, 1933, in Pride, Louisiana.

Education: St. Gerard High School, Louisiana.

Family: Parents, Emmett and Elma Smith; married Roland John Bourgeois, Jr. (1949–1954); Robert M. Leeds (1971–1980). She has one son, Danny P. Bourgeois.

Most Memorable TV Role: Elly May Clampett on *The Beverly Hillbillies* (CBS, 1962–1981).

Benchmarks: She was a tomboy and loved animals in her youth (just like Elly May); won beauty contests; was Miss Baton Rouge and Miss New Orleans; appeared in *The Twilight Zone* episode "Eye of the Beholder"; starred in *Frankie and Johnny* with Elvis Presley in 1966. She is semiretired and living in Louisiana. Donna frequently performs as a gospel singer and speaks at churches across America. She has recorded several gospel albums, the first being released in 1982.

Prime Quotes: "*The Beverly Hillbillies* was a story about the American Dream. No matter who tried to slicker us or take advantage of us, we always came out on top. We were never the losers. So the right attitude was important. We set a good example. The hillbillies set high standards." * "I really love pets. They're like children. They know if you really love them or not. You can't fool them." * "I was offered to do a nighttime soap after *The Beverly Hillbillies*. There was so much I didn't want to do because of family values. It was a big hit in a couple weeks, but it didn't matter to me, because I wanted to do a certain caliber of work and didn't want to do garbage." * "Today, I am busy giving back. I speak at churches, ladies groups, and schools; I've done two children's books and my cookbook, my life is full and busy. I still have large turnouts wherever I go to speak. Afterward I visit with the fans, sometimes for hours, which I enjoy. It's nice to hear which episode [of *The Beverly Hillbillies*] people enjoyed or related with."

A Living Legend.

19

Inger Stevens
(The Farmer's Daughter)

> The most horrifying thing for a child is to be different. I fit
> nowhere. I was awkward, shy, clumsy, ugly with freckles and had no
> chance of winning a beauty contest.
>
> —Inger Stevens

She seemed to fit the typical Hollywood star profile, but she was no typical
Hollywood star.

Blond, bright, and sex all over, Inger Stevens possessed a tantalizing appeal
that was defined by both her above-average appearance and intelligence. Her
personal life remained a mystery, which, on one hand, merely lent to her allure. But
on the other hand, she clearly had emotional issues, as evidenced by her apparently
taking her own life by way of a drug overdose. According to John Austin's book
Hollywood's Babylon Women (S.P.I. Books, 1994), in the early hours of April 30,
1970, Stevens's periodic roommate and companion, Lola McNally, found her on
the kitchen floor of her Hollywood Hills home. When her friend called out to
her, Inger opened her eyes, raised her head, and tried to speak but was unable

to say a word. McNally told authorities that she had conversed with Stevens the evening before without any cause for concern. Stevens died in the ambulance en route to the hospital, whereupon medics removed a bandage from her chin that revealed a small portion of what appeared to be fresh blood oozing from a cut that was allegedly relatively fresh. Los Angeles County Coroner Dr. Thomas Noguchi attributed her demise to "acute barbiturate poisoning."

It was a sad ending to the life and career of a promising actress and a sweet but clearly complex human being. As writer Gary Brumburgh has documented in *Classic Images Magazine* (June 16, 2011), Stevens had once offered some keen insight into her psyche, saying: "Once I felt that I was one person at home and the minute I stepped out the door I had to be somebody else. I had a terrific insecurity and extreme shyness that I covered up with coldness. Everybody thought I was a snob. I was really just plain scared."

Maybe so, but Stevens had little fear of performing on stage or in front of the camera, as she had made several appearances on television series, commercials, and in plays until she received what turned out to be her big break in the 1957 feature film *Man on Fire* (starring Bing Crosby). Roles in a few more major movies followed, but she came to prominence on the big screen just as the studio system was collapsing, and when it appeared that her film career was heading south, she had wisely maintained a strong presence on the small screen with heralded performances on respected shows like *The Alfred Hitchcock Hour*, *Route 66*, and (as with fellow female icon Donna Douglas) *The Twilight Zone*, in which she appeared in two episodes: "Lateness of Hour" (originally airing 12–2–60) and "The Hitch Hiker" (1–22–60).

In "Hiker" she played a young woman who, during a cross-country drive alone, becomes increasingly frantic when she sees the same man, thumbing for a ride, mile after mile. In the end, the man turns out to be Death itself. No matter how fast she drives the man is always up ahead, hitching her for a ride.

The paranoid-geared premise for "Hiker" may have resonated with Inger's "fears" offscreen, not to mention her early and untimely appointment with her real-life demise.

Inger later accepted more upbeat roles. One in particular was the perfect TV vehicle for her talents: a small-screen adaptation of the 1947 motion picture *The Farmer's Daughter* (for which Loretta Young had earned an Oscar) that aired on ABC from 1963 to 1966, with the renowned William Windom as her costar.

But it was Inger who took the stellar lead: a quiet, seemingly old-fashioned Minnesota farm girl named Katrina "Katy" Holstrum, who gets a job working in the home of her local congressman, Glen Morley (Windom). Katy's physical allure, gentle heart, and keen mind and instincts worked their magic on the widowed Steve Morley, the congressman's son (played by Mickey Sholdar), his mother (Cathleen Nesbitt), and the household staff (which during just the first season included Philip Coolidge as Cooper, the butler).

As author John Austin pointed out, the lyrics for the show's opening theme posed an intriguing question that may have held and revealed not only the secret to Inger's particular appeal as Katy, but to her allure in general: "Who can resist that gal?"

ICONIC FACTS

Birth Data: Born Ingrid Stensland on October 18, 1934, in Stockholm, Sweden.

Education: Attended Manhattan High School in Manhattan, Kansas, and the Actors Studio in New York.

Family: Parents, Per Gustaf, a high school teacher, and Lisbet Stensland; married Anthony Soglio (1955–1958); Ike Jones (1961–1970, until her death).

INGER STEVENS (*THE FARMER'S DAUGHTER*)

Most Memorable TV Role: Katy Holstrum on *The Farmer's Daughter* (ABC, 1963–1966).

Benchmarks: At 16, worked in burlesque shows in Kansas City, Missouri; worked as a chorus girl and in the Garment District of New York while taking classes at the Actors Studio. She and Rod Steiger were nearly asphyxiated by carbon monoxide fumes while filming a scene from *Cry Terror!* (1958) in a tunnel. (Years later, Steiger said she initially refused medical treatment at the scene and wanted to die.) She once leaped from a crash-landing jet liner minutes before it exploded; ended up committing suicide on April 30, 1970, at the age of 35. After her passing, it was revealed that she had been long married (from 1961) to African American bit actor Ike Jones. The marriage was kept secret to protect her career. The couple was estranged at the time of her death.

Prime Quotes: "A career, no matter how successful, can't put its arms around you. You end up being like Grand Central Station with people just coming and going. And there you are—left all alone."

Passing: April 30, 1970, in Los Angeles of "acute barbiturate intoxication." The Los Angeles County coroner ruled her death a suicide.

20

Linda Kaye Henning, Lori Saunders, Meredith MacRae

(Petticoat Junction)

> I loved being on *Petticoat Junction*.
>
> —Lori Saunders

"Lots of curves, you bet . . . even more when you get—to the junction."

"Petticoat . . . Junction," that is.

So sprang the lyrics from the opening theme song of *Petticoat Junction*, the cozy country comedy that ran on CBS from 1963 to 1970.

The charmingly catchy tune was written by show creator Paul Henning and Curt Massey, who also performed it. Joining Massey were a bevy of female background vocalists who the TV audience could only assume was made up of Billie Jo, Bobbie Jo, and Betty Jo, the three Bradley sisters and daughters of Bea Benaderet's Kate Bradley. Along with older relative Joseph P. Carson (a.k.a. Uncle Joe), played by Edgar Buchanan, they ran the Shady Rest Hotel in the small country town of Hooterville, vaguely located somewhere in the middle part of the country.

Following the success of Henning's *The Beverly Hillbillies*, CBS wanted another similarly bucolic hit series. The writer-producer recalled his wife Ruth's stories of visiting a relative's hotel in Eldon, Missouri, which was located next to a few railroad tracks. Thus, the *Petticoat* premise was born.

In the show's musical theme lyrics, the underlined implication or "train of thought" that ran through the *Junction* like "curves" was manifold. First, there was indeed an actual train, called the Cannonball, that curved around the tiny town on a twisting railroad track (and trains, at least according to Sigmund Freud, have long held erotic undertones). The term "curve" could later be attributed with a wink and a nod to the *curvaceous* Bradley siblings, who, as healthy young women, were blessed with particularly attractive physical traits that were slyly referenced in the title of their hometown (i.e., Hooterville). The girls are clearly skinny-dipping in Hooterville's water tower, which is located next to the Shady Rest. As their mother Kate warns them in the pilot episode, "Someday that train is going to come along, drain your swimming pool, and leave you high, dry, and bare!"

From 1963 to 1965, the first two black-and-white seasons, the Bradley girls were played by Jeannine Riley as Billie Jo, Pat Woodell as Bobbie Jo, and Linda Kaye (later Linda Kaye Henning) as Betty Jo. By the third season, the show's first year in color, Riley and Woodell had left, and Gunilla Hutton and Lori Saunders stepped into the roles of Billie Jo and Bobbi Jo, respectively. By the fall of the fourth season, Meredith MacRae (daughter of Sheila MacRae, *The Jackie Gleason Show*) replaced Hutton as Billie Jo.

It's unclear why Riley exited the show, but it's been said she left to pursue a career in feature films. Woodell has gone on record saying she departed the series to pursue a singing career, which she said was her true calling. Hutton apparently was late responding to calls to the set for the fourth season, When Meredith joined Saunders and Henning they ultimately became the best-known female threesome of the entire six actresses cast on the series.

Each actress delivered her own unique interpretation of the young female Bradley persona, at times intermingling reality with fantasy. Following are some good examples of how actors can influence the writers on a continuing series.

Linda Kaye Henning says on the Henning Estate's *Petticoat Junction* DVD that the original choice for the role of Billie Jo was a young Sharon Tate (who was tragically murdered at the hands of Charles Manson). But when her earlier—and controversial—posing for *Playboy* came to light, the producers thought it best to look elsewhere. However, they did give Tate a small recurring role on *The Beverly Hillbillies* as a sexy secretary who is chased by Jethro, much to Nancy Kulp's Miss Hathaway's dismay (a still photo showing Sharon as Billie Jo alongside Pat and Linda is among the DVD's bonus extras).

Jeannine Riley and Gunilla Hutton, with their Kewpie-doll good looks, portrayed Billie Jo as a healthy, boy-crazy young flirt, which was how the character was originally conceived. When Meredith MacRae came aboard, Billie Jo's interest in boys moderated just a bit and the desire for a career in show business came to the fore.

Pat Woodell played Bobbi Jo as an introverted bookworm who was a bit too studious to attract boys. This too was how the role was originally conceived and how Lori Saunders initially played it when she joined the cast. But it soon became apparent that Lori had a different flair for comedy than Pat. She would give a line a slightly daffy delivery and before you know it, Bobbi Jo became a high-spirited, delightfully ditzy extrovert.

Either way, the petticoats for each of the six Bradley girls perfectly fit each actress to a T (and A) at the junction.

Petticoat Junction.

ICONIC FACTS

Linda Kaye Henning

Birth Data: Born Linda Kaye Henning on September 16, 1944, in Los Angeles, California.

Education: Attended San Fernando Valley State College.

Family: Parents, Ruth and Paul Henning (*Petticoat Junction* producer); married *Petticoat Junction* costar Mike Minor (1969–1973); Ashby Adams (1994–present).

Most Memorable TV Role: Betty Jo (Elizabeth Josephine) Bradley/Elliot on *Petticoat Junction* (CBS, 1963–1970).

Benchmarks: Linda was a dancer in the feature film *Bye, Bye Birdie* (1963). Her father, *Petticoat Junction* creator Paul Henning, made her audition for the role of Betty Jo. She became the only actress to remain on the series for its entire seven-year run, appearing in 222 episodes; provided the voice of Jethrine Bodine, Jethro's sister, played in drag by Max Baer, Jr., on *The Beverly Hillbillies* (also produced by Paul Henning); portrayed Mrs. Mallory in the TV series *Sliders* (SyFy, 1995–2000). Her Betty Jo character on *Petticoat* loved animals, as does Linda in real life. Today, she is a Los Angeles Zoo docent.

Prime Quotes: Her father created *Petticoat Junction* for the show's main star Bea Benaderet. As she once recalled, "He had worked with her for many years, and Bea went with him to see me in a play I was doing at a neighborhood playhouse. She said, 'Paul, why in the world won't you let your daughter try out for Betty Jo?'" * Regarding Jeannine Riley, Gunilla Hutton, and Pat Woodell (all of whom left the series): "They wanted to pursue other careers. It was tough. But we all got along, and I tested with the [other] girls, and they asked me my opinion." * "The people who watched [*Petticoat Junction*] really identified with it because they lived those lives."

A Living Legend.

Lori Saunders

Birth Data: Born Linda Marie Hines on October 4, 1941, in Kansas City, Missouri.

Family: Married Bernard Sandler (1961–present); children: Ronald and Stacy Sandler.

Most Memorable TV Role: Bobbie Jo (Roberta Josephine) Bradley, the middle sister on *Petticoat Junction* (CBS, 1965–1970).

Benchmarks: She began her career in television on several episodes of *The Adventures of Ozzie & Harriet*; played Betty Gordon, Mr. Drysdale's secretary, in the last season of *The Beverly Hillbillies*; has been featured in over 100 commercials, including for Fantastik! All Purpose Cleaner. She retired from acting in 1980 and now works as a painter, sculptor, and photographer. She enjoys creating art-sculpture and oil paintings, and working for various charities, including Flower Power, Animal Rights, Beauty Without Cruelty, Feed The Children, and Make-A-Wish Foundation. Her current project is helping to establish full sponsorships for many students who are interested in environmental studies for the future of our planet.

Prime Quotes: From her website: "I was in five movies before retiring to the 'good life.' I love working with various charities, creating art-sculpture and oil paintings. I have been married forty years to my wonderfully supportive and fun-loving husband, Bernard. He retired as Owner and Agent of Commercial Talent Agency. We are blessed to live in beautiful Montecito, California."
A Living Legend.

Meredith MacRae

Birth Data: Born Meredith Lynn MacRae on May 30, 1944, on an army base in Houston, Texas, where her father was stationed.

Education: Attended UCLA and obtained a bachelor of arts degree in English.

Family: Parents, actor/singer Gordon MacRae (Curly in the 1955 film *Oklahoma*) and actress Sheila MacRae (Alice Kramden on "The Honeymooners" segment of *The Jackie Gleason Show*, CBS, 1966–1970). She married Richard Berger (1965–1967); Greg Mullavey (1969–1987), with whom she had one daughter, Allison; Phil Neal (1995–2000).

Most Memorable TV Role: Billie Jo (Willimena Josephine) Bradley, the eldest sister on *Petticoat Junction* (CBS, 1966–1970).

Benchmarks: Played Mike's fiancée, Sally Ann, on *My Three Sons* (CBS, 1963–1965); created and hosted the 1987 PBS series *Born Famous*, where she interviewed other children of celebrities.

Prime Quotes: "In a way, that was probably the most fun we had was when we traveled. We just . . . were devils. We would order room service with hot fudge sundaes and things, and wine. We were all over 21 by then, and we just had a ball." * "One good thing about *Petticoat Junction*, it gave me a chance to establish my identity in my own right. . . . I was no longer known as Gordon and Sheila's daughter. I was finally Meredith MacRae."

Passing: July 14, 2000, in Manhattan Beach, California, from complications of brain cancer.

21

Dawn Wells

(Gilligan's Island)

DAWN WELLS (*GILLIGAN'S ISLAND*)

Just because a woman is over 50 does not mean she no longer has
anything to offer. If anything, we have so much more to offer! We
have lived life, we get better with age. . . . Sure, I could retire; but
what would I do? Play Bingo? I think not!

—Dawn Wells

Mary Ann Summers—the name screams down-home charm—the very core of who
Dawn Wells is in real life.

Mary Ann may have been stranded for three years on *Gilligan's Island* (CBS,
1964–1967), but Dawn did her justice and did it with style—and a strong sense of
community and heart.

For "a three-hour tour" on the S.S. *Minnow*, captained by the Skipper
(Alan Hale) and first mate Gilligan (Bob Denver), Mary Ann was joined by an
additional cast of castaways that included the wealthy Thurston Howell (Jim
Backus) and his wife Lovey (Natalie Schaefer), the intelligent Professor (Russell
Johnson), and movie star (and Mary Ann opposite) Ginger Grant (played by
fellow female TV icon Tina Louise).

But it was Mary Ann who kept them together like a family—like only a good
and kind farm girl could. And that only added to her appeal in the role, which, of
course, was accented by her short-shorts, checkered halter top, and the ribbons in
her adorable brunette pigtails.

Fred Freeman cowrote (with Lawrence J. Cohen) five episodes of *Gilligan's
Island* for its first season (1964–1967), and he also briefly dated Tina Louise. Who
better to add his two cents to the great Mary Ann–Ginger debate? The Mary
Ann character, he says, "was more grounded, real, and down-to-earth. I was more
attracted to her than I was to Ginger, quite honestly. Ginger was a showgirl. And
Mary Ann was just more . . . normal. She was more of a subtle beauty with a subtle

attractiveness. But they were both comical characters. In general, the show was over the top to a degree. It was what it was."

The sitcom remained so, on into the reunion movies of the 1970s. But as far as Dawn Wells was concerned, her only preoccupation with returning to the role of Mary Ann was, "I gotta wear shorts again?!" The only difference was she wore panty hose for the reunions—and of course, too, there was a different Ginger. Tina Louise had not signed on for the reunions. As a result, Wells says, the chemistry between Mary Ann and Ginger "was just not there. The other two girls didn't have the comedy timing that Tina had." But it was exciting to be back with everybody because when [the show] was cancelled, we didn't get a chance to say good-bye. We went on vacation, and when we came back, Sherwood [Schwartz, the show's creator] called and said, 'I'm sorry—it's over.' So, it was really fun to get together and do it again."

Then or today: "It's just too bad there really isn't a Mary Ann," Wells says. "Her values and everything she stood for, family and community, and so much more, were [and remain] so sincere."

Indeed. For the innocent, youthful, and yes—virginal—spirit of Mary Ann on *Gilligan's Island* is nowhere to be seen in any new television show or character today. "And that's sad," Wells said. "I still don't think [any man] wants to follow a dozen men. He may not tell you that. He may want the woman he gets involved with to have experience, and yet he doesn't want to be with someone that everyone else has had."

"I love what [talk show] host Steve Harvey has said. 'Ladies . . . men look at three things: your hair, your hands, your legs. But show it.' He said, 'peacocks have plumes. So attract us. Tempt us. But that doesn't mean you have to be a slut."

Dawn has remained in good shape with her head on straight, even after years of taxing long hours that series or film work usually requires (sometimes six days a week, 18 hours a day). "You can't party all the time. You just can't," she says.

DAWN WELLS (*GILLIGAN'S ISLAND*)

ICONIC FACTS

Birth Data: Born Dawn Elberta Wells on October 18, 1938, in Reno, Nevada.

Education: Attended Reno High School; majored in chemistry at Stephens College in Columbia, Missouri; graduated from University of Washington in Seattle with a degree in theater arts and design.

Family: Parents, Joe and Betty Wells; married Larry Rosen (1962–1967).

Most Memorable TV Role: Mary Ann Summers on *Gilligan's Island* (CBS, 1964–1967).

Benchmarks: In 1960, represented Nevada in the Miss America Pageant in Atlantic City; has had a successful career in theater, appearing in nearly 100 productions; presides over the Wishing Wells organization, which makes clothing for people with disabilities. As the spokeswoman for Idaho Potatoes since 2004, Dawn's publicity video, demonstrating the perfect way to peel an Idaho potato, went viral and has over ten million views. She once performed in a musical based on *Gilligan's Island*, although not as Mary Ann but as Mrs. Howell—playing opposite Barry Williams (*The Brady Bunch*) as Mr. Howell. She owns an acting school.

Prime Quotes: "Mary Ann has been such a big part of my life these past 40 years, it's really impossible to get away from it. But why would I want to? Everywhere in the world that I go I am greeted with love. Some kids who watched the show back then are still watching, but with their grandchildren now. That is a really wonderful thing! As an actress I have succeeded, I created a character that meant something to some people and it has lasted. So I refuse to ignore it and run away from it."

A Living Legend.

22

Linda Evans

(The Big Valley)

LINDA EVANS (*THE BIG VALLEY*)

> Nobody's got it made . . . no matter what they look like.
>
> —Linda Evans

Linda Evans was the ethereal beauty of *The Big Valley*, which aired on ABC from 1965 to 1969. While the matriarchal senior female of the series was represented by Miss Barbara Stanwick (as she was billed on the show), Evans as her onscreen daughter Audra Barkley offered a feast for the eyes belonging to anyone who could appreciate her various wonders. That milk-and-honey complexion, her piercing blue eyes, her athletic and shapely form, her luscious blond flowing locks, and her sweet disposition; all of that and more was on evident display.

Linda's first speaking part on television was for a guest-starring role on the ABC sitcom *Bachelor Father* (CBS/NBC/ABC, 1957–1962), playing opposite that show's male lead John Forsythe. Decades later, that moment would foreshadow one of her longest-running roles playing opposite Forsythe again, but this time on more of a steady basis—on *Dynasty*, the hit ABC prime-time soap that ran from 1981 to 1989.

But it was between *Bachelor* and *Dynasty* when Evans first found fame on *Big Valley*, which also featured future *Six Million Dollar Man* Lee Majors (who would later marry future *Charlie's Angels* star and fellow female TV icon Farrah Fawcett).

ICONIC FACTS

Birth Data: Born Linda Evanstad on November 18, 1942, in Hartford, Connecticut.

Education: Attended Hollywood High School, in Hollywood, California.

Family: Parents, Alba and Arlene Evanstad, both of whom were professional dancers; married film producer John Derek (1968–1974); Stan Herman, a property executive (1976–1981).

Most Memorable TV Role: Audra Barkley on *The Big Valley* (ABC, 1965–1969).

Benchmarks: Appeared in the *Beach Party* feature film sequel, *Beach Blanket Bingo* (1965), in which her vocals were dubbed by Jackie Ward (then known as Robin Ward), who was one of the most popular studio singers of the 1960s–1970s; decided to change her last name from Evanstad to Evans after being cast in *The Big Valley*; has made guest appearances on many detective shows like *Mannix*, *Banacek*, *McCloud*, and *McMillan & Wife*. In 1971, then-husband John Derek suggested she appear in *Playboy* magazine, the photos for which were published a second time in 1982 when she turned 40. In 1981, she was cast as Krystle Carrington on *Dynasty*, which aired on ABC until 1989; the same year she began a relationship with New Age musician Yanni (with whom she remained until 1998). In 2009, she competed in and won the British TV program *Hell's Kitchen*. She is frequently listed as one of the most beautiful women in America, which is ironic, as a junior high school English teacher suggested she take acting classes to overcome extreme shyness.

Prime Quotes: "If there's no inner peace, people can't give it to you. The husband can't give it to you. Your children can't give it to you. You have to give it to you." * "Find out what you don't want to know about yourself, what you're afraid of." * "I never saved my money. Whenever I worked in the past, I would spend it on my family or my husbands." * "It doesn't matter if I don't succeed in something, what matters, is that I learn from my mistakes." * "I played with dolls until I was 15. My mother encouraged it because my older sister got married when she was 15, so Mom thought that the longer I stayed with dolls, the better." * "You can take Elvis. You can take Marilyn Monroe. Success and fame will not be the answer if something inside of you is bothering you, if things in your mind aren't going right."

A Living Legend.

PART IV

THE SUPERSLEUTHS

23

Barbara Feldon

(Get Smart)

I've always supported myself. I like the sense of knowing exactly
where I stand financially. But there is a side of me that longs for a
knight in shining armor.

—Barbara Feldon

There are at least 99 reasons to love Barbara Feldon as Agent 99 on *Get Smart*,
NBC's James Bond–inspired 1960s spy-spoof created by Mel Brooks and
Buck Henry. Right-hand woman to series lead Don Adams's Maxwell "Max"
Smart, former model Feldon's particular appeal on the show rested with her
enticingly long legs, her deep, inset brown eyes, that sultry voice—and the
highest cheekbones this side of Mount Rushmore. All of it certainly added up
to more than just a mere 99, leaving so much more to the imagination, if only
commencing with the uncovering of her *Smart* character's "real" name.

"As an old pro looking back at *Get Smart*," opines Larry Brody, "I get all.
That show couldn't have existed without Barbara Feldon's 99. But at the time
it was on the air, Larry Brody the beginning writer who'd just moved to LA just

looked at her and . . . snorted. To me then she brought nothing to the table. I was wrong. Way wrong . . . which is why 23-year-olds shouldn't be making important showbiz decisions . . . which is why I wish someone would point that out to the powers that be now."

According to John Javna's *Cult TV*, the long-held debate among *Get Smart* fans (Smarties?) about 99's true moniker has long been resolved: she didn't really have one. She may have been introduced in one episode as Susan Hilton, but she later tells her spying partner Maxwell Smart (the show's lead character played by Don Adams) that it was just a fake name. So, ultimately, the show's writers once confirmed that 99's real name was never revealed.

"Sorry about that, Chief!" as Max was prone to say to his supervisor (Edward Platt) at CONTROL, the CIA-type agency that battled the evil KAOS organization (both organization names, like 99's narrative name, were also never revealed).

"Sorry," was also the one thing Maxwell most likely was not after he finally wised up, got smart, and married 99 in the show's final season.

Offscreen, however, Feldon felt quite differently about the married life fulfilling or validating a woman's existence.

In 2003, Touchstone Books published her memoir *Living Alone & Loving It: A Guide to Relishing the Solo Life* (which took its main title from another one of the show's catchphrases). As a press release for the publication explained:

> After a relationship impasse, Barbara Feldon—universally known as the effervescent spy 99 on *Get Smart*—found herself living alone. Little did she know that this time would become one of the most enriching and joyous periods of her life. Now Feldon shares her secrets for living alone and loving it. Prescribing antidotes for loneliness, salves for fears, and answers for just about every question that arises in an unpartnered day, she covers both the practical

and emotional aspects of the solo life, including how to: Stop imagining that marriage is a solution for loneliness • Nurture a glowing self-image that is not dependent on an admirer • Value connections that might be overlooked • Develop your creative side • End negative thinking. Whether you are blessed with the promise of youth or the wisdom of age, *Living Alone & Loving It* will instill the know-how to forge a life with few maps and many adventures.

Library Journal cautiously called the book a "breezy memoir," discussing how Feldon "came to understand that she could be perfectly—even radiantly—happy living alone. (Indeed, she sometimes sounds a bit desperate as she hammers home her theme.) Astute and optimistic, she notes the problems inherent in regarding 'single status as inferior to being married' and advocates consciously embracing the solo life so as to live life on one's own terms."

The review went on to note how Feldon's "wise words (e.g., 'Stop believing that marriage is the solution to loneliness') will be useful to anyone, single or otherwise. For public libraries and the night stand, along with Wendy Burt and Erin Kindberg's lighthearted and upbeat *Oh, Solo Mia! The Hip Chick's Guide to Fun for One*."

ICONIC FACTS

Birth Data: Born Barbara Anne Hall on March 12, 1933, in Bethel Park, Pennsylvania.

Education: Graduated from Bethel Park High School and Carnegie Mellon University, Pittsburgh, with a BA in theater arts in 1955.

Family: Parents, Ray and Julia Hall; married Lucien Verdoux-Feldon (1958–1967); had 12-year relationship with *Get Smart* producer Burt Nodella.

Most Memorable TV Role: Agent 99 in *Get Smart* (NBC, 1965–1970), for which she received two Emmy Award nominations.

Benchmarks: Barbara was once a chorus girl at the Copacabana nightclub in New York City; won $64,000 on the TV quiz show *The $64,000 Question*. Her category was Shakespeare. After modeling for Pauline Tregiere, she moved on to Revlon, where she appeared in the Top Brass ads for which she became well known with lines like, "I want a word with all you tigers."

Top Brass led to television, where she made early appearances on shows like *Flipper* and *The Man from U.N.C.L.E.*, and as an industrial spy on a series called *East Side, West Side*; the latter two led to her most famous role as 99 on *Get Smart*. Since the show's male lead Don Adams was two inches shorter than Feldon, she was forced to wear flat shoes and slouch for the entire run of the series. In 1982, at age 50, she began hosting a syndicated cable talk show titled *The 80s Woman*. In 1995, she reteamed with Adams for the new *Get Smart* series that featured Andy Dick as their onscreen son (the show lasted one season). Her other non-*Smart* TV appearances included *Slattery's People*, *The Red Skelton Hour*, *Medical Center*, *McMillan & Wife*, *Cheers*, *Mad About You*—and in 1967—she did the pilot for NBC's *Rowan & Martin's Laugh-In* (though as a guest star, more or less promoting *Get Smart*). That same year, she costarred with fellow classic TV legend Dick Van Dyke in the feature film *Fitzwilly*, while her TV-movies include *Of Men and Women* (1973), *Let's Switch* (1975), and *A Guide for the Married Woman* (1978). She also provided the voice of Patti Bear in the classic 1973 animated TV special *The Bear Who Slept Through Christmas*, which is considered by some to be one of the most poignant animated Christmas specials in history. She later became an active supporter of the Equal Rights Amendment.

Prime Quotes: "I was a very loving and good friends with Don Adams in the years after *Get Smart* and until he died. We never really bonded during the show

except as characters. He was preoccupied with the role. We just thought of ourselves as congenial business colleagues. Yes. There was an extra sweetness about them, a sense of nostalgia. And you never know when something will turn into art. I don't think it's pretentious to say it was art, maybe pop art." *
"There's not a day when somebody doesn't smile and say, 'Oh, you're Agent 99.' I like being in a world that regards me in a friendly way."

A Living Legend.

Anne Francis

(Honey West)

A lot of people speak to me about Honey West. *The character*
made young women think there was more they could reach for. It
encouraged a lot of people.

—Anne Francis

"Anne Francis was fabulous," says Margaret Wendt without restraint. "She was a
television person who could have been a movie star. And I don't why she wasn't."

Enamored with Anne's deep blue eyes and staple beauty mark on her
lower lip, Wendt would watch and closely analyze the actress on *Honey West*, a
30-minute crime series that aired on ABC for just one season from 1965 to 1966.
Francis first appeared as the West character on an episode of the TV detective
show *Burke's Law* that aired on April 21, 1965. Her impression in that singular
performance as a sleek, martial-arts-moving pre–Mrs. Peel/*Avengers* and pre–
Charlie's Angels female lead was so strong she received a series of her own, playing
a private eye who inherited the family business after her father died. Wendt
elaborates on Anne's unique look:

> Her eyes were sort of *catish* and she had her beauty mark before Cindy Crawford.
> She didn't come off as particularly friendly . . . or as someone that you wanted to
> know. But you certainly wanted to watch her. She may have been playing a part,
> but you really never knew what she was thinking, in interpreting her character
> . . . or what she was thinking as a person, in real life. So, none of that really
> matched. You thought something else was going on with her inside while she
> was acting . . . but you really weren't sure exactly what was going on. There was a
> great mystery to her.

Wendt stresses the importance for such female TV icons to make a strong
impression in order to stand out from the overcrowded abyss of Hollywood

starlets. "You either watch their show or their performance and you remember them, or you forget about them. Anne Francis made you remember who she was . . . because she was memorable."

As Francis once explained, although her show was highly rated it was cancelled because the network purchased another series, *The Avengers*, "which was imported from England, for less than it cost to produce our show."

Entertainment historian Rob Ray weighs in:

I would describe Anne Francis with the phrase blonde with a brain. In other words, she was the antithesis of the stereotypical dumb blonde. Unlike say, [an early performance from] Farrah Fawcett in *Charlie's Angels*, it was not at all difficult to totally believe [Francis] as successful private detective in *Honey West*. She was smart, savvy, and commanded your respect while remaining very, very beautiful.

The actress also impressed Ray with her other performances, most notably as Marsha White, the mannequin who came to life on the *Twilight Zone* episode "The After Hours," which originally aired on CBS, June 10, 1960. As Ray succinctly concludes:

I guess the thing that's interesting about her turn in ["Hours"] is her vulnerability. As she enters the store, she's poised, self-assured, and seems to know where she wants to go. And it slowly unravels as the truth to her true identity is slowly revealed. It's an astonishingly nuanced performance that must have resonated with viewers. Nearly 50 years later, people were still telling her how well they remembered that one role.

ICONIC FACTS

Birth Data: Born Ann Lloyd Marvak on September 16, 1930, in Ossining, New
York (which is near Sing Sing prison).

Education: After her first MGM contract, during which she attended studio
school with Elizabeth Taylor, Jane Powell, and Natalie Wood, she returned to
New York.

Family: She was the only child of Phillip and Edith Francis. She married Bamlet
Lawrence Price, Jr. (1952–1955); Robert Abeloff (1960–1964). Children: Jane
Elizabeth Abeloff and Margaret West (whom she adopted as a single mother
in 1970).

Most Memorable TV Role: The lead in *Honey West* (ABC, 1965–1966), for which
she received a Golden Globe for Best Female Star, and an Emmy nomination.

Benchmarks: Became a model for John Robert Powers at age 6, and performed
on radio and TV in New York. By age 11, made her Broadway debut as the
younger Gertrude Lawrence in that star's 1941 hit play "Lady in the Dark."
Around the same time, attended New York's Professional Children's School;
was later contracted with MGM in Hollywood for a few somewhat obscure
films. Determined to play against her voluptuous type, she returned to New
York, worked in countless respectable TV shows like *The United States Steel
Hour*, and performed in summer stock productions like "My Sister Eileen."
In 1950, played a troubled, pregnant but provocative teen in the feature film
So Young So Bad and was subsequently discovered and signed by 20th Century
Fox's Darryl F. Zanuck. Following a few other ingénue roles, she finally took
the female lead in movies like *Bad Day at Black Rock* (1955) and *Forbidden Planet*
(1956), a sci-fi cult classic, in which she played the alien Altaira. By the 1960s,
TV became her focus with her notable guest spots and *Honey West*. After the

show ended, she went back to the big screen with movies *Funny Girl* (1968) and *The Love God* (1969). She returned once again to the small screen with guest spots on shows like *Banacek, Ironside, Kung Fu, The Golden Girls* (playing a strong-willed foil to Bea Arthur's Dorothy Zbornack), and a series of TV-movies like *Haunts of the Very Rich* (1972), *A Masterpiece of Murder* (1986), and more. A spiritual person, she authored the book *Voices from Home: An Inner Journey*, published in 1982. She was also involved with several charitable organizations, including Direct Relief, Angel View, and the Desert AIDS Project, among others. In 2005, *TV Guide* ranked her number 18 on its "50 Sexiest Stars of All Time" list. She made her final performance in 2004 for an episode of TV crime-drama *Without a Trace*, titled "Shadows."

Prime Quotes: "Producers and writers I work with, young women in their 30s and 40s, tell me all the time, 'You have no idea what an influence you had on me with *Honey West*. You showed that I could do something unusual with my life, that I could have my freedom and not be dependent on another human being for my livelihood.'" * "Most young blondes in those days [1950s] were not taken too seriously. I had wanted to work on a project [directing] all my own from beginning to end for many years. I had managers who said, 'Look, you're an actress. You're not supposed to do that other business.' And now I look at all the women today who are doing it, and no one's batting an eyelash."

Passing: Diagnosed with lung cancer in 2007, the actress sadly died on January 2, 2011, from complications of pancreatic cancer in a Santa Barbara, California, retirement home.

Barbara Bain

(Mission: Impossible)

BARBARA BAIN (*MISSION: IMPOSSIBLE*)

The entire thing was glorious because I got to play [on *Mission: Impossible*], which was very glamorous and exciting. And within each script it was an actress's dream to play different parts each week. What could be better? I was royally awarded and it was a great launch of a career.

—Barbara Bain

Her eyes are deep-set, and her voice is just plain deep. Photogenic beyond compare, former model turned Emmy-winning actress Barbara Bain has never taken a bad picture. Bain most notably played Cinnamon Carter on TV's *Mission: Impossible* (CBS, 1966–1973), where she was drop-dead gorgeous.

Performing opposite then-husband Martin Landau, as well as Peter Graves, Peter Lupus, and Greg Morris, among others, Bain's slinky style of allure spoke to the 60s state of mind and yet ventured beyond the era. Throaty yet refined, her vocal cords and presence were *impossible* to turn away from. Hypnotic to say the least, it was Bain's bewitching steel-gray blue eyes that proved to be one of her most compelling traits.

As author John Javna explains in his book *Cult TV*, Bain and Landau had been married about one decade when they were cast for their first *Mission*. While modeling in New York, she had enrolled in one of his acting classes, and it was hate at first sight. Although now divorced, after their first encounter they eventually fell in love and married. She went on to win three Emmys for *Mission*, but left the series shortly after her husband. A few years later, she and Landau moved to England to costar in the syndicated sci-fi series from the 70s titled *Space: 1999* (which became a cult classic).

As she once told a reporter, Bain became involved with *Impossible* because her role was interconnected with Landau from the outset. "It was written for Martin and 'The Girl,' as she was first called." Bruce Geller, the show's creator, didn't tell her at the time that she had "kind of crept into his consciousness" as he was penning the pilot. He envisioned a female character that possessed certain qualities. "[Gellar] wanted her to be terribly sexy and terribly smart," Bain said, "and the combination was not sort of exactly running around in Hollywood at the time. You were either the dumb blonde, or the intellectual nice person that lived next door."

Gellar then laid his eyes on Bain and, as she relayed, "There I was. He never told me that he actually wrote it for me until after I was cast, and I auditioned over and over and over with all kinds of other folks."

In an exclusive interview for this book, Bain explains "The role of Cinnamon Carter was a groundbreaking [character] that was written for me. It was a woman doing work with the boys and there wasn't any separation between us. Women do stop me and tell me they were named after Cinnamon or that they were inspired to pursue law or medicine or all kinds of work that women didn't do back then."

As to the secret of her appeal? "You know, it's an elusive thing. When you're drawn to a performer there's something compelling about them that's a part of that person's nature. It makes you want to be in that person's presence. But I can't answer a question like that about myself. I wouldn't be able to say what it is."

Defining beauty in general, Bain concludes:

The poets have been trying to do this for centuries. I would say a sunset over the ocean is beautiful. For visual beauty, it might be the look in someone's eye. It must be something in our DNA that compels us to be attracted to something. What people think is beautiful changes though the ages. When I was a kid I would see beautiful women on the screen and they were just wondrous creatures. The people walking down the street in Chicago didn't look that way. When I was fairly little, I saw a movie with Rita Hayworth and the last shot at the end of the picture was a close-up of her with one tear coming down her cheek, and it was so still and absolutely perfect . . . a moment of feminine beauty. And I thought, "When you grow up, you cry neat."

ICONIC FACTS

Birth Data: Born on September 13, 1931, in Chicago, Illinois; and while sources list different birth names for her, she says these are incorrect. She's very private about her family history and prefers not to share that information.

Education: Graduated from the University of Illinois with a bachelor's degree in sociology.

Family: Married Martin Landau (1957–1993), with whom she has two daughters: Juliet Landau and Susan Landau.

Most Memorable TV Role: Cinnamon Carter on *Mission: Impossible* (CBS, 1966–1969), for which she won three consecutive Emmys (1967, 1968, 1969), the first actress to do so. She also starred as Dr. Helena Russell on the British import science-fiction series *Space: 1999* (syndicated, 1974–1976, although it was formally released in the United States in 1975).

Benchmarks: Once had aspirations to be a teacher, inspired by her first grade teacher; became interested in acting at the University of Illinois when she didn't want to take a PE class and took dance instead. She studied dance under Martha Graham and worked as a fashion model after moving to New York City; enrolled in acting classes with Lee Strasberg at the Actors Studio, where she met her future husband, Martin Landau. In 1992, she founded a literacy program called BookPals, where celebrities visit local schools and read to children to encourage reading. In 2010, she appeared in the feature film *Nothing Special*, and in 2014, the movie *Silver Skies*.

Prime Quotes: Regarding her audition for *Mission: Impossible*: "The ultimate decider was Lucille Ball, who owned the property [Ball's studio, Desilu, was the show's proprietor]. I went in and the last interview was with [her]. And I walked in shakily and all she did was look me up and down and say, 'Looks alright to me,' and that was it. It was kinda neat." * "I was the first woman with the guys. I was one of the big boys playing on that turf. No questions asked. I was capable of being on this turf. I wasn't saying 'yes, dear, no, dear' and stirring a pot. I did become in many, many ways a role model for many, many young women who stop me still on the street or in supermarkets, all sorts of places, and tell me that I was instrumental in them going for a career or for some such thing that they wanted in life, whatever it was. It's very gratifying."

A Living Legend.

Stefanie Powers

(The Girl from U.N.C.L.E.)

I wasn't one of the beautiful girls. I was a tomboy. I never got chased
around the table.

—Stefanie Powers

No female in the history of classic television ever pursed her lips so sensually as
Stefanie Powers as April Dancer on *The Girl from U.N.C.L.E.* (NBC, 1966–1967),
whose form-fitting and stylish outfits uniquely combined the dynamic darling
appeal of Diana Rigg's Mrs. Emma Peel from *The Avengers* and Marlo Thomas's
mod wear from *That Girl*.

Powers posed her mouth and other assets in many other roles over the years,
including Jennifer Hart opposite Robert Wagner's Jonathan Hart on *Hart to Hart*
(ABC, 1979–1984). But it was on *Girl* that Powers made her sumptuous mark. *The
Man from U.N.C.L.E.* was bound to spawn *The Girl from U.N.C.L.E*, which the
actress once described as a "markedly different" series from the fraternal series
that gave it birth. In one interview, she described her show as "a satire," citing as
its inspirations the 1960s TV editions of *Batman* and *The Green Hornet*, the styles
for which she believed were "incorporated a bit . . . into our show, which was
adorable. But it irritated NBC, who thought we looked as if we were having too
much fun. That was their big criticism."

Girl was cancelled after only one season. But having Powers cast in the lead
was nothing but a treasure for those who appreciated the show, and its early
cancellation certainly did not prevent her from attaining a solid following.

A combination of Joey Heatherton, Ann-Margret, and Lindsay Wagner,
Stefanie's manifold powers of charismatic persuasion are in full force throughout
each frame, smile, and distant cry of *U.N.C.L.E.*, and every other performance in
her career.

STEFANIE POWERS (*THE GIRL FROM U.N.C.L.E.*)

ICONIC FACTS

Birth Data: Born Stefania Zofia Federkiewicz on November 2, 1942, in Hollywood, California.

Education: Attended Hollywood High School.

Family: Mother, Julianna Dimitria Golan; married actor Gary Lockwood (1966–1972), who appeared in the second pilot episode of the original *Star Trek* (titled "Where No Man Has Gone Before"); Patrick De La Chenais (1993–1999).

Most Memorable TV Role: April Dancer on *The Girl from U.N.C.L.E.* (NBC, 1966–1967).

Benchmarks: Also played Jennifer Hart in *Hart to Hart* (ABC, 1979–1984); had a key role in an arc of episodes on *The Six Million Dollar Man* and *The Bionic Woman*, for which she was at one time considered for the lead. Another popular series role from the 1970s was as Toni "Feather" Danton on the *Feather and Father Gang* (ABC, 1976–1977); she also played Jane Powers in *Doctors* (2001). She made countless TV guest-star appearances, including *The Ann Sothern Show*, *Bat Masterson*, *Bonanza*, and *Please Don't Eat the Daisies*. She later performed in *Owen Marshall, Counselor at Law*, *The Mod Squad*, *The Bold Ones*, *Medical Center*, *Cannon*; made numerous segments of *Love, American Style*; and made a host of TV-movies, such as the compelling *Five Desperate Women* (1971), *Family Secrets*, and *Hollywood Wives*, both of which aired in 1984. In the mid-1990s, she reconnected with Robert Wagner for a series of successful *Hart to Hart* reunion movies. She recently took over the role of Tallulah Bankhead for her friend Valerie Harper in the live stage play "Looped." She dated actor William Holden, and after his death in 1981 became president of the William Holden Wildlife Foundation and a director of the Mount Kenya Game Ranch in Kenya. Before acting, she started out as a dancer, making all more appropriate her most famous TV character's name on *The Girl from U.N.C.L.E.* (April Dancer).

Prime Quotes: "I act now only when and if I can enjoy it. That's more important to me than any other part of this. I only care about the rewards of the work, not the celebrity. I only indulge myself in parts that I normally wouldn't have done previously. I only focus on the things that are going to give me pleasure."

* "[*Hart to Hart*] came at the right time. It proselytized a kind of romance and relationship that really were ideal. They were two people who didn't have to qualify their relationship and didn't seem to have to in any way sacrifice anything in order to be together. They were on equal footing, and they regarded each other as partners in everything they did."

A Living Legend.

Diana Rigg

(The Avengers)

I hope there's a tinge of disgrace about me. Hopefully, there's one good scandal left in me yet.

—Diana Rigg

Diana Rigg has guts, and she always did.

Decades before Jennifer Garner played Sydney Bristow in ABC's *Alias* (2001–2006) or even Elektra in the 2003 *Daredevil* feature film (or its subsequent stand-alone sequel); and eons before Scarlett Johansson played a similarly dressed Black Widow in Marvel's *The Avengers* megasuccessful feature film of 2013, Rigg was working her sleek cat-like superspy suit and moves as Mrs. Emma Peel on the classic TV series from the 1960s called *The Avengers*. Not to be confused with the Marvel superhero franchise of the same name (although it most likely always will be), the small-screen *Avengers* was a British import that ABC aired in America from 1966 to 1969.

Alongside Rigg's Mrs. Peel was distinguished actor Patrick Macnee, who portrayed the debonair sleuth John Steed. But whereas Macnee's Mr. Steed utilized the special gadgetry of his jacked-up cane to battle various villains, Rigg's Mrs. Peel employed martial arts and her sleek feminine wiles and ways and form to fight the bad guys. And no one complained, maybe not even the bad guys.

NBC's famous promotions writer Dan Holm offers his insight into what made Rigg so "a-Peeling":

What comes to mind when I think Emma Peel? Worldly, witty, sexy, smart, sexy, stylish, strong, and oh, yeah . . . sexy.

Diana Rigg's Emma Peel was the perfect fantasy girlfriend for a young boy [like myself] growing up in Wisconsin. An independent woman and devoted partner, Emma Peel was a bridge between traditional television females of the 50s and the empowered self-assurance of the 60s. She could take care of business, take care of herself, and look out for her partner. She did it all with a swagger and a sly smile.

As John Javna documented in *Cult TV*, by the time Rigg appeared on *The Avengers* she was already a five-year veteran of the Royal Shakespeare Company. In 1964, she toured Europe and America in a live stage production of "King Lear" and appeared on American TV's *A Comedy of Errors*. She then opted for a more mainstream path to performing to avoid being typecast as "a lady actress."

Rigg was actually the second actress to costar as Macnee's right-hand woman. Before Rigg, Honor Blackman was cast as the also-all-leather-clad and judo-chopping Peel-like character called Cathy Gale; after Rigg left to pursue a career in films, Linda Thorson joined the series as yet another hot side-kicker named Tara King.

But it is Rigg's dynamic female presence that is most remembered, as her iconic Mrs. Peel fit her like one of those leather gloves she wore on the series. According to www.imdb.com, Rigg once said, "Society was so much more prudish in the 1960s. In one episode of *The Avengers*, I played a belly dancer and I had to stick a jewel in my navel because the Americans wouldn't tolerate them. In those days, you didn't flash the boobs at all. What you did do to look glamorous was jack the boobs up and probably wear something quite low-cut." As to the famous leather, svelte, cat-like garb that she donned on the series, it "was a total nightmare. It took a good 45 minutes to get unzipped to go to the loo. It was like struggling in and out of a wetsuit."

Rigg left the wetsuit behind for good in an episode titled "The Forget Me Knot," a portion of which transpires in John Steed's apartment, where a newspaper headline clarifies how the show's producers opted to have Rigg exit the series. It read: "Peter Peel, Air Ace, Found Alive in Amazonian Jungle," a reference to her long-lost husband who, as it turned out, was waiting for her downstairs in his car. Consequently, she resigned from all her assignments with Mr. Steed. Tara King, meanwhile, was ready and waiting to take her place. The two women meet on the stairway when Tara trips up the stairs, as Mrs. Peel makes her exit. They give a once-over to one another and Mrs. Peel says sweetly, "Remember—he likes three lumps in his tea and you stir it anticlockwise."

Mrs. Peel was quite versed in Mr. Steed's prime refreshments, and she was known to invite him out to dinner (when she was likely to offer him a bottle of Côte de Beaune with quails). Offscreen, Ms. Rigg liked to stay home and cook more than get out and kick, and frequently invited Mr. Macnee over for a hot meal in real life (they were just good friends). According to *The Limelight Edition of the International Press Bulletin* of 1968 (vol. II, no. 3), she described her then-contemporary home kitchen as "gadget ridden," with then-modern appliances like an electric carving knife and a food mixer. A few favorite dishes of this British dish were roast beef and Yorkshire pudding, and a garlicky leg of lamb.

Sounds like an appropriate meal for Mrs. Peel, too.

ICONIC FACTS

Birth Data: Born Enid Diana Elizabeth Rigg on July 20, 1938, in Doncaster, England, then located in the West Riding of Yorkshire; today it's South Yorkshire.

Education: Attended boarding school at Moravian School in Fulneck; theatrically trained at the Royal Academy of Dramatic Art.

DIANA RIGG (*THE AVENGERS*)

Family: Parents, Louis Rigg and Beryl Helliwell; married Menachem Gueffen (1973–1976); Archibald Stirling (1982–1990), with whom she had daughter Rachael Stirling.

Most Memorable TV Role: Mrs. Emma Peel on *The Avengers* (ABC, 1965–1968).

Benchmarks: At two months old, Diana moved with her family to India, where she learned to speak Hindi, and remained there until she was eight years old; played Countess Teresa di Vicenzo in the 1969 James Bond film *On Her Majesty's Secret Service*. In the fall of 1973, she starred in a short-lived one-season sitcom on ABC titled *Diana*; was Olenna Tyrell in the HBO series *Game of Thrones*; portrayed Mrs. Gillyflower in the BBC series *Doctor Who*. In 1994, she was made Dame Commander of the British Empire. In 2005, *TV Guide* voted her the sexiest ever TV star in America. She sued Britain's *Evening Standard* and *Daily Mail* newspapers for libel and won when they wrote that she was an embittered woman who held British men in low regard.

Prime Quotes: "I think I was quite daring. I was once escorted out of a restaurant because I was wearing a trouser suit. It wasn't considered good breeding for a woman to go around in trousers after 6:00 pm, especially in smart restaurants and bars such as the Connaught Hotel, which served the best cocktails." * "They do say that the profession gets increasingly difficult, but my career seems to have been inside out. I'm playing the biggest parts now that I'm older. That's probably right, because I wasn't ready for them before." * "I hope there's a tinge of disgrace about me. Hopefully, there's one good scandal left in me yet."

A Living Legend.

Peggy Lipton

(The Mod Squad)

PEGGY LIPTON (*THE MOD SQUAD*)

> Anybody who lived in that time [the 1960s] knew it was pretty
>
> sexual times. Even in the late 60s, if you met somebody and you were
>
> attracted you didn't wait; you'd go straight to bed.
>
> —Peggy Lipton

She was a heroine, but not masculine. She was in control, but retained her femininity. In fact, she was the Bionic Woman—but without the super strength. She was groovy, solid, hip, and hot.

If you haven't figured it out by now, we're talking about Peggy Lipton and her performance as Julie Barnes on *The Mod Squad*, the initial 1960s partnership detective series that sprang from the producing team of Aaron Spelling and Leonard Goldberg. Their other shows included *Charlie's Angels*.

However, whereas Charlie assigned his Angels to the more high-reeling adventures of high-society types, Captain Greer (played by Tige Andrews) on *The Mod Squad* instructed the fair-haired Julie and her partners, Pete (Michael Cole) and Linc (Clarence Williams III)—all of whom added up to "one white, one black, one blond" (so voiced the show's promotional spots)—to go incognito in schools, colleges, and community organizations . . . to uncover the crimes and passions of the younger set.

Debuting in the drug-infused, Vietnam War–ridden 60s, *The Mod Squad* catered to a younger TV demographic, who were attracted to Lipton's multidimensional emotional performance and her *earthy* appearance as Julie.

From the exciting chase scene in the opening credits (which was punctuated with pulsating theme music), it became clear that Julie would ever be protected by Pete and Linc.

But viewers take note and don't be fooled: Julie was no wallflower, and Lipton stepped up to the plate with her performance. Julie may not have been a karate/judo-chopping supercop (like any one of the *Charlie's Angels*), and she skewed younger than Angie Dickinson on *Police Woman* (predating that show about seven years), but she was no less influential and memorable. Pete and Linc may have rescued her one too many times on a weekly basis, but what and where would they have been without her?

Notable TV promotions writer and producer Dan Holm sums up Lipton's appeal as Julie:

> She was young, oh-so-cool, and head-snappingly beautiful. Her street-wise background never interfered with her innate sincerity. But Peggy Lipton's Julie Barnes in *The Mod Squad* was so much more than a pretty face. It was her struggle between navigating life as she believed it should be—and life as she experienced it—that made her so vulnerable and relatable. The character of Julie Barnes was the kind of woman you not only wanted to spend time with but to look deep into those incredible eyes and get to know. In Julie Barnes, there was an immediate familiarity. She was someone you knew, thought you knew, or wanted to know.

ICONIC FACTS

Birth Data: Born Margaret Ann Lipton on August 30, 1946, in New York, New York.

Education: Attended Lawrence Junior High School and the Professional Children's School.

Family: Parents, Harold and Rita Lipton; married Quincy Jones (1974–1990), with whom she had children Rashida Jones (actress) and Kidada Jones.

Most Memorable TV Role: Julie Barnes on *The Mod Squad* (ABC, 1968–1973).

Benchmarks: Had a brief singing career in the late 60s and early 70s and landed three singles on the billboard charts; once had a tryst with Paul McCartney and dated Elvis Presley. After her marriage to composer Quincy Jones, she took a decade-long hiatus from acting to concentrate on her family; then played Norma Jennings in David Lynch's TV show *Twin Peaks* (ABC, 1991–1992). Recently guest-starred in several TV series including *House of Lies* and played Susie in the TV show *Crash*. She once had a hit record that reached number 102 on the Billboard Singles Charts: it was titled "Lu."

Prime Quotes: "[*The Mod Squad*] was the first of its kind and everything was up to date, the clothes were in style, the words, the expressions, the issues."

A Living Legend.

Farrah Fawcett, Kate Jackson, Jaclyn Smith

(Charlie's Angels)

> I was a sex symbol who wanted to be an actress.
>
> —Farrah Fawcett

Magic!

That's the best word to describe what took place each time Farrah Fawcett, Kate Jackson, and Jaclyn Smith shared the screen as the original daring and darling troika of *Charlie's Angels*, ABC's hit 1970s action-adventure series created by Douglas S. Cramer and Aaron Spelling. As with *Petticoat Junction*, there was a changing of the guard on *Angels*. Cheryl Ladd, Shelley Hack, and Tanya Roberts joined the series after subsequent exits from Fawcett and Jackson.

But it was the initial angelic threesome of Farrah, Kate, and Jackie that are best remembered and loved by *Charlie's* fans the world over. Debuting in the fall of 1976, the series could have easily been retitled *Glamour's Angels*.

Margaret Wendt says:

I loved *Charlie's Angels*, and the fact that we never saw Charlie, even though we all knew he was at least voiced by John Forsythe. So, I think they did a really good job. They were sexy and beautiful, and they really had the moves. You really believed they were beating up the bad guys. And Farrah Fawcett was so beautiful . . . and Jaclyn Smith so elegant . . . and Kate Jackson . . . such sophistication . . . you just couldn't touch those girls when it came to class and distinction. Jill Munroe [Farrah's character] and Kelly [Jaclyn Smith] would turn on the charms, and were sly and cunning. . . . They lured the bad guys in—and Sabrina [Kate Jackson] would finish them off or place the handcuffs on them. *Charlie's Angels* . . . they came along at a time when if you looked like any one of them, you were just plain blessed.

ICONIC FACTS

Farrah Fawcett

Birth Data: Born Farrah Leni Fawcett on February 2, 1947, in Corpus Christi, Texas.

Education: Graduated from W.B. Ray High School, Corpus Christi, Texas (where she was voted Best Looking); attended University of Texas at Austin, originally a microbiology major until changing her major to art.

Family: Parents, James and Pauline Fawcett; married Lee Majors (1973–1980); for 17 years lived with actor Ryan O'Neal, with whom she had one child, a son, Redmond O'Neal.

Most Memorable TV Role: Jill Munroe on *Charlie's Angels* (ABC, 1976–1980).

Benchmarks: Made TV appearances in the 60s on shows like *I Dream of Jeannie* and *The Dating Game*, and in the 70s on David Jansen's detective show *Harry O*. Was a strong presence in commercials, as with Wella Balsam shampoo and Ultrabrite toothpaste. In 1976 came *Charlie's Angels*, but then-husband Lee Majors wanted Farrah home by 6:30 pm to have dinner on the table. After the show debuted, the number of baby girls named Farrah significantly increased in America. In 1977, it was the 177th most popular name. That same year, Farrah became dissatisfied with *Angels* and abruptly left the series after the

first season. Her character was replaced by Kris Munroe, Jill's younger sister (played by Cheryl Ladd), and Farrah agreed to return to the show in guest spots for six episodes: three for the 1978–1979 season, and three for the 1979–1980 season. In 1980, she had a memorable opening night while appearing on stage in "Butterflies Are Free" in Jupiter, Florida: a heavyset woman in the first row started heckling and making bird calls during the performance. She later lifted her dress and flashed the performers, causing costar Dennis Christopher to take notice, though his character was supposed to be visually impaired. A male patron vomited and another fainted. Despite it all, the reviews for Farrah's performance were positive. In 1984, she appeared as abused wife Francine Hughes in the TV-movie *The Burning Bed*. Her performance was critically acclaimed and earned her an Emmy nomination. Following that she delivered several more critically acclaimed performances on screen and on stage. Her other TV-movies include *Murder in Texas* (1981), *Between Two Women* (1986), *Poor Little Rich Girl: The Barbara Hutton Story* (1987), and *Children of the Dust* (1995). Her feature films include *Logan's Run* (1976), *Somebody Killed Her Husband* (1978), *Sunburn* (1979), *Saturn 3* (1980), *Extremities* (1986), and *The Apostle* (1997). In 1991, she partnered onscreen with offscreen love Ryan O'Neal for the short-lived CBS sitcom *Good Sports*. In 1998, she was severely injured by James Orr after she spurned his proposal of marriage. Ryan O'Neal's daughter, actress Tatum O'Neal, disapproved of her father's relationship with Farrah. She and Ryan O'Neal split in 1997, but reunited in 2001 after he was diagnosed with leukemia. In 2004, she received her third Emmy nomination for her performance in *The Guardian*, on which she made semiregular appearances, as she did on the ABC Michael J. Fox series *Spin City*. In 2005, she reteamed onscreen with O'Neal for her *Chasing Farrah* reality show on TV Land. The two remained a couple until her death in 2009. Her famous feathered flip became an international trend for women around the globe. Her poster in a red one-piece bathing suit sold 8 million plus copies; the suit she wore was donated to the Smithsonian's National Museum of American History in 2011. Farrah was actively involved in charity work with the Cancer Society, in addition to her work against domestic violence. *Playboy* founder Hugh Hefner said: "Farrah was one of the iconic beauties of our time. Her girl-next-door charm combined with stunning looks made her a star on film, TV, and the printed page."

Prime Quotes: "The reason that the all-American boy prefers beauty to brains is that he can see better than he can think." * "Marriages that last are with people who do not live in Los Angeles." * "God gave women intuition and femininity. Used properly, the combination easily jumbles the brain of any man I've ever met." * "When you do bad things, bad things happen to you." * "I don't think an actor ever wants to establish an image. That certainly hurt me, and yet that is also what made me successful and eventually able to do more challenging roles." * "My number one goal is to love, support, and be there for my son." * "I became famous almost before I had a craft. I didn't study drama at school. I was an art major. Suddenly, when I was doing *Charlie's Angels*, I was getting all this fan mail, and I didn't really know why. I don't think anybody else did, either." * "As I've gotten older, I've found that I can have men as friends. I used to not be able to."

Passing: June 25, 2009, in Santa Monica, California, after waging a three-year battle with anal cancer.

Kate Jackson

Birth Data: Born Lucy Kate Jackson on October 29, 1948, in Birmingham, Alabama.

Education: Attended the Brooke Hill School for Girls, the University of Mississippi, and the American Academy of Dramatic Arts in New York.

Family: Parents, Hogan and Ruth Jackson; married Andrew Stevens (1978 to 1982); David Greenwald (1982–1984); Tom Hart (1991–1993). Children, Charles Taylor (whom she adopted).

Most Memorable TV Role: Sabrina Duncan on *Charlie's Angels* (ABC, 1976–1979).

Benchmarks: Worked as a page for NBC, performed in summer stock in Vermont, and made her TV debut as Daphne Harridge on *Dark Shadows*

(ABC, 1966–1971). Had a regular role on *The Rookies* (ABC, 1972–1976), was the first Angel to be cast in *Charlie's Angels*, and was responsible for creating the show's title. Due to a scheduling conflict with the *Angels* filming, she was forced to reject the starring role in *Kramer vs. Kramer*, for which Meryl Streep went on to win her first Oscar. The feature films in which she did appear include *Making Love* (1982), *Loverboy* (1989, with a teen Patrick Dempsey), and *Grey's Anatomy*, among others. Her TV-movies include both the original 1973 and 2000 remake editions of *Satan's School for Girls*, as well as *Armed and Innocent* (1994) and a 1979 small-screen remake of the *Topper* feature films (in which she costarred with then-husband Andrew Stevens, a pilot for a series that did not sell). She also appeared in the pilot film for the *James at 15* TV show (that did sell, but she did not continue on when the project went to series). Beyond *Charlie's Angels*, she starred in three other prime-time TV series: *The Rookies*, *Baby Boom*, and *Scarecrow and Mrs. King*. In 1987, Kate had her long, shapely legs insured for $8 million. *FHM Magazine* has ranked her number 18 on their list of the 100 Sexiest Women of All Time. She recently wrote a memoir, *The Smart One*, which was scheduled to be released in 2011 but has since been delayed to February 1, 2015. She's survived two battles with breast cancer, in 1987 and 1989. She has since dedicated herself to speaking out on the subjects of breast cancer and heart health.

Prime Quotes: Regarding *Charlie's Angels*: "It was good when it was good; and when it wasn't good, it was bad." * "I'd rather share the glory of a hit than star by myself in a flop." Regarding the *Charlie's Angels* feature films: "I think [they] missed the mark. In the TV show, Farrah, Jaclyn, and I were best friends who cared for each other and I think that came through in the acting. In the movies, they were too busy competing with each other, trying to see who could jump the highest or wear the tightest clothes." * "I'm married now, so I have a life. I had to get a life. That's one thing I really had to do, you know. You do that kind of work on television series after television series and you don't have a life. So, that's part of what I did while I was gone, I got a life." * "I don't see how I can go about a directing career and be a good mom at the same time. And if I'm not a good mom, I don't think it matters much what else I do well." * "Sometimes the better an actor is, the less he's noticed." * Regarding her health challenges: "The range of emotions you go through is amazing," she says. "But I made a conscious decision to be positive."

A Living Legend.

Jaclyn Smith

Birth Data: Born Jacquelyn Ellen Smith on October 26, 1945, in Houston, Texas.

Education: Graduated from Mirabeau B. Lamar High School in Arlington, Texas; attended Trinity University in San Antonio.

Family: Parents, Jack and Margaret Ellen Smith; married actor Roger Davis (1968–1975); actor Dennis Cole (1978–1981); Anthony B. Richmond (1981–1989, with whom she had two children: Gaston and Spencer Margaret Richmond); pediatric surgeon Brad Allen (1997–present).

Most Memorable TV Role: Kelly Garrett in *Charlie's Angels* (ABC, 1976–1981); she was the only original female lead to remain with the series for its complete run.

Benchmarks: Starred in several highly rated TV-movies. In 1985, she entered the business world with the introduction of her collection of women's apparel for Kmart, and pioneered the concept of celebrities developing their own brands rather than merely endorsing others. In 1990, she was chosen by *People Magazine* as one of the 50 Most Beautiful People in the World. In 1999, made a cameo appearance as Kelly Garrett in the first *Charlie's Angels* feature film, and in March 2010, she returned to acting after a five-year absence, with a guest role on the NBC television drama *Law & Order: Special Victims Unit.* In 2002, Jaclyn underwent treatment for breast cancer after a lump was detected during a routine examination, and in March 2012, Smith guest-starred on *CSI: Crime Scene Investigation.*

Prime Quotes: "I'm an old-fashioned girl, and I didn't believe in living with people, so I guess I married for the wrong reasons at times." * "After having children, life becomes about living beyond yourself; about being bigger and better." * "It's not about me, it's about my family. You don't answer questions for you, but for us. You learn to live beyond yourself." * "Just because something is three months away and seems far off, doesn't mean you will want to be there when the time comes." * "Time whizzes by when you have children; they make you aware of the passing of time, but also help keep you young." * "You have to be reasonable with yourself and not feel guilty when things aren't perfect." * "Farrah Fawcett had courage, she had strength, and she had faith. And now she has peace as she rests with the real angels." * "Angels are like diamonds; they can't be made, you have to find them. Each one is unique."

A Living Legend.

PART V

THE WONDER WOMEN

30

Elizabeth Montgomery

(Bewitched)

GLAMOUR, GIDGETS, AND THE GIRL NEXT DOOR

Actors are supposed to be prepared.

—Elizabeth Montgomery

Who doesn't love Elizabeth Montgomery—and what's not to love?

A performer with multiple awards and nominations to her name, Montgomery not only acted, but also sang, danced, and was even an artist (who once had aspirations to work for Walt Disney). She began her professional career on Broadway, made her name in feature films, and went on to appear in over 200 guest-starring roles on television before she created her most famous small-screen sorceress: Samantha "the-witch-with-a-twitch" Stephens on *Bewitched*.

After Samantha became Queen of the Witches on *Bewitched*, Montgomery was then designated Queen of the TV-movies, with groundbreaking and Emmy-nominated performances in television films like *A Case of Rape* (NBC, 1974) and *The Legend of Lizzie Borden* (ABC, 1975). Offscreen, she donated much of her time, money, and personal efforts to numerous charitable causes and, in the process, became one of the most beloved, down-to-earth, and likable performers in the history of the entertainment industry (on and off screen).

Montgomery as Samantha has remained nothing less than enchanting since *Bewitched* debuted more than five decades ago (September 17, 1964). As was expressed in *The Bewitched Book* (Dell, 1992), *Twitch Upon a Star* (Taylor, 2012), and *The Essential Elizabeth Montgomery* (Taylor, 2013), she made witches likable and believable because she was so likable, sincere, and pure. Elizabeth brought a down-to-earth sincerity to every role she played in her vast career, be it for the stage, the big screen, or television. But certainly it was with Samantha that she knocked it out of the park.

Margaret Wendt was good friends with Elizabeth, whom she had met through a mutual acquaintance upon first moving to Los Angeles. She offers her insight on Elizabeth's spellbinding ways, on screen and off, as both shared (with other noteworthy public personalities) an interest in metaphysical thought beyond the fabricated magical realm of *Bewitched*:

I just loved Elizabeth Montgomery. She was a woman who was a class act from the word *go*. She was gorgeous, but different from the Farrah-Fawcett-homecoming-queen-type gorgeous. Elizabeth was of a sophisticated, cotillion status. I loved her when she was on *Bewitched*, and everything she did before or after the show. She was very convincing as an actress. She could never be typecast, even as many years as she played Samantha. And in real life, she enjoyed many conversations about the metaphysical world, which we discussed at length—along with Martha Mitchell, wife to John Mitchell of the White House. Elizabeth, myself, Martha, and a couple agents at CAA from the past—we all believed in the paranormal. But we didn't talk about it because at that time, it wasn't okay to talk about it. And Elizabeth, in particular, really enjoyed playing Samantha partly because of her interest in the metaphysical.

Peter Ackerman is the son of TV female icon Elinor Donahue (*Father Knows Best*) and *Bewitched* executive producer Harry Ackerman, who also oversaw production for many other classic TV hits (such as Sally Field's 1960s *Gidget*). Peter frequently visited the sets of many legendary shows and befriended various stars, including Elizabeth. "Sometimes," he muses, "I think I could write a book about this period, as [*Bewitched*] was the first of either of my parent's shows where I spent significant time on the set." He shares his memory of Elizabeth not only as Samantha—but in her dual role on *Bewitched* as Serena, Samantha's more mischievous look-alike brunette bombshell cousin:

I loved Auntie Liz, as we Ackerman boys called her. She was wonderful. She was bright, loving, pixie like, and "alive." I always remember her with a slight crooked smile on her face and a glint in her eye; she truly was like an aunt to me. . . . During the time of the show our families were close. Bill Asher [Elizabeth's then-husband and *Bewitched*'s main director/producer] and Liz and their kids Willie, Robert, and Rebecca came over to our house all the time. Bill and Dad would place wagers on football games and sometimes we'd all get into a limo and head to Rams games. Sometimes it was just the guys as my mom and Liz stayed home together, perhaps with some of the younger kids in the house. Fun times they were. Auntie Liz WOULD wiggle her nose for us if asked, and never denied the request. The *Bewitched* set is the one I visited the most often. I have memories of Liz when dressed as Serena, and she played the trick she would on anyone and pretended that she was not Liz, and I believed her. That, and two different signed pictures on the wall in my dad's office, one from Liz and one from Serena, made me think that Liz and Serena were two different actresses!

ICONIC FACTS

Birth Data: Born Elizabeth Victoria Montgomery on April 15, 1933, in Los Angeles, California.

Education: Attended the Westlake School for Girls in Los Angeles; graduated from the Spence School for Girls in New York City; also attended the American Academy of Dramatic Arts in New York City (for three years).

Family: Parents, actor Robert Montgomery and Broadway actress Elizabeth Bryan Montgomery; one brother, Robert "Skip" Montgomery, Jr. Married Frederick Gallatin Cammann (1954–1955); actor Gig Young (1956–1963); *Bewitched* director/producer William Asher (1963–1973), with whom she had three children: William Asher, Robert Asher, and Rebecca Asher; actor Robert Foxworth (1993–1995, with whom she lived from 1974).

Most Memorable TV Role: Samantha Stephens on *Bewitched* (ABC, 1964–1972), for which she was nominated for an Emmy five times.

Benchmarks: Debuted in "Late Love" on Broadway in 1963 and received the Daniel Blum Theatre World Award for Most Promising Newcomer. Made three major motion pictures, including *The Court-Martial of Billy Mitchell*, released in 1955 (also starring Gary Cooper) and *Who's Been Sleeping in My Bed?*, released in 1963 (costarring Dean Martin and Carol Burnett, who became a good friend). Also released in 1963 was *Johnny Cool*, directed by William Asher, with whom she would fall in love, marry, and later partner with on *Bewitched* (in 1964). Before playing her most famous TV role as Samantha, she made over 200 guest-star appearances on television, including over 28 appearances on her father's anthology series, *Robert Montgomery Presents*; received her first Emmy nomination for playing a prostitute in "The Rusty Heller Story" episode of *The Untouchables*; and made famous the "Two" episode of *The Twilight Zone*, costarring Charles Bronson (neither spoke a word of dialogue). After *Bewitched* she became first Queen of the TV-movies, with small-screen films like *The Victim* (ABC, 1972) and *A Case of Rape* (NBC, 1974), the latter for which she received her first post-*Bewitched* Emmy nomination. *Rape* was also the first issue-oriented TV-movie and became one of the top ten highest-rated TV-movies in history. In 1975, she took the lead in *The Legend of Lizzie Borden* (ABC), for which she garnered yet another Emmy nod, as she would in 1977 for the acclaimed NBC miniseries *The Awakening Land*. After making the *Borden* film, she insisted on being called Lizzie! Liberal in her politics, Elizabeth spoke out against the Vietnam War, despised the Reagan administration, and was one of the first celebrities to offer her public support and personal funds for gay rights and those suffering from AIDS. She was also a strong supporter of women's rights and those with disabilities, as well as a volunteer for Learning Ally, a nonprofit organization which records educational books for disabled people. Her final TV-movies based on the adventures of Miami crime reporter Edna Buchanan were to continue, but she died shortly after the second film aired. In 1995, Women In Film bestowed her, posthumously, with the Lucy Award (named for Lucille Ball) "in recognition of excellence and innovation in creative works that have enhanced the perception of women through the medium of television." Her daughter, Rebecca, accepted the award. In 2005, TV Land erected an honorary statue of her likeness as Samantha Stephens in Salem, Massachusetts (which *TV Guide* once called the "witch capital of the world"). In 2008, Elizabeth finally (if again, posthumously) received her star on the Hollywood Walk of Fame.

Prime Quotes: "I get letters from people saying one of the things they like best about what I've done since *Bewitched* is that they never know what I'm going to do next." * "The minute someone says 'Oh God, you could never do that; you can't get that kind of stuff on the air' . . . that's the kind of stuff I want to do." * "Like most people, I secretly hope that it's true—that there are witches like Samantha; and that families like hers really do exist."

Passing: May 18, 1995, in Beverly Hills, California, of colorectal cancer.

31

Barbara Eden

(I Dream of Jeannie)

If gentlemen prefer blondes then I'm a blonde that prefers gentlemen.

—Barbara Eden

For Barbara Eden, it's always been about the belly button, if maybe a few other noteworthy assets too.

From 1965 to 1970, she played the happy-go-lucky though mischievous magical genie to Larry Hagman's astronaut master Major Anthony Nelson on the hit NBC sitcom *I Dream of Jeannie* (created by future novel and TV miniseries king Sidney Sheldon).

In March of 2012, Eden was interviewed by writer Sandi Berg for *Life After 50 Magazine*, in which she recalled her Hollywood days and shared her thoughts on her career, health and fitness, and aging. "I've always been kind of 'what you see is what you get.' I don't think there's anything too obtuse about me."

As Berg went on to detail, the actress was raised in San Francisco and had aspirations to act when she was just a young girl. Her first real break arrived when she won a role on *The Johnny Carson Show*, a 1955 summer replacement series. From there, Eden began to create a reputation as a reliable, hardworking performer, which, in turn, paved the way for guest-starring roles in dozens of TV shows in the late 1950s. That included winning a lead in the small-screen edition of the feature film *How to Marry a Millionaire*, in which she played Loco Jones, the role played by Marilyn Monroe in the big-screen version. Eden continued to get regular work through the early 1960s, and then, in 1965 she was cast as Jeannie. As she relayed to Berg:

> I had been reading about *I Dream of Jeannie* in the trades and I saw that they were testing every gorgeous brunette in town—Miss Syria, Miss Lebanon, Miss Greece, Miss Turkey, Miss Israel—actresses from every Middle Eastern country. I thought: "Well that's not for me." Then my agent sent me the script and I read

it and I thought it was odd that they were sending it to me. He asked me what I thought of it, and I said: "It's really wonderful, but are you sure they know what I look like?" He said they knew very well what I looked like because they were interested in giving me an offer for the part if I liked it and would meet with Sidney Sheldon who was in town for three days.

As Berg explained, Eden won the role of Jeannie without a screen test or audition, and credited writer Nat Perrin. Perrin was a friend of Sidney Sheldon's who also happened to be one of the writer/producers on *The Johnny Carson Show*; he was well aware of Eden's comedic ability and particular appeal.

ICONIC FACTS

Birth Data: Born Barbara Jean Morehead on August 23, 1934, in Tucson, Arizona.

Education: Graduated from Abraham Lincoln High School in San Francisco, California; studied for a year at City College of San Francisco.

Family: Parents, Alice Mary and Hubert Henry Morehead; married actor Michael Ansara (1958–1974), with whom she had son Michael (who passed away in 2001); Charles Fegert (1977–1982); Jon Eicholtz (1991–present).

Most Memorable TV Role: The fun-loving, carefree genie named Jeannie on *I Dream of Jeannie* (NBC, 1965–1970).

Benchmarks: Made many guest appearances on TV before *I Dream of Jeannie*, including *Burke's Law*, *Route 66*, *The Andy Griffith Show*, and an episode of *I Love Lucy* that was directed by future *Bewitched* director William Asher. In 1964, she starred with Tony Randall in the feature film *The Brass Bottle*, which was about a genie living in a bottle. Although Burl Ives played the genie, and Eden was Randall's onscreen love, the film inspired Sidney Sheldon to create *I Dream of Jeannie*. Jeannie's belly button wasn't an issue on *I Dream of Jeannie* until its existence was questioned by columnist Mike Connolly. When *Rowan & Martin's Laugh-In* producer George Schlatter decided to premiere her belly button on his show, NBC issued a "No Navel Edict." In 1980, Barbara starred in the NBC TV show *Harper Valley PTA*, based on the feature film of the same name. Her other TV series include *How to Marry a Millionaire* (1957–1959) and *A Brand New Life* (which aired for only one season in 1989–1990). She reunited with her *Jeannie* costar Larry Hagman on several occasions over the years, including the 1971 TV-movie *A Howling in the Woods* and for a few-episodes arc on Hagman's hit CBS series *Dallas*. However, he opted not to join her when she decided to return to the Jeannie role for a series of TV-movies: *I Dream of Jeannie: 15 Years Later*, in 1985 (directed by *Bewitched*'s William Asher) and *Still Dreaming of Jeannie* in 1991. The same year of the second Jeannie movie, and during the Persian Gulf War, Barbara traveled to the Middle East with Bob Hope to perform for the combat troops on an around-the-world USO tour entertaining servicemen during the Christmas season. Her other TV-movies include *The Feminist and the Fuzz* (1971) and *Your Mother Wears Army Boots* (1989). She made several guest-star appearances on TV over the years, including playing a witch in an episode of *Sabrina, the Teenage Witch*, and on shows like *Army Wives* and *George Lopez*. In 2009, she portrayed Mary Anderson in the TV movie *Always and Forever*. In 2011, Barbara published a memoir, *Jeannie Out of the Bottle,* which debuted at number 14 on the New York Times Best Seller list. On May 25, 2013, she donned her famous Jeannie garb at the Life Ball City Hall event in Vienna, Austria, and the audience—along with former President Bill Clinton beside her on stage—was blown away. When there is time in her crowded schedule, she works actively on behalf of numerous charities including the Trail of

Painted Ponies, Breast Cancer Research, American Cancer Society, the Wellness Community, the Make-A-Wish Foundation, the March of Dimes, the American Heart Association, Save the Children, and Childhelp USA.

Prime Quotes: "Out of all the actors I have worked with, I love working with Larry Hagman the most. We were very close and it was just a wonderful time." * "[Jeannie's] very easy to live with; actually, I think I'm more restricted by her now than when she was on the air, or 20 years after. I was just so busy." * "If gentlemen prefer blondes then I'm a blonde that prefers gentlemen." * "I would embrace the character, because it won't do any good if you don't. And another thing: Don't whine or talk trash about it. I don't think you ever demean to your public what you've done. You're insulting them if you demean your work." * "I've never stopped working. If you're active, you can appreciate what you did in the past, you don't feel like it's gone."

A Living Legend.

32

Julie Newmar

(My Living Doll / Batman)

Never mind changing the world. Make everything you have better.
People will notice.

—Julie Newmar

In 2011, Julie Newmar granted an exclusive interview to David Laurell, editor in chief of *Life After 50 Magazine*. She talked about what it was like to play Catwoman on the legendary TV series *Batman* (which originally aired on ABC from 1966 to 1969), appearing in 12 half-hour episodes for the first two seasons. She admitted to knowing very little about the series or the character and only accepted the part because her brother John, who was attending Harvard University, told her the series was a huge hit on the Ivy League campus.

Upon her arrival at the 20th Century Fox wardrobe department, Newmar was then presented with the glittery, skintight Catwoman costume. "Some people think I created the costume," she said. "That was not the case, although I did re-create it. I moved the belt from the waist to the hips because that worked better for my figure. It gave it a more sensual, feline look."

The elegant actress went on to label her Catwoman days "as a fabulous time of my life . . . the show and the characters were high camp, the writing by Stanley Ralph Ross was brilliant. So good in fact, all I had to do was show up and put the costume on."

She very much enjoyed portraying Catwoman, but forfeited the part after the show's second season due to a prior film commitment and was replaced by Eartha Kitt. Lee Meriwether (*Time Tunnel*, *Barnaby Jones*) also played the part on the series, while Michelle Pfeiffer and Halle Berry later interpreted the character on the big screen. Either way, Newmar opined, "the part of Catwoman will always be one of the most desirable roles for an actress to play, because she's sexy and sensual and there is so much variety—so many levels on which she can be played. Catwoman is not a one- or even two-dimensional character. She is playful and sassy, although she is out for danger. Batman always knew that, but he was still caught up in her allure and sexiness."

As to Anne Hathaway's most recent Catwoman (in the 2012 superhit feature film *The Dark Knight Rises*), Newmar offered only her highest praise, calling the young actress gorgeous. "It's . . . a very physical role," she said. "Being a dancer helped me with the physical part of the role—it helped me move like a cat."

Certainly, Newmar herself is "elevated," graceful, and multitalented.

In addition to playing Catwoman, she portrayed the lead opposite Robert Cummings in *My Living Doll*, which premiered on CBS in 1964. Here she played Rhoda, the robot, a little more than a decade before fellow female TV icon Lindsay Wagner played Jaime Sommers on *The Bionic Woman* (on which Newmar later made a guest appearance).

In December 2013, Julie (along with Angie Dickinson) received the Golden Halo Lifetime Achievement Award (for Excellence in Acting) that was bestowed upon her by the Southern California Motion Picture Council. Renowned classic TV historian, DVD producer/director, and radio host Stu Shostak presented Newmar with the award. As he commented about Julie's unique brand of appeal:

> I've always had a thing for tall, beautiful women . . . and when you add immense talent, charm, and a wicked sense of humor to the mix, you come up with the ever-stunning Julie Newmar. I first became aware of Julie when she played a robot in *My Living Doll*. I was eight years old at the time and even then, seeing this "mechanical woman" wrapped only in a towel gave me a feeling that . . . well . . . it DEFINITELY gave me a feeling! But for me, she was, is, and always will be the best—and the ONLY—Catwoman. Nobody else who's played that part since has even come close to what Julie Newmar did in that role . . . and she looked just as stunning in that feline outfit as she did in that towel two years earlier.

ICONIC FACTS

Birth Data: Born Julia Chalene Newmeyer on August 16, 1933, in Los Angeles, California.

Education: Graduated from John Marshall High School in Los Angeles at age 15; attended UCLA.

Family: Parents, Don Newmeyer, a professional football player who headed the Physical Education Department at Los Angeles City College, and Helen Jesmer, a former Ziegfeld Follies beauty; married J. Holt Smith (1977–1983), with whom she has one son, John Jewl Smith, who was born with Down syndrome.

Most Memorable TV Roles: Rhoda Miller, the robot on *My Living Doll* (CBS, 1964–1965); Catwoman on *Batman* (ABC, 1966–1969).

Benchmarks: She studied classical ballet and piano early on. After graduating
from high school in June 1951, she toured Europe for a year with her mother
and brother John. Upon returning to California, she was accepted by the LA
Opera Company as prima ballerina and also worked as a staff choreographer
for Universal Studios while studying philosophy, French, and classical piano
at UCLA. By the mid-1950s, she used her original name "Julie Newmeyer"
and had danced, uncredited, in several feature films. In 1955, she moved to
New York to perform on Broadway, which she did as Vera the ballerina
in "Silk Stockings." Other stage roles followed, including Stupefyin' Jones
in "Li'l Abner," that of the Swedish vixen in a 1961 production of "The
Marriage-Go-Round," for which she won Broadway's Tony award. In
1964, she was cast in *My Living Doll*. She also made several TV guest-
star appearances on shows like *Route 66*, *The Twilight Zone*, *F Troop*, *Star
Trek*, and *Get Smart*. She also had roles in movies like *For Love or Money*
(1963), *Mackenna's Gold*, and *The Maltese Bippy* (both released in 1969). She
was later featured in *Playboy* magazine and performed on more TV shows
like *Bewitched*; *Love, American Style*; *McCloud*; *McMillan & Wife*; *Columbo*;
Fantasy Island; and *Hart to Hart*. Besides acting, she became a successful
businesswoman and inventor, holding the patents for an "invisible" bra and
Nudemar pantyhose (which became renowned for their strategically placed
elastic back seam that gave shape and lift to a woman's derrière). While
raising a son with special needs, Julie returned to UCLA and enrolled in real
estate courses in order to have more flexible and accessible hours for her
son. She later returned to stage in a production of "The Women" and made
a cameo appearance as herself in the feature film cult classic *To Wong Foo,
Thanks for Everything, Julie Newmar* (1995). In the 2008, she provided the
voice for Martha Wayne in the animated series *Batman: The Brave and the*

Bold. That same year, she was diagnosed with Charcot-Marie-Tooth (CMT), an incurable neurological disorder that affects equilibrium and the ability to walk. Consequently, she commenced a new career: writing. She is now the author of *The Conscious Catwoman Explains Life on Earth* (Eleven Books, 2011).

Prime Quotes: All from *The Conscious Catwoman Explains Life on Earth*: "Tall girls, don't slump. Think of how many short guys out there would love to have your offspring. Stand up for them." * "Good manners are wisdom practiced backwards. Bad manners are the throne of selfishness claiming to be individuality." * "Every profession has its scullery duty." * "I hide my annoyance when people tell me: 'But you can wear anything!' Anything . . . is what I don't wear." * "Women bloom later in life. Some of them like roses, bloom, and re-bloom and re-bloom." * "Lack of responsibility lands you in the hospital, the poor house, or with 'friends' who hurt you." * "Forgive yourself first. You'll have reserves when you want others to forgive you." * "Responsibility is the home base of great women and men. Greatness is to take responsibility for your feelings, your acts, and their consequences." * "When entering a restaurant—drop the attitude. People have too much attitude these days, a lot of it is mendacious. Just put one foot quietly in front of the other." * "Words, thoughts, eventually have a life of their own. Never say something you don't want to be true." * "On criticizing others . . . don't hear it, see it, or respond to it unless . . . you're in an outdoor cafe Via Veneto style, and then it's prodigious fun."

A Living Legend.

33

Nichelle Nichols
(Star Trek)

> You didn't really want to mess with Uhura. She was always graceful
> and respectful, but she also held a very responsible position as one of
> the commanding officers of the *Enterprise*.
>
> —Nichelle Nichols

There is an exterior and interior ethereal beauty that's immediately evident each time one views Nichelle Nichols as Communications Officer Lt. Uhura, on the original *Star Trek* series (which initially aired on NBC from 1966 to 1969), or in any of her later feature film performances in the role.

As author John Javna explains in *Cult TV*, Nichols portrayed Uhura (which is Swahili for *freedom*) as sensitive, intelligent, and sexy.

Suffice it to say, Nichols became a television trailblazer within an elite group of fellow legendary African American actresses, including Ethel Walters (*Beulah*, ABC, 1950–1953), Diahann Carroll (*Julia*, NBC, 1968–1971), Gail Fisher (*Mannix*, CBS, 1967–1975), Esther Rolle (*Maude*, CBS, 1972–1974; *Good Times*, CBS, 1974–

1979), and Isabel Sanford (*All in the Family*, CBS, 1971–1975; *The Jeffersons*, CBS, 1975–1985), among others.

African American actor Lloyd Haynes (later of ABC's *Room 222*) was the first communications officer in the initial *Star Trek* pilot titled "The Cage," which featured Jeffrey Hunter as Captain Christopher Pike. When "Cage" failed to fly, Nichelle replaced Haynes on the *Enterprise* as the all-new character named Nyota Uhura in a second pilot, "Where No Man Has Gone Before," in which William Shatner's Captain Kirk unseated Hunter's Pike. She had auditioned for the series by reading lines for Mr. Spock (ultimately represented in both pilots by Leonard Nimoy). Once the series went weekly, however, Nichols and Shatner shared what became TV's first interracial kiss in the third season episode "Plato's Stepchildren" (which originally aired November 22, 1968).

Although induced by alien interplay, the Kirk-Uhura moment became both monumental and controversial in the history of classic television. In her autobiography, *Beyond Uhura, Star Trek and Other Memories*, Nichols references a letter from one Caucasian Southerner who said, "I am totally opposed to the mixing of the races. However, any time a red-blooded American boy like Captain Kirk gets a beautiful dame in his arms that looks like Uhura, he ain't gonna fight it."

On a more intellectual and substantial level, former NASA astronaut Mae Jemison has credited Nichelle's performance as Uhura as inspiring her career choice, while actress Whoopi Goldberg had sought a role (which became the all-knowing bartender Guinan) on *Star Trek: The Next Generation* (an episode in which Jemison also appeared).

Approximately three years after the original network demise of the first *Trek* series, Nichelle reprised the Uhura role, if in voiceover only, for *Star Trek: The Animated Series* (which NBC aired on Saturday mornings from 1973 to 1975). In one episode of this show, "The Lorelei Signal," Uhura takes command of the *Enterprise*, a development Nichols had desired for the initial live action series. "But such was not meant to be," she says today with a new peace about the issue, a mere portion of the grace and dignity that has come to be her staple over the years.

TV writing legend Larry Brody penned an episode of the animated *Star Trek* series that later aired on NBC in the early 1970s for which Nichelle voiced the role of Uhura. As Brody recalls:

> I've met Nichelle a couple of times. She's a very warm, nice person. Her Lt. Uhura was a totally admirable woman as well as a beautiful one. But no one was trying to make a statement about women's rights or women's personalities when she was cast. I didn't take her nearly as seriously as I did the "Big Three" of Kirk, Spock, and Bones [i.e., Dr. Leonard McCoy, played by DeForest Kelley]. She did, however, seem much more important to the running of the *Enterprise* than Sulu [George Takei] or Chekov [Walter Koenig].

Star Trek, in many of its forms, remains special for countless individuals, cast members, writers, producers, and fans alike. For Nichelle Nichols, the show was a blessing.

Nichelle had considered leaving the series to pursue a career on the Broadway stage. But a conversation with Dr. Martin Luther King, Jr., altered that plan. As she reveals today, King had personally encouraged her to remain on board the *Enterprise* crew of *Star Trek*, of which he was a significant fan:

> Dr. King told me I should not "give up the ship," if you will. He believed I was an important role model for young black children and young women around the country. But not only that, he also thought I was a positive image for people, young and old, of every color, heritage, and culture who would now see blacks as equals. After hearing that, I knew I could not leave the series. I realized just how

responsible and important a role I had as Uhura . . . a part that to this day has proved to be a blessing not only in my life—but in the lives of countless others. And for that, I am deeply grateful, humbled, and honored.

ICONIC FACTS

Birth Data: Born Grace Dell Nichols on December 28, 1932, in Robbins, Illinois.

Education: From age 12 to 14, she studied classical ballet at the Chicago Ballet Academy and also pursued Afro-Cuban dancing under the tutelage of Carmencita Romero.

Family: Parents, Lishia and Samuel Earl Nichols, a factory worker and town mayor; married (and divorced) Foster Johnson in 1951, with whom she had one son, Kyle Johnson; Duke Mondy (1967–1972).

Most Memorable TV Role: Lieutenant Nyota Uhura on the original *Star Trek* series (1966 to 1969).

Benchmarks: She sang with Duke Ellington at age 16; later became the first African American to place her handprints in front of Hollywood's Chinese Theatre; served on the Board of Directors for the National Space Institute, where she helped to recruit three of the astronauts on the *Challenger* mission. Her early, pre–*Star Trek* performances include the stage play "The Fantasticks," and on TV's *Peyton Place*, *The Lieutenant*, and *Tarzan*. In 1994, she published her autobiography, *Beyond Uhura: Star Trek and Other Memories*, in which she said the role of Peggy Fair on TV's *Mannix* was offered to her during the final season of *Star Trek* but producer Gene Roddenberry refused to release her from her contract. Between the end of the original series and the *Star Trek* animated show and feature films,

Nichols appeared in several TV and film roles. In 2002, she played mother to Cuba Gooding, Jr., in the comedy *Snow Dogs*. In 2006, she took the film lead as a madam of a legal Nevada brothel in *Lady Magdalene's*, for which she also served as executive producer, choreographer, and sang three songs (two of which she composed). She has twice been nominated for the Sarah Siddons Award as best actress and is an accomplished dancer and vocalist. Her first Siddons nomination was for her portrayal of Hazel Sharpe in "Kicks and Co." and the second for her performance in "The Blacks." In addition to her voiceover work for the animated *Trek* series, she offered her vocal talents in other cartoon shows, such as *Spider-Man*; the "Simple Simpson" segment of *The Simpsons* (in which she played herself); two episodes of *Futurama* ("Anthology of Interest," in which she was one of Al Gore's Vice Presidential Action Rangers, and "Where No Fan Has Gone Before"). She also provided the recurring voice of Diana Maza, Elisa's mother in the animated *Gargoyles* series, and vocally portrayed Thoth-Kopeira in an episode of *Batman: The Animated Series*. Beyond the *Trek* movies, her other feature films include *The Torturer* and *Tru Loved*, both of which were released in 2008. Her TV-movies include *Scooby-Doo: Curse of the Lake Monster* (2010). In 2014, she worked in four feature films: *Omaha Street*, *Unbelievable*, *The White Orchid*, and *Escape from Heaven*.

Prime Quotes: "I was very blessed in always knowing what I wanted to do, and by the grace of God I've been able to succeed in my chosen career." * "I'm a fan of the fans. I love them. They're fabulous. I love being around them. I love their madness and their caring. I love watching them take off for a weekend, don the costumes, and become characters from the 23rd century and beyond. I thank the fans for giving us—me—so much support and love. I want them to know I love them. They'll always be my friends. I'll see the fans, always. They can rest assured of that." * "I think anybody with any intelligence sits down and sees *Star Trek* not as a kids' show." * "All the people in *Star Trek* will always be known as those characters. And what characters to have attached to your name in life! The show is such a phenomenon all over the world."

A Living Legend.

34

Lindsay Wagner

(The Bionic Woman)

The more together I was as a person, the more I was going to be able
to give as an actress.

—Lindsay Wagner

The natural beauty, charm, and what was later defined as emotional intelligence
of Lindsay Wagner took the television world by storm in the 1970s. Following a
successful modeling career, Lindsay ventured into TV and a contract with Universal
that secured her guest spots on shows like *The Rockford Files*, *Marcus Welby, M.D.*,
and *Owen Marshall, Counselor at Law*, on the latter of which she prophetically
performed with Lee Majors.

A few years after *Marshall*, Lindsay would work with Majors again in a two-
part episode of his hit series, *The Six Million Dollar Man*. Here, she played Jaime
Sommers, a former flame of Majors's Col. Steve Austin, an astronaut and test pilot
fitted with superpowered body parts following a horrific flight accident. Shortly
after their reunion, Sommers also falls prey to a terrible mishap, this time a skydiving
accident. At which time, Steve, now a special agent for the Office of Strategic
Intelligence (OSI) makes a demand to his superior Oscar Goldman (stoically
played by Richard Anderson): "rebuild" Jaime to save her life. Goldman reluctantly
agrees, but unlike with Steve's surgery, Jaime's body rejects her superpowered parts
(including a bionic ear, in comparison with Steve's bionic eye), and she dies.

The audience was outraged, and the "Bring Back Jaime" campaign had begun.
Universal was flooded with phone calls and mail, demanding that the superpacked
Sommers character return. The issue: Lindsay was no longer under contract with
Universal. As was explained in *TV Guide* at the time, both studio and network
executives suggested replacing her with another actress. Names like Sally Field,
Stefanie Powers, and even Majors's wife, Farrah Fawcett (pre–*Charlie's Angels*),

were among the choices. But the powers-that-be were having none of it. The battle cry was: "Get [us] Lindsay Wagner!"

The audience fell in love with Lindsay Wagner as Jaime Sommers, and they would accept no substitute. As such, Lindsay's manager Ron Samuels, then married to fellow feminine superhero star Lynda Carter (*Wonder Woman*), bartered a deal to have her return as Jaime for another two episodes of *Six*, with a storyline in which Jaime miraculously returned to life; she never really "died." The ratings for this second two-part segment went through the roof, and Samuels negotiated a second superdeal for Lindsay to play Jaime once again, but this time on a regular weekly basis in a series of her own.

Consequently, *The Bionic Woman* TV show was born in the same breath that a new TV star was born in the form of Lindsay Wagner, who earned an Emmy Award for playing Jaime, becoming the first female performer in a science-fiction series to win the coveted accolade for Best Actress in a Dramatic Role.

In September 2013, journalist David Laurell profiled Lindsay in *Life After 50 Magazine*. In an article titled "The Perceptive Woman," Wagner defined *The Bionic Woman* series as "a cutting-edge show that brought about the concept of women as superheroes. It was such a success that *Wonder Woman* came shortly thereafter." She talked about agreeing to play Jaime on a weekly basis only if the producers, including Kenneth Johnson (*The Incredible Hulk*) and Harve Bennett (*The Mod Squad*, and later the first, best batch of *Star Trek* feature films) worked diligently to inject both family values and humor into the show:

> I didn't just want to be a cop in a skirt. I really wanted [the series] to be
> something that reflected the culture of the feminine rise of the time. To me, the
> show had the opportunity to be a part of the rebalancing of the consciousness of
> our culture—about women branching out into a new and more independent and

productive role in society. We addressed a lot of social issues and always made sure the character was, first and foremost, using her mind to solve situations, and then used her bionic strength to carry out what came from her head and her heart. I was very happy with how the team accomplished that—the different approach they took to presenting a female lead. Jaime was never just a woman with a push-up bra and a gun. That, to me, is not what a heroine is.

ICONIC FACTS

Birth Data: Born Lindsay Jean Wagner on June 22, 1949, in Los Angeles, California.

Education: Graduated from David Douglas High School in Portland, Oregon; was a graduate student at the University of Oregon.

Family: Parents, Marilyn Louise and William Nowels Wagner; married Allan Rider (1971–1973); Michael Brandon (1976–1979); Henry Kingi (1981–1984, with whom she had two children: Dorian and Alex Kingi); Lawrence Mortorff (1990–1993).

Most Memorable TV Role: Jamie Sommers on *The Bionic Woman* (ABC, 1976–1978), for which she won an Emmy (in 1979), the first for a lead female actress in a science-fiction series.

Benchmarks: In 1969, she made an early TV appearance as a contestant on *The Dating Game*, and later performed in single guest appearances on shows like *The Rockford Files*, *Marcus Welby, M.D.*, and *Owen Marshall, Counselor at Law* (which costarred Lee Majors). She's made countless, highly rated TV-movies over the years, many of which have accrued a strong following since their debut. Beyond *The Bionic Woman*, she also starred in other weekly TV shows, including *A Peaceable Kingdom* and *Jessie*. And she appeared in a two-episode arc of *Kate & Allie*, which was intended as a pilot for a sitcom (but it never sold). In 2011, she guest-starred as Dr. Vanessa Calder in the SyFy channel's *Warehouse 13* and its sister show *Alphas*. Lindsay gives seminars and workshops for her self-help therapy, "Quiet the Mind and Open the Heart," promoting spirituality and meditation. In 2013, she began teaching acting and directing at San Bernardino Valley College in Southern California.

Prime Quotes: On playing Jaime Sommers: "I was very insistent about not using my bionics in an aggressive or offensive way. No offensive moves were done by her. It was all in defense. I continuously encouraged the writers to find ways for her to use her mind and her bionics as an extension of her mind." * "I find that most people who've followed my whole career don't see me as the physical, strong *Bionic Woman*. They relate more to the types of stories I've always gravitated to and/or generated; stories that have to do with people transcending circumstances in their lives, which we call all relate to." * "No matter who rejects you, don't lose touch with your higher self, with the higher powers, with anything that you can find which is of the light, that will give you strength in those times when you feel so lonely."

A Living Legend.

35

Lynda Carter

(Wonder Woman)

I never meant to be a sexual object for anyone but my husband. I
never thought a picture of my body would be tacked up in men's
bathrooms. I hate men looking at me and thinking what they think.
And I know what they think. They write and tell me.

—Lynda Carter

Upon viewing any episode of the *Wonder Woman* TV series (ABC, 1975–1977; CBS,
1977–1979), it becomes evident just how suited statuesque star Lynda Carter was
for the super role of Amazon Diana Prince, a.k.a. Wonder Woman. Not only
did Carter's physical appearance match perfectly with Charles Moulton's original
comic book vision, but Diana's warm heart and soul was made crystal clear through
Carter's sparkling blue eyes, which gleamed with intelligence and compassion, in
both the most intimate and adventurous scenes of the series.

In watching the show, whether in the first season's 1940s-based episodes or
the later 1970s-premised segments, Carter's natural wonders fit like a glove with
Wonder Woman's see-through plane, bullet-defying bracelets, American eagle
gold breastplate, star-studded boomeranging tiara, and magic truth-inducing lasso.

Bringing Diana to life and Wonder Woman to believability was a tall order, but Carter was up to the task. She made credible a sci-fi/fantasy character and, in the process, retained a sleek femininity (right beside Lindsay Wagner's *The Bionic Woman*), representing with elegance and leadership the growing women's liberation movement.

As Diana, Carter also showcased the proper and balanced amount of humanity that allowed her to connect with the home viewers, both female and male. Carter's *Wonder* persona also attained a strong following in the gay community, while her onscreen love for Lyle Waggoner's Steve Trevor merely contributed to her accessibility to the audience, all of whom could identify with matters of the heart.

Lynda Carter brought a sincere reality to the superhero set of the 1970s, which had included more straitlaced performances like Lee Majors as *The Six Million Dollar Man* or, to a lesser extent, Nicolas Hammond as *Spider-Man*. Other TV superheroes before that included Adam West's genius-across-the-board interpretation of *Batman*, in prime time, while on Saturday morning, Joanna Cameron delivered a stylish performance as *Isis*, and Deidra Hall and Judy Strangis were electric as *Electra Woman and Dyna Girl*, respectively.

Carter's more straitlaced Diana Prince was superhuman with her physical prowess and intelligence, but was merely human in the ways of the heart. Her love for the Steve Trevor character, whether in the 40s or the 70s edition, was portrayed with earnest by Carter, thus adding dimension to a superhero character that might have easily become a caricature in the potentially incapable hands of another actress. Carter's innate compassion and understanding offscreen imbued Diana's dynamic makeup onscreen, and combined to create a more than credible interpretation of an iconic female character.

LYNDA CARTER (*WONDER WOMAN*)

In 1978, shortly after the series switched networks and eras, Carter shared her thoughts on playing Wonder Woman with author Peggy Herz. "I grew up on comic books," the actress revealed. "Wonder Woman was my heroine. My sister and I loved her!"

As a teen, Carter said she was tall and had "big feet and freckles." At one point, she was five feet five inches tall and weighed 100 pounds. A good student in high school, she very much wanted to be a pom-pom girl, but she didn't make it. Around the same time, her father was facing a few financial challenges, and her parents subsequently divorced. While still in school, she became a professional singer, performing in pizza parlors, supper clubs, and other such establishments. "I always loved singing and dancing," she said. As to dating during her early academic days, "the boys all seemed kind of short and skinny," she recalled with a smile. "I always wanted to fit in with all the kids, but I never really did."

But as Herz pointed out, by the time Carter graduated, she had blossomed—and decided to enter a beauty pageant. In 1973, she was named Miss USA and became a finalist that year in the Miss World contest. "It was a terrific experience," she said, "like playing out a big fantasy. You feel you're really the princess of your dreams when you're chosen to be a beauty queen! A little girl from nowhere becomes someone."

In 2013, Carter shared additional thoughts about portraying Wonder Woman in *The 100 Most Influential People Who Never Lived*, a special magazine published by Time Home Entertainment. Upon first auditioning for the role, she was greeted with a great deal of skepticism within the entertainment industry. More than a few network and studio executives "wondered" if it was possible for a female lead to carry a prime-time television series—and if a female superhero would register with the home viewer. Adding to the skepticism was the fact that she was then an unknown actress.

Fortunately, the show's producers, headed by Douglas S. Cramer (*Mission: Impossible*; *Mannix*; *The Brady Bunch*; *Love, American Style*), fought diligently to have Carter star in the series and insisted that the pilot's premise remain faithful to Charles Moultan's original comic book mythology. "Their creative vision," Carter said, "struck a chord with the audience and endeared the show to longtime Wonder Woman fans."

From a personal perspective, she said her performance proved to be "life-altering." She was proud to portray a character that "crashed through intellectual and physical gender types. I love how Wonder Woman epitomized and became a symbol of the empowerment of women," she intoned. "I never viewed her strength as constituting an attack on men or as an attempt to diminish them in any respect but, rather, saw her as representing women as equals. To this day, I view the character as a voice for equality as we continue the real-world fight for civil rights for all. Not surprisingly, Wonder Woman's fans, and my fans, are drawn from the entire population: female, male, straight, gay, old, and young."

"When an actor is fortunate enough to portray an iconic figure like Wonder Woman," she concluded, "one's persona become inextricably tied to the character. I try to live harmoniously with my inner Wonder Woman and hope that the character will continue to impact lives in a positive way for generations to come."

ICONIC FACTS

Birth Data: Born Linda Jean Córdova Carter on July 24, 1951, in Phoenix, Arizona.

Education: Attended Globe High School in Globe, Arizona, and Arcadia High School in Phoenix, as well as Arizona State University.

Family: Parents, Colby and Jean Carter. Married Ron Samuels (1977–1982) and Robert A. Altman (1984–present), with whom she has children James Clifford Altman and Jessica Carter Altman.

Most Memorable TV Role: Wonder Woman, alias Diana Prince, in *Wonder Woman* (ABC/CBS, 1975–1979), on which she performed many of her own stunts, including hanging from a helicopter.

Benchmarks: Before *Wonder Woman*, she made guest appearances on shows like *Starsky & Hutch* and *Matt Helm*. She won the title of Miss World USA representing her home state of Arizona in 1972. In 1978, she was voted the Most Beautiful Woman in the World by the International Academy of Beauty and the British Press Organization. While filming *Wonder Woman*, she was cast as a Playboy Bunny in the 1979 film *Apocalypse Now*, but her scenes had to be cut when shooting was delayed and she had to get back to the *Wonder Woman* set. She made several noteworthy TV-movies, including *Rita Hayworth: The Love Goddess* in 1983 and *Family Blessings* in 1998. An accomplished singing and recording star, Lynda started performing in bands when she was in high school and college. In 2009, she released a jazz album, *At Last*, which peaked at number 6 on the jazz charts. In recent years, she has guest-starred on various TV shows, including on *Two and Half Men* and *Smallville*.

Prime Quotes: "I'd like to think I had something to do with it, but it's a phenomenon unto itself. And it's not too bad to be a sort of pop icon, you know? It's not too tough to handle." * "I had become isolated by fame. I longed for a family and some substantive relationships. Fame is a vapor. You can't grab hold of it."

A Living Legend.

PART VI

THE LIBERATED SOULS

36

Gale Storm

(My Little Margie)

I'm eternally grateful that God has given me much more than I could have expected out of life. I feel He's been responsible for all the wonderful things I've had, and continue to have. I wouldn't feel right asking for more.

—Gale Storm

Gale Storm was Gidget before Gidget was Gidget.

"I liked Gale Storm," says Margaret Wendt. "I think she was exotic . . . and she certainly died too young. Sometimes the actors are so interesting to look at, that what they look like becomes more interesting than whatever business they're doing or performing as their characters. I remember I used to talk about how she would wear her hair . . . she was like an Eartha Kitt [type] to me. There was something very different about her face . . . and you become so enthralled with the way they look or how they achieved that particular look as that particular character or in that particular performance that you actually miss what they were doing in the scene as that character. I think of her show as a little show . . . but she was a big deal."

Her hybrid charm as an actress stemmed from that fine and rare mix of an adorable and approachable beauty that was enhanced by an inspired magnetism and eternally youthful mind-set. Young at heart but wise beyond her years might be the best way to describe Storm, who started acting while still in her teens.

Classic cinema and television historian and author Steve Randisi was good friends with the actress in her later years. As he recalls, from the time Storm made her big-screen debut in 1940's *Tom Brown's School Days*, she "won over audiences with her exuberant personality and wonderful sense of comedic timing."

However, Randisi says it was on the small screen that in-home viewers were privy to Storm's initial and significant success with *My Little Margie*, the 1952 summer replacement for CBS's *I Love Lucy*:

GALE STORM (*MY LITTLE MARGIE*)

It was a quiet source of pride for Gale to realize that audiences devoted to Lucy's antics were now watching her character in the same timeslot—with nearly the same level of constancy and affection. So much so that *Margie* evolved into a permanent weekly series [albeit on a different network, NBC] and would later spawn a radio version utilizing the same cast. Margie was cute and vivacious and, like Lucy, was more than willing to be bruised by taking a pratfall or a pie in the face. And like many other female characters in fifties sitcoms, Margie had a knack for getting herself in and out of an array of disasters. This she often did independent of the men in her life, including her wealthy widower dad (aptly portrayed by former screen heartthrob Charles Farrell) and her spiritless boyfriend Freddy [Don Hayden]. It was her show and, in most cases, the writers had Margie one or two notches ahead of her male stalwarts.

After *Margie* had been relegated to daytime reruns in 1956, Randisi explains how "a more mature Gale" embarked on a second sitcom, *The Gale Storm Show*, more commonly known by its syndication title, *Oh! Susanna*. "This second series was something of a departure in that Susanna Pomeroy [Storm] embodied certain qualities of the independent woman that were becoming more and more commonplace on television. She held down a glamorous job [as the entertainment director of a luxury liner] and often stood up to, and got the edge on, a male superior [in this case, Captain Huxley, played by veteran character actor Roy Roberts].

Susanna didn't surpass *Margie* in popularity, but it did in terms of longevity. "*Margie* spanned 126 episodes over two and half years," Randisi intones, "while *Susanna* ran for 143 episodes over four years." Moreover, every third episode of the second series was a musical, "thus enabling audiences to enjoy Gale's magnificent singing voice." (By this time, too, Storm had become a popular recording artist for Dot Records. Her 1955 hit, "I Hear You Knockin'," sold over one million copies.)

As to the *Susanna/Gale Storm Show*, Storm once said during production, "We're trying to make the jokes more motivated, and we're trying to make Susanna more intelligent."

Of all the recognition Storm received during her extensive career in film, television, and theater, she most often recalled a comment from *Margie* director Hal Yates. According to Randisi, Yates was a "no-nonsense perfectionist" whose career dated back to the silent era. "And he told Gale that she reminded him of Mabel Normand, one of the screen's earliest and finest purveyors of slapstick. 'Considering his expertise in comedy,' she said, 'that was one of the finest compliments I ever received.'"

ICONIC FACTS

Birth Data: Born Josephine Owaissa Cottle on April 5, 1922, in Bloomington, Texas.

Education: Albert Sidney Johnston Junior High School and San Jacinto High School.

Family: Parents, William Walter and Minnie Corina Cottle; married Lee Bonnell (1941–1986, until his death) and Paul Masterson (1988–1996, until his death). Children: Peter, Phillip, Paul, and Susanna Bonnell.

Most Memorable TV Roles: Margie Albright on *My Little Margie* (CBS, 1952–1955), which was only supposed to be a summer replacement series for *I Love Lucy* but became one of the most popular sitcoms of the early 50s; also played Susanna Pomeroy (the first name which she passed on to her daughter in real life) on *The Gale Storm Show* (a.k.a. *Oh! Susanna*, CBS/ABC, 1956–1960).

Benchmarks: One of her sisters gave her the middle name "Owaissa," which is a Norridgewock Amerindian word meaning "bluebird." When she was 17, two of her teachers urged her to enter a contest on *Gateway to Hollywood*, which was supervised by Jesse Lasky, Sr., and broadcast from the CBS Radio studios in Hollywood, California. The first prize was a one-year contract with a movie studio. She won and was immediately given the stage name Gale Storm. All four of her children appeared on her hit sitcoms. Her performing partner and future husband, Lee Bonnell (from South Bend, Indiana), became known as Terry Belmont, who had also at one point won the *Gateway to Hollywood* competition, which is how he got his name (although he has been periodically billed as Lee Bonnell). On September 28, 1970, Gale appeared on *The Merv Griffin Show* and talked about how her husband changed his name to Lee from Terry, the latter of which she said "wasn't a strong name for a man." She made a few successful B movies, including *Where Are the Children* (1943) and *The Kid from Texas* (1950), and she was best known in westerns as Roy Rogers's leading lady. For a short but popular recording career, she had several hit songs like "Dark Moon," "Memories Are Made of This," and "Ivory Tower." She also recorded covers of Smiley Lewis's R&B hit, "I Hear Your Knockin'" and Frankie Lymond's "Why Do Fools Fall in Love?" Throughout it all, she battled and won a bout with alcoholism and became an outspoken and committed lecturer in helping to remove the stigma attached to alcoholism, particularly as it applied to women.

Prime Quotes: "My successes have certainly not been without problems. During the 1970s I experienced a terribly low and painful time of dealing with alcoholism." * "I found myself needing a drink when I woke up in the morning. So I had a drink before breakfast. And lunch. And dinner. It just got away from me. Before I knew it, I was drinking all the time." * "[Medical] tests showed that my liver had become enlarged to three or four times its normal size. I looked as though I were six months pregnant. [The] tests proved that I was drinking myself to death."

Passing: June 27, 2009, in Danville, California, from natural causes.

37

Barbara Hale

(Perry Mason)

I liked playing women with an independent streak.

—Barbara Hale

Raymond Burr played Perry Mason, TV's top attorney (who never lost a case!) on the extremely popular series of the same name that ran on CBS from 1957 to 1966. But Perry would have been nothing without his secretary and right-hand gal Della Street, as portrayed with grace and subtle allure by the elegant Barbara Hale. Unlike the audience, Perry's affection for Della was not so obvious. "Circumstantial evidence" is how he may have defined and defended his alleged attraction, although many wondered how he could turn away from her numerous charms.

Hale's Street was one of television's first single professional working women, and the story of how she came to play the part is just as monumental. Close friends with two of the show's producers, Corny and Gail Patrick Jackson, Hale had worked with Corny at an advertising agency in Chicago, and with Gail on a doll-making venture. The doll project never panned out, but Hale remained friends with Corny and Gail, who later remembered her for a part in a certain new legal series she was developing.

"Oh, Gail," Hale said, "bless your heart for thinking of me. But I just can't do a show right now," mostly because she had three children to care for, the youngest of whom was only three years old. "I need to be home."

"Well," Gail replied, "this won't take much time—and Barb, we're only going to do 18 episodes."

Upon learning of the limited workload, Hale was intrigued, and then hearing it was *Perry Mason*, based on the famous Erle Stanley Gardner books—and with Burr as the star—she was elated. "Raymond, God love him," she recalls, "was one of the first people I met at RKO," the studio she was first contracted with as an actress. "I had known him since the day I first arrived in Hollywood. We were both under contract with RKO, and we got to know each other very well. He was a wonderful actor and a dear friend."

Hale stayed with the series for nine seasons, and 332 episodes, certainly more than the initial 18 segments promised to her by Gail Patrick. After *Mason* ended in 1966, Hale found herself working with Burr a few more times: first in his second hit series, *Ironside*, in the 70s, and in 1994—for the TV-reunion movie titled *Perry Mason Returns*, which spawned a series of TV-movie sequels based on the original series.

These new Mason movies also starred William Katt, who played Paul Drake, Jr., the son of the character made famous by William Hopper on the original series. By the time *Perry Mason* returned in the 90s, Hopper had unfortunately succumbed to lung cancer, but the producers, namely Dean Hargrove, wanted to keep the Drake family presence in the new films. And just as Hale was familiar with Burr when she was first cast as Della in the original series, the actress was also somewhat familiar with the actor who replaced Hopper in the reunion movies: William Katt—her son in real life, who had previously starred on *The Greatest American Hero* (ABC, 1981–1983). (Katt later left the film series and was replaced by William R. Moses; Burr died in 1993, and in stepped David Ogden Stiers until the airing of the final film, *A Perry Mason Mystery: The Case of the Jealous Jokester*, which aired in 1995.)

Although she was excited about the new *Mason* movies, Hale was concerned as to how they were going to mesh with the storyline of the original series, considering that all the original actors, beyond Hale and Burr, were no longer living, including Hopper, William Taylon (who played prosecutor Hamilton Burger), and Ray Collins (Lt. Arthur Tragg). "They were my boys," she says a bit wistfully. "I loved each of them dearly. They were like four of my brothers . . . my loves—and to this day, along with Raymond, of course, I miss them terribly."

As to her portrayal of Della, one of TV's first single professional working women, Hale remains both humbled by the reception and proud of her positive influence as a role model:

> I received so much fan mail from young ladies who were trying to decide what
> to do. This is when young women were more involved with finding a career that
> would suit them, rather than their husbands, so to speak. It's when women were
> just starting to think about their occupation in the workforce. And I cannot
> tell you the number of letters I received saying how pleased they were with the
> show because they were looking for a profession to follow . . . to study. And they
> were smitten with anything that had to do with the legal profession because of
> the show. And they were all in love with Raymond, and wanted to study law and
> work for someone just like Perry Mason.

As Perry's right-hand executive secretary, Barbara's Della added the perfect blend of feminine mystique to the show, which of course, charmed viewers, but Hale had to follow a strict train of thought that was laid down by Erle Stanley

Gardner on the *Mason* set. For one thing, the definition of Della's relationship with Perry had to remain a mystery, which of course was mind-boggling to the viewers, if fitting to the very premise and popularity of the series. Essentially, there could be no romance between the characters.

Hale remembers one time in particular when Gardner was not pleased when the director had placed Della on Perry's lap. "He didn't like that at all," she recalls with a sly smile.

The actress remembers another onscreen moment that did not sit well with Gardner, this time when she and Burr were filming a scene in a restaurant and they ordered a daiquiri cocktail. The following day, Gardner had reviewed the scene in the dailies or "rushes" (regular filmed sequences) and said, "No. We have to do that over."

Both Barbara and Burr wondered why.

"It doesn't fit."

As Hale explains today, because the show was somewhat based on Gardner's life and career "Perry had to order what Erle drank and Erle never drank a daiquiri."

Such attention to detail played into every measure of the series, adding to its quality—even down to the design of Hale's wardrobe as Della, for which Hale credits executive producer Gail Patrick Jackson. Prior to her *Mason* gig, Jackson had been known professionally as simply Gail Patrick and had a fairly successful career in the 1930s and early 40s as an actress specializing in playing the sophisticated (if sometimes cold) best friend, sister, or romantic rival of the female lead (in films like *My Man Godfrey*, *Stage Door,* and *My Favorite Wife*).

Consequently, Patrick knew of what she spoke—and Hale listened. With Barbara as Della, Gail did not seek so much to represent the fashions of the day exactly, but instead to keep that aspect a blur. Hale explains:

Della was fashionable, but always just a step ahead of the times. If women were wearing their skirts long, Della would wear them a little longer. When they were wearing them shorter, Della would wear them shorter still . . . but not to the extent that it became unfashionable . . . only to a certain degree . . . which essentially meant that my wardrobe never changed. And that was because we knew the show was going to run for a long time . . . and we wanted to give the show a timeless look. The early episodes don't look extremely 50s and the later ones don't look extremely 60s. In many ways, people could [watch] episodes of the show and not pinpoint exactly what year they were filmed.

Meanwhile, Burr's continuous weight gain was a sensitive issue for the actor, whom Hale affectionately referred to then and now as "Big Daddy." But she would make every attempt to temper his discomfort with humor, by telling him, "Honey—don't you worry one bit about how big you get. You just get as big as you want . . . because the bigger you get—the smaller I look."

So were Della and Perry in love?

"That's audience participation," Barbara replies, "because the girls or the guys that didn't want them to be lovers could accept them as very appreciative loving partners at work. In other words, if women viewers liked Perry, they didn't want to see him married. And if they liked her, they didn't want to see her married—even some of the gals didn't want to see Della married. . . . We would always receive letters that said, 'When are you going to get married?'" In fact, she adds, some fans thought that she and Burr were already married—in real life. This reminiscence offers one such example:

Our trailers were across the street from the courthouse. And one day, as I was making my way down the steps of the courthouse to my trailer for lunch, this little guy from about a block ran over to me and said, "Oh, Mrs. Mason! Mrs. Mason! Wait! Wait!"

When *Perry Mason* began production, she approached her superiors with a suggestion: she didn't want more lines or more "business" (character interaction and action), or anything of that ilk. "No," she clarified. "I don't want more to do. I just want Della to have reaction shots in response to Perry's dialogue . . . so that she could be looked upon as the silent partner."

"I think that's what women do," she explains. "I think that's an extremely key quality and value of a woman. It's just like in marriage . . . the male is the 'Big Daddy,' so to speak. But the woman is the one that is dependable, standing by his side . . . around the corner [wherever] . . . ready to help him. If he needs a pill she gives him a pill . . . that kind of support . . . combining intelligence and sensitivity. And that's [a unique quality] that women have in business that men, in general, tend to lack . . . not every man . . . but many . . . because it isn't in their nature . . . as a rule . . . and certainly not in the areas of [being] a CEO."

"In other words," she adds, "behind every great man is an even greater woman. . . . And that's the extreme value of a woman in business. Because anyone with any true sense of power doesn't parade it . . . they know they have the power and all they have to do is give a look or support . . . because they don't have anything to prove. And that's what helped the Della character and the empire with Perry Mason . . . that she had the chance to display how she felt with subtle reaction shots, instead of action shots. That's the way she should have been portrayed . . . because I thought that her sense of *quiet knowing* was her strength."

As to her status as a television icon, Hale responds with a wink and a smile: "I had to make an impact or Raymond would have put me in the back room!"

BARBARA HALE (*PERRY MASON*)

ICONIC FACTS

Birth Data: Born Barbara Hale on April 18, 1922, in DeKalb, Illinois.

Education: Graduate of Rockford (Illinois) High School, class of 1940; attended the Chicago Academy of Fine Arts.

Family: Parents, Luther Ezra Hale and Wilma Colvin; married Bill Williams (1946–1992, until his death, and whom she met in 1945 during the filming of *West of the Pecos*). They had three children: Jody Katt, actor William Katt (*The Greatest American Hero*, ABC, 1981–1983), and Juanita Katt.

Most Memorable TV Role: Legal secretary Della Street in more than 250 episodes of the long-running *Perry Mason* television series (CBS, 1957–1966); later reprising the role in 30 made-for-TV movies for NBC.

Benchmarks: She originally wanted to be an artist at a time when magazines and newspapers utilized drawings instead of photographs. She was then discovered at the Drake Hotel in her favorite red coat and started modeling for a comic strip called "Ramblin' Bill." From there, she became one of the original "Dr Pepper" girls featured in the soda company's calendars in the 1940s and 50s. She then became an actress and performed in feature films like *Higher and Higher* (1943, which was Frank Sinatra's first movie), *West of the Pecos* (1945, with Robert Mitchum), and *A Lion in the Streets* (1953, with James Cagney), among many others. Raymond Burr once named one of his orchids after her. A cancer survivor, Hale is retired, a grandmother, and a follower of the Bahá'í Faith.

Prime Quotes: After the original *Perry Mason* series ended, she was the TV commercial spokeswoman for Amana Radarange, during which she said things like, "If it doesn't say Amana, it's not a Radarange." * On working with

Sinatra: "I played his sweetheart. And I even sang with him. But I was never so terrified in my life. My friend [soap star] Jeannie Cooper said, 'My God, Barb—you're the first person I'd ever seen bend a microphone.'" * On working with Cagney: "He was a doll, and I got to know his entire family. They were very close and just lovely, wonderful people . . . very family-oriented." * And Robert Mitchum: "We were good friends. But he was such a bad boy. You know what Bob used to do to me, that crazy fool. I'd be in the Commissary [at RKO, where they filmed *West of the Pecos*], having lunch, and he'd scream across the room from the front door, 'Hey, Hale!' And I'd say, 'Yeah . . . ?' And he'd say, 'Are you gettin' any?!' He just about blew me away, that boy." * During her time on *Perry Mason*, Barbara was known industry-wide for her screams. As Raymond Burr once said, "She has the best shriek in Hollywood."

A Living Legend.

38

Tina Louise

(Gilligan's Island)

It's entirely my name. To me it means joy. Nobody in my family can
be hurt if anything happens to this name because it's my name only.

—Tina Louise

Television writer Fred Freeman is about to become one of the most envied men in
America and most likely the world because of this one particular revelation.

Ten years after *Gilligan's Island* finished its original run on CBS (1964–1967)
he dated Tina Louise, who played movie star Ginger Grant on the mere three-
season TV series that went on to become one of the most popular programs ever
produced for the small screen. Of their now-famous romantic interlude, Freeman
recalls: "An actress friend of mine introduced us. We had one date, and it was
absurd. She wouldn't even remember if I ran into her. I knew *immediately* she
wasn't interested at all in me. We had dinner, and we were back at her house for
about an hour and a half and that was it. She wasn't attracted to me. She wasn't
interested in me in the least."

As to Tina's performance as Ginger onscreen, Freeman is more upbeat. "She
was fine in the role," he says, ". . . very good, actually. And of course, pretty. Very
pretty."

For his book *Sweethearts of '60s TV* (S.P.I. Books, 1993), Ronald L. Smith
asked Tina if she was considered a "pretty child." She laughed, thought for a
moment, and said, "I don't know. I think I was okay. . . . My stepmother once
said I was homely, and teased me. I don't think I was ravishing, but I think I
was pretty."

No matter how many times or in how many ways it's stated, "pretty" just
doesn't seem to cut it when describing Tina's allure, certainly when it came to
playing Ginger on *Gilligan's Island*. She was as beautiful as those long, slinky,
glittery gowns that the beautiful actress donned on the series. Combined with her

fiery red hair and the sexiest mouth mole this side of supermodel Cindy Crawford, Tina was get-out gorgeous as Ginger!

While her *Island* costar, Dawn Wells, as Mary Ann, was considered a Gidget-type or the girl next door, "glamour" could have easily been Tina's middle name.

She studied at the Actors Studio in New York with Lee Strasberg because she believed it was time to "develop and deepen" the knowledge of her craft. Strasberg, she said, "had the most dynamic effect" on her, influencing her life "as no other man ever has."

Another man who impacted Tina's life was Sherwood Schwartz, creator and producer of *Gilligan's Island* (as well as *The Brady Bunch*). As he explained to author David Story in *America on the Rerun: TV Shows That Never Die* (Citadel Press, 1993), Schwartz was ultimately pleased with casting Tina as Ginger. "Sometimes you get lucky," he said. "Tina could play a languorous, feminine, sexy woman . . . I give [her] enormous credit for that characterization. . . . She made it work."

Actress Connie Forslund was one of the two replacements for Tina in the *Gilligan's Island* TV-movies of the 70s and, according to what Story chronicled in his book, even she was impressed with Louise's take on Ginger. "I think Tina Louise created a totally original and unique character. I don't think she was imitating Marilyn Monroe [as many had commented]—it's just that their two characters were sort of in the same category . . . beautiful, sexy and kind of [unexpectedly] funny ladies, a kind of innocence mixed with sexuality—they both had that. I loved Tina Louise on *Gilligan's Island*."

Dawn Wells played Mary Ann Summers opposite Tina's original Ginger on the series; and she greatly missed Louise when the cast regrouped for the reunion-movies. "Tina was absolutely perfect for the part," she says.

Undoubtedly, countless millions would agree.

ICONIC FACTS

Birth Data: Born Tatiana Josivovna Chernova Blacker on February 11, 1934, in New York, New York.

Education: Miami University in Oxford, Ohio.

Family: Parents, Betty Horn Meyers, fashion model, and Joseph Blacker, candy store owner and accountant; married Les Crane (1966–1974), gave birth to Caprice Crane.

Most Memorable TV Role: Ginger Grant on *Gilligan's Island* (CBS, 1964–1967).

Benchmarks: Tina's parents never gave her a middle name, so her high school drama teacher picked the name "Louise" and it stuck. In 1957, she released a musical album titled *It's Time for Tina*. In 1959, she posed for *Playboy* magazine. She made her Broadway debut in "Li'l Abner," playing Appassionata Von Climax, during which she shared a dressing room with another up-and-coming actress making her Broadway debut (fellow future female TV icon Julie Newmar). After several more films, Tina returned to Broadway to star with Carol Burnett in "Fade in, Fade Out." She then went to Hollywood for *Gilligan's Island*, and later worked on TV's *Bonanza*, *It Takes a Thief*, *Mannix*, *Police Story*, and *Marcus Welby, M.D.*, among others, and was a first-season regular on *Dallas*. Although she opted not to participate in the *Gilligan* reunion movies of the 70s, she reunited with Dawn Wells, Bob Denver, and Russell Johnson for an *Island* dream sequence on the sitcom *Roseanne*. Some of her TV-movies include *Look What Happened to Rosemary's Baby*, *Don't Call Us*, and *Nightmare in Badham County*, all of which aired in 1976. A few years later she appeared in *Friendships, Secrets and Lies* (1979) and *The Day the Women Got Even* (1980). Her feature films include *The Happy Ending* (1969, directed by Richard Brooks), *The Stepford Wives* (1975, with Katharine Ross), and *Dog Day* (1984, with Lee Marvin). And

in 1991 she appeared in *Johnny Suede* (costarring Brad Pitt). In 2004 she received
the coveted TV Land Pop Culture Icon Award in Los Angeles. In 2005, she
bartered a deal with IGT (International Game Technology) and Warner Bros.
Consumer Products: 80 lines of voiceover work for a highly publicized gaming
machine, a MegaJackpots product with the chance to win $1 million. The slot
machines appeared in casinos from coast to coast as well as internationally. She
is an active member of the Academy of Motion Picture Arts and Sciences and
a lifetime member of the Actors Studio. As a literacy and academic advocate,
she became a volunteer teacher at Learning Leaders, a nonprofit organization
dedicated to providing tutoring to New York City schoolchildren. It has
been her passion to help young students gain not only literacy skills but also
confidence, self-determination, and proof of their own potential. Besides
continuing her volunteer work in literacy, she has written several books.
Her first book, a personal memoir on her first eight years titled *Sunday*, was
published in 1998. A children's book, *When I Grow Up*, was published in 2007.
Her third book, *What Does a Bee Do?*, was published in 2009 and was inspired
by the colony collapse disorder, otherwise known as honeybee depopulation
syndrome. She's also recorded the album *It's Time for Tina*; and in 2014, she
worked on two feature films: *Tapestry* and *Late Phases*.

Prime Quotes: "The best movie you'll ever be in is your own life, because that's
what really matters in the end." * "People walk up to me and say: 'Are you
Ginger?' and I say: 'No. I'm Tina.' I do that to keep my sanity." * "Teaching
children the skill of reading and a love for the written word is important
because this will remain with them throughout their lives. If we can reach
children at an early age, I believe it will make a difference. This thought
brings me tremendous joy."

A Living Legend.

39

Karen Valentine

(Room 222)

KAREN VALENTINE (*ROOM 222*)

I hate that word [cute]. It's the most awful word in the language.

—Karen Valentine

"Miss Johnson is here to dry the area behind her ears. She's going to spend the rest of this semester with you, student teaching."

Thus spoke Michael Constantine as Principal Seymour Kaufman—of the fictional Walt Whitman High School—in the pilot episode of TV's first half-hour dramedy, ABC's *Room 222* (which first aired from 1969 to 1974). Kaufman was introducing student-teacher Alice Johnson, as played by Karen Valentine, to veteran faculty member Pete Dixon (Lloyd Haynes).

In a subsequent scene from the pilot, Dixon tells an eager Johnson, "You know, Alice, you can't expect to be a great teacher in one day."

"Oh, I don't," she replies with a laugh. "I'm going to give it a week."

An early ABC voiceover promo for the dram-com summarized its core: "Walt Whitman High—where teachers will understand their students . . . where students are eager to learn. Business goes on as usual in *Room 222*."

There was clearly nothing usual about Valentine's unique appeal and darling personality. To this day, she remains one of the most likable actresses in the history of classic television, certainly with regard to legendary females of the genre. As Alice on *Room 222*, she became Gidget for the twentysomething set (actually taking the lead in the TV-movie *Gidget Grows Up*, which aired in 1969—the same year *222* debuted). Ageless as the sun is warm, Valentine, as her name so succinctly implies, has heart.

In 1997, she was interviewed by Donny Osmond, who admitted what most baby-boomer guys had felt as a youngster: that he once had a crush on Valentine. After they both shared a smile over that revelation, the actress went on to chat about how much she enjoyed working on *Room 222* and detailed the events that led up to her audition for the series. She was voted the Apple Blossom Queen of Sebastopol, California, and later represented California in the Miss Teenage America pageant. TV variety show host Ed Sullivan caught her act in the talent competition, in which she danced in a flamboyant costume while lip-syncing to Eydie Gormé's "Blame it on the Bossa Nova."

Sullivan then said, "I want that girl on my show!" The following week, she went on to make what would become the first of two appearances on the legendary variety show hosted by TV's top master of ceremonies. While she would win over the Sullivan audience a second time (with her performance of the song "I Can't Get a Man with a Gun"), Valentine quite inadvertently would also later earn praise—and laughter—from director Gene Reynolds (*M*A*S*H*), who was supervising the auditions for *Room 222*. Valentine was quite nervous during the reading for Alice Johnson. But Reynolds thought such anxiety only added to her charm and perceived her awkwardness as the essence of the character. Consequently, Karen won the part of Alice.

Of her general association with *Room 222*, which addressed many political and racial issues long before *All in the Family* and other such programming hit the airwaves, Valentine once concluded:

> I think why the show did so well is that all the [serious issues] it addressed were couched in humor. There was a tone about the show that it got the message across but it didn't hit the audience over the head with it. And it made it very palatable.

ICONIC FACTS

Birth Data: Born Karen Lynne Valentine on May 25, 1947, in Sebastopol, California.

Education: She graduated from Analy High School in Sebastopol, where she was a member of the Future Teachers of America.

Family: Married Carl MacLaughlin (1969–1973); Gary Verna (1977–present).

Most Memorable TV Role: Alice Johnson on *Room 222* (ABC, 1969–1974), for which she was twice nominated for an Emmy, winning in 1970.

Benchmarks: She was born and raised on a chicken farm; and before she became an actress, she worked as a model, waitress, and switchboard operator during her salad days. In 1969, she was cast in *Room 222* and *Gidget Grows Up*. She later starred in the critically acclaimed true story *Muggable Mary, Street Cop*, and headlined her own TV sitcom *Karen* (which debuted on ABC in the fall of 1975). In 1976, she appeared on *The Donny & Marie Show* and performed in a satire of the school-com *Welcome Back, Kotter* (which was ultimately inspired by *Room 222*). She made guest appearances on many other shows, like *Starsky & Hutch*; *McMillan & Wife*; *Love, American Style*; and later on *The Love Boat*; *Murder, She Wrote*; and the Hallmark Channel series *Mystery Woman*. In 2004, she costarred with John Larroquette in the Hallmark Channel TV-movie *Wedding Daze*. Valentine has also starred in many live stage productions, including the Broadway and National Tour editions of "Romantic Comedy," an Off-Broadway and National Tour edition of "Breaking Legs," and an LA production of "Steel Magnolias."

Prime Quotes: "[*Room 222*] was a real forerunner for integrated shows. It was the first show, I think, that showed blacks and whites interacting so well together, and role models in teachers and counselors. It was so well accepted that in certain parts of the country, *Room 222* was required viewing by some of the teachers and principals and administrative staffs around different schools." *
"It was exciting to be in that cast, because we were all so very different. And yet, we all respected and cared for one another. We grew up together. We all

became married and divorced during the course of that show. Talk about a life experience." * About appearing on *The Hollywood Squares* with Paul Lynde (via Donny Osmond interview): "Sitting next to Paul was a scream because he was just such a funny, funny man. And we'd tape five shows in [one] night. We'd do three shows, and then we'd go to dinner. And there'd be wine at dinner, and so the last two shows were very funny."

A Living Legend.

Adrienne Barbeau

(Maude)

When I see myself on film it makes me smile. I mean, making a good living doing what I enjoy is so much fun. I just hope that everyone has the chance to enjoy life like I do.

—Adrienne Barbeau

Beyond Adrienne Barbeau's obvious physical attributes, her intelligent and spirited interpretation of Carol Findlay Traynor on *Maude* (CBS, 1972–1978) is legendary and a significant benchmark in the history of television.

Carol was the first divorced single mother on TV. She was bright, forthright, and held her own against the world, certainly, of course, against her equally strong-willed mother (as determinedly played by the domineering and endearing Bea Arthur). The high grade of likability that Barbeau brought to the role, with her great smile, witty spark, and twinkle in her eyes, added texture to the character that sealed her performance and made it accessible for the viewers. She played against type and never allowed Carol to be defined only by her physical allure.

"As to Carol having sex appeal," Barbeau says, "that never crossed my mind. I just wanted her to be believable and honest and, as often as possible, funny."

The actress recalls one particular episode of *Maude*, "not necessarily because it was a favorite, but because it dealt with an important topic—manic depression. And of course, it helped that we had Henry Fonda guesting. That was memorable by itself!"

Other segments featured additional big-name guest stars like John Wayne, while several more allowed for the cast to sing and dance—when the characters were put on shows for various charitable events. These episodes allowed the cast, including Bill Macy as Maude's (fourth!) husband, Walter, a break from the show's regular format. "I think we all enjoyed the musicals a great deal," Barbeau says. "Bea and Bill and I had come from musical theater, so it was great fun to be back in our milieu. It was always a joy to go to work, but even more fun to be singing and dancing."

There were many unique moments on the series and certainly various transitions as well, including several cast changes, one involving Carol. Before Barbeau joined the series, Marcia Rodd first played the part in the show's pilot. Barbeau explains:

> Marcia did play the role in the pilot, but she was based in New York and when the show went to series and was to be filmed in LA, I believe she didn't want to relocate. I was doing "Grease" [on Broadway] at the time, having just been nominated for a Tony for my role as Rizzo, and Norman Lear's casting director came to see the show and asked me to meet with Norman. Carol had already been established as having a seven-year-old son and when we met, Norman felt I looked too young to play the role. He went back to LA and continued auditioning actresses there. A month later, my agent showed up backstage at a

Saturday matinee and said they hadn't been able to find what they were looking
for and asked would I fly to LA the next day and audition for them there. I am
forever indebted to the producers of "Grease" and my understudy, Joy Rinaldi,
who allowed me to miss two performances. I auditioned on Tuesday, flew back
to NY that night, and was hired four days later.

Barbeau's final scenes in *Maude* transpired in the second to last episode
when Carol and her young son Philip (first played by Brian Morrison, 1972–1977;
and then by Kraig Metzinger, in this final season) move away because of her
new job opportunity. The characters of Arthur and Vivian Harmon (played by
Conrad Bain and Rue McClanahan) also move, leaving Maude and Walter alone,
until they relocate to Washington, where Maude becomes a congresswoman. As
Barbeau recalls, the emotions were strong in those final episodes. But most of all,
she remembers "what a joy it was to go to work every day. I had the greatest job
in the world."

ICONIC FACTS

Birth Data: Born Adrienne Jo Barbeau on June 11, 1945, in Sacramento, California.

Education: Attended Del Mar High School in San Jose, California, and Foothill
College in Los Altos Hills, California.

Family: Parents, Armene and Joseph Barbeau, public relations executive; married
director John Carpenter (1979–1984), with whom she had one son, John Cody
Carpenter; Billy Van Zandt (1992–present), with whom at age 51 she gave birth
to twin boys named Walker Steven and William Dalton Van Zandt.

Most Memorable TV Role: Carol Findlay Traynor on *Maude* (CBS, 1972–1978).

Benchmarks: Barbeau was the original Rizzo in the live stage musical version of "Grease" in 1972, and has worked consistently in every entertainment venue since leaving *Maude* in 1978. In 1980, she was cast as the lead in the feature film *The Fog*, directed by husband John Carpenter; she made other big-screen horror movies like *Creepshow* (1982) and other features such as *Escape from New York* and *The Cannonball Run* (both in 1981). From 1992 to 1995, she was the voice of Catwoman in *Batman: The Animated Series*. She played Suzanne Stanwyck on the soap opera *General Hospital* from 2010 to 2011; has made recent appearances in TV shows like *Revenge* and *Sons of Anarchy*; returned to the New York stage for the first time in 34 years to portray Judy Garland in "The Property Known as Garland," which was written by her husband Billy Van Zandt. In 2006, she penned the memoir *There Are Worse Things I Could Do* and is also the author of several novels.

Prime Quotes: "I loved doing Ruthie, the snake dancer in *Carnivale*. I loved everything about the show, from the producers to the cast to the crew to the caterers! Ruthie was spiritual, sensual, and strong—not the typical role for a woman in her fifties. And I loved doing Rizzo in the original Broadway production of "Grease" . . . and Stevie Wayne in *The Fog*, Maggie in *Escape from New York*, and especially Billie—the outrageous bitch—in *Creepshow*. Oh—and Golde in "Fiddler on the Roof." Sort of an eclectic group [of characters], but [playing] each one brought me great joy."

A Living Legend.

Meredith Baxter

(Bridget Loves Bernie)

MEREDITH BAXTER (*BRIDGET LOVES BERNIE*)

I really hope other people will take . . . as . . . a vote of hope and
confidence . . . that their life can change and be okay after coming out.

—Meredith Baxter

In the 1970s, she was the Catholic Bridget who loved the Jewish Bernie on the
controversial hit (if abruptly cancelled) CBS sitcom *Bridget Loves Bernie* (1972–1973),
and on ABC's groundbreaking drama *Family* (1976–1980) she was the young
divorced mother named Nancy Lawrence Maitland who was devoted to her little
baby boy. In the 80s, she was front and center as the liberal mom Elyse Keaton
who adored her entire brood on NBC's superhit comedy *Family Ties* (which made a
star of Michael J. Fox, who played her son).

A beauty with brains and heart, her name is Meredith Baxter, a.k.a. Meredith
Baxter Birney when she was married to *Bridget* costar David Birney (and yes, his
last name sounds the same as his character's first name). Blond and built like a
brick house, Meredith was sexy, but not in the obvious freewheeling ways of other
female stars of her era.

A working actress since she was a child, she was the daughter of actress
Whitney Blake, who also holds an interesting place in classic TV history. From
1961 to 1966 Blake starred as Dorothy Baxter, married to Don DeFiore's George
Baxter, employers to Shirley Booth's lovable housekeeper on the NBC/CBS
sitcom *Hazel*. After *Hazel* folded, Blake went on to cocreate (with Norman Lear)
One Day at a Time, the first weekly comedy series to feature a divorced mother (in
the guise of Bonnie Franklin). As Baxter once said of Blake, "More than anything
else, my mother wanted to be an actress—a famous actress—which in the 1950s
was all about being young, sexy, and available. She was all that, and more. She had
big blue eyes, alabaster skin, a heart-shaped face, a beautiful figure. She was just a
knockout."

Baxter clearly cherished her mother, and for a time she also held her relationship with David Birney in equal high regard. Unfortunately, as she conveyed in her book *Untitled: A Memoir of Family, Fame and Floundering* (Three Rivers Press, 2012), Birney was allegedly emotionally and physically abusive (allegations he has denied). She also explained in her book how she used alcohol as a coping mechanism for her marital issues and that she's been sober since 1990.

According to an *ABC News* online article by Susan Donaldson James (via *Good Morning, America*), the thrice-divorced Baxter said it was years before she changed her "victim" mentality. She also described herself as "mousey, quiet, and retiring," which some psychology professionals believe is the classic match for a dominating husband.

Baxter has recently stepped out of the closet (during an appearance on NBC's *Today Show* in 2009). In early December 2013, she tied the knot with longtime partner, contractor Nancy Locke (whom, according to *People Magazine*, she had been dating for seven years). "Now, I understand why marriage caught on," the actress told *People*.

In an interview with AOL News in 2012, she concluded, "I thought it [coming out] was going to be the end of my career. I thought it was setting myself on fire. I thought it was the end. And it turned out to be the best possible thing I could ever have done. I didn't know to want the freedom that came, but it was glorious."

ICONIC FACTS

Birth Data: Born Meredith Ann Baxter on June 21, 1947, in South Pasadena, California.

Education: Graduated from Hollywood High School.

MEREDITH BAXTER (*BRIDGET LOVES BERNIE*)

Family: Parents, Tom Baxter and actress Whitney Blake (*Hazel,* CBS, 1961–1965); married Robert Lewis Bush (1966–1969); David Birney (1974–1989); Michael Blodgett (1995–2000); and Nancy Locke (2013–present). Children: Theodore Justin and Eva Whitney Bush; Kathleen Jeanne and twins Mollie Elizabeth and Peter David Edwin, with husband David Birney.

Most Memorable TV Roles: Bridget Fitzgerald in *Bridget Loves Bernie* (CBS, 1972–1973); Nancy Lawrence Maitland in *Family* (ABC, 1976–1980), the latter for which she received two Emmy nominations.

Benchmarks: In 1981, she starred with Annette O'Toole and Shelley Hack in *Vanities*, a comedy-drama stage play that aired on HBO. In 1982, she was cast as Elyse Keaton, mother to Michael J. Fox on *Family Ties*. More recently, she played Liz Stevens on TV's top show *Glee*, as part of a lesbian couple with fellow female icon Patty Duke. In 1994, she won a Daytime Emmy Award for "Other Mothers," a *CBS Schoolbreak Special* in which she played a lesbian mother raising a young son. Baxter's other notable TV performances include regular roles on *The Faculty* (1996) and *Cold Case* (2006–2007). She's made several highly regarded TV-movies, including *A Woman Scorned: The Betty Broderick Story* (1992), *A Mother's Fight for Justice* (2001), and more. In 1994, she received a special award for public awareness from the National Breast Cancer Coalition for her work in the TV-movie *My Breast*. She's also made several appearances connected to *Family Ties*: she played Michael J. Fox's mother in his 1990s sitcom *Spin City*, and lent her voice for two animated series. First, from 2009 to 2011 to *Family Guy* (twice as her *Ties* character Elyse and once as herself); then she played a character called Elise, Sr., for the 2011–2012 season of *Dan Vs.* In recent years, she created a skincare line called Meredith Baxter Simple Works, which raises funds for her breast cancer research foundation.

Prime Quotes: On *Family Ties*: "It was wonderful. It gave me a place to go. I was terrified when the show was going to be over. I signed up for a seventh season and I never discussed it with David [Birney] because I could not imagine my life with having no place to go. It was just so hard at home and I had no friends. I would compartmentalize. I could just be a different person there. I had someone waiting at home who had such contempt for me." * "I didn't realize when I was younger. I was so shut down. It wasn't until this young sports woman moved into my guest house and I knew she was gay and she was very attractive and I realized I wanted to know where she was all the time. Once in a while we'd go to the movies and it was like, 'Whoa, I'm having a big reaction to this.' Then, I was away working and a flurry of texts started back and forth between us and I thought, 'OK, I'm not making this up.' So, I had to go back home and address it and I guess that's when it started."

A Living Legend.

42

Suzanne Pleshette

(The Bob Newhart Show)

Telephone operators have called me 'Sir' since I was six.

—Suzanne Pleshette

It's been more than four decades since Suzanne Pleshette was first introduced to millions of viewers as Emily Hartley, the smart and sassy TV wife with the sexy gravelly voice on *The Bob Newhart Show*, which originally aired on CBS from the fall of 1972 to the spring of 1978.

The sultry brunette with large "bedroom eyes" (which is explained later), Pleshette played Emily as a hip and hot television spouse, much differently than, say, Florence Henderson interpreted Carol Brady on *The Brady Bunch*. Pleshette's Emily was kind of like a steroid-induced Laura Petrie, Mary Tyler Moore's character from *The Dick Van Dyke Show*. But whereas Laura engineered the Petrie household, and made certain to have dinner on the table for her TV writer husband Rob (Van Dyke), the wise-cracking Emily was a schoolteacher by day, and was sure to entertain her TV psychologist hubbie Bob Hartley (played by Newhart), especially after a long day's journey into work with his therapy group of patients.

The *New York Times* critic Frank Rich once described Pleshette's Emily as "the sensible yet woolly wife" on the *Bob Newhart* sitcom, the star of which once appeared with her on *The Tonight Show* shortly before they were paired in the series. A few of the *Bob Newhart* producers had seen the segment and they had found their Emily.

Pleshette earned two Emmy nominations for the role and, according to *TV Guide* at the time, Bob Newhart was finding himself "outtalked" by Pleshette on the set about 12 to 1 but professed to be unperturbed by the phenomenon. "I don't tangle with any lady who didn't give Johnny a chance to exercise his mouth—even to sneer—for 10 whole minutes."

Besides Pleshette's voice, one of her other most appealing physical traits was her significantly groundbreaking and relatively short brunette locks. In the first season or so of *The Bob Newhart Show*, Emily's hair was coifed in a shag or mullet cut, the style made popular by David Cassidy on *The Partridge Family*. But also like Shirley Jones, Cassidy's TV *Partridge* parent and stepmom in real life, Pleshette's short do was reminiscent of Mia Farrow—during her *Rosemary's Baby* days— although clearly in a much happier way.

"Now—THAT'S a woman who could wear short hair," says Margaret Wendt. "Some women can wear short hair and others should not. Suzanne made short hair sexy. She had that whole look down—the dark hair, the bangs, and those thick eyelashes. When I was growing up, everybody wanted a Suzanne Pleshette hairstyle. The first time my friends and I each cut our hair we wanted it to look like hers. We were all California girls with the long hair and all that, and we never really wanted to cut our hair. The closest we came to getting any kind of haircut was knowing Vidal Sassoon. We attended prestigious Catholic schools and we all thought we were 'it' . . . everyone's cup of tea, and more. But then all of a sudden, we saw Suzanne Pleshette and everything changed. So all the Catholic school girls in my class went and had their hair cut just like her."

Pleshette's short hair as Emily represented a straightforward confidence. Her performance as Emily both embraced and personified television's first working-professional wife of her generation with a clear-cut mind of her own. Although she had flaws and fears (of flying, for one), Emily didn't pull any punches, and Pleshette didn't hold back in playing the part. It was more than clear on several occasions that she and Bob had a very strong and consistent sexual relationship, evidenced by the coy but subtle and frequent seductions ignited by Emily.

Although they had one too many people in their lives (including Bill Daily's very bold, lonesome, and childlike airline pilot Howard Borden, who lived next door to the Hartleys in their high-rise apartment building), that did not stop Emily and Bob from playing in the sheets; and play they did . . . at one particular moment in TV history that is like no other (i.e., the "bedroom eyes" reference now comes into play).

From 1982 to 1990, Bob appeared in yet another CBS sitcom with his name on it; this one simply titled *Newhart*, in which he played a Vermont innkeeper named Dick Loudon. This time, his onscreen wife was Joanna Loudon, played by Mary Frann (who died in 1998). Although Pleshette was not a regular fixture on the series, her future husband Tom Poston played the inn's fix-it man, and she ended up making a memorable surprise cameo in *Newhart*'s final episode—a motion and a notion that, although it did not sit well with Frann, somehow fit with Pleshette's gutsy persona.

Legendary TV scribe Arnie Kogen cowrote two episodes of *The Bob Newhart Show* and he regrets not writing for *Newhart*. He elaborates:

Emily Hartley was the perfect TV wife for Bob Hartley. She could be bubble-headed but she was smart. She had an IQ higher than her psychologist husband. Pleshette herself once described the TV couple this way, "They loved each other but didn't denigrate each other." Whatever else Suzanne Pleshette is known for, and she's known for a lot, *The Bob Newhart Show*, the movie *The Birds*, she'll probably be best remembered for that final episode of *Newhart* when innkeeper Dick Loudon (Bob Newhart) wakes up and discovers he's in bed with his wife from his previous TV series (Emily Hartley, as played by Pleshette) and that whole innkeeper series, all nine seasons of it, was a dream. A bad dream.

[And that moment received] one of the biggest laughs in TV history. It was a great idea . . . one of the strongest final episodes of a TV series—ever. It was a few years after I left *Newhart* but I wish I was involved.

Dan Holm, who created NBC's famous "Must See TV" campaign, remembers watching *The Bob Newhart Show* when he was just a teenager.

Suzanne Pleshette as Emily Hartley first came on my radar when I was in high school. Emily was a woman who was a mature kind of hip. She was educated, successful . . . had a great sense of humor and always effortlessly sexy. She was a devoted big city wife with a practical quality. Her house was always in order and her head was screwed on straight. Her insight and no-nonsense approach made her the perfect antithesis to her TV husband Bob.

Pleshette shared her own observations about playing Emily with author Joey Green, who, in 1996, published *Hi, Bob!*—a companion book to the first *Bob Newhart Show*. In the book Green posed the question, "What does Emily Joyce Hartley, a beautiful, affectionate, sophisticated and vivacious pillar of strength, see in bottled-up Bob Hartley?" Pleshette didn't believe that Emily was particularly intelligent, carefree, sweet, sexy, or even consoling in any way. She did, however, believe that Emily cared a great deal for her husband. In fact, Pleshette thought Emily was "crazy about him." But she also felt that Emily enjoyed her job as a schoolteacher. Suzanne appreciated the depth of the character and how the show's writers gave Emily flaws. (For example, she had certain phobias, including a fear of flying.). Emily would also periodically lose her patience with Bob, and Pleshette believed her TV persona could have been somewhat more empathetic toward her spouse.

Also, Pleshette believed Emily was Bob's therapist, and that their marriage allowed for such interrelating, especially when one or either partner is a psychologist. In this sense, Pleshette believed that Emily and Bob had "a very equal marriage," and that she contributed to that union, from a financially independent perspective. She didn't envision Emily as a feminist, because that's not how she perceived herself offscreen in real life. However, her interpretation of Emily did seem to be a natural extension of her own personality. Initially, Pleshette was attempting to infuse her entire personality into the character, but when she just started playing the character as honestly as she could—within the confines of what the writers created—she believed "the character really took off." At first, she was receiving more laughter from the audience as a result of Emily's behavior, more so than the actual dialogue she was given to say, lines of which she believed were better suited for an ingénue. But again, when the writers started adding more depth to Emily, adding to her imperfections—and Emily's texture—the actress could not have been more pleased. Pleshette was especially taken with the idea that Emily had failed romances in the past. Just because she was attractive didn't mean she was always lucky in love, and, as Pleshette said, "that's not the conventional thing to do." "The conventional thing," she concluded, "would have been to give me a historically successful dating background and to have made Carol [Bob's less attractive receptionist, played by the delightful Marcia Wallace] the girl who never got the guy. But they went against the convention, and I think it was wonderful. Absolutely wonderful."

ICONIC FACTS

Birth Data: Born Suzanne Pleshette on January 31, 1937, in Brooklyn Heights, New York.

Education: Graduated from Manhattan's High School of Performing Arts; attended Syracuse University and Finch College, and a prestigious acting school called The Neighborhood Playhouse School of the Theater.

Family: Parents, Geraldine Kaplan and Eugene Pleshette; was briefly married to teen idol Troy Donahue (1964); Texas oil millionaire Tom Gallagher (1968–2000); and actor Tom Poston (2001–2007, until his death).

Most Memorable TV Role: Emily Hartley on *The Bob Newhart Show* (CBS, 1972–1978).

Benchmarks: Played teacher Annie Hayworth in Alfred Hitchcock's *The Birds* (1963). She appeared in many heralded classic TV shows, such as *Route 66*, and was producer William Dozier's original choice for the role of Catwoman on *Batman* (ABC, 1966–1969); briefly starred in the 1984 CBS sitcom *Suzanne Pleshette Is Maggie Briggs*. In 1989, she starred in the NBC series *Nightingales*. In 1990, she performed a tour de force in the TV-movie *Leona Helmsley: The Queen of Mean*. She made countless more noteworthy television appearances before and after *The Bob Newhart Show*.

Prime Quotes: "I'm an actress, and that's why I'm still here. Anybody who has the illusion that you can have a career as long as I have and be a star is kidding themselves." * "I don't sit around and wait for great parts. I'm an actress, and I love being one, and I'll probably be doing it till I'm 72, standing around the back lot doing *Gunsmoke*."

Passing: January 19, 2008, from respiratory failure at age 71.

43

Valerie Harper

(Rhoda)

VALERIE HARPER (*RHODA*)

I like to see women shown as full human beings.

—Valerie Harper

Valerie Harper is best known for her multiple Emmy and Golden Globe winning performance as Rhoda Morgenstern on TV's *The Mary Tyler Moore Show* and the subsequent spin-off series *Rhoda*. By far one of the most likable characters in the history of television, Rhoda runs a close second on the likability meter to Valerie the actual human being, whose career is as expansive as her heart.

In recent years, Valerie's made notable guest appearances on TV shows like *'Til Death*, *Drop Dead Diva*, and *Hot in Cleveland*. In 2013, she lent her "animated" vocal techniques to an episode of *The Simpsons*, in which she played the Department of Standardized Testing Proctor. But it was as Rhoda that she found her true "voice."

In 2013, Gallery Books published her memoir, *I, Rhoda*, in which she addressed her battle with lung cancer in 2009. Within weeks of that diagnosis, she was back rehearsing on Broadway for "Looped," where she portrayed stage icon Tallulah Bankhead, a role that earned her a Tony Award nomination. Then, shortly after *I, Rhoda*'s release, Harper revealed her life-threatening and valiant struggle with terminal brain cancer. Later that year, and against the odds, she competed on ABC's *Dancing with the Stars*, becoming nothing less than inspirational to all those who face the various challenges of life.

Upon meeting the actress you can't help but commend her integrity and courage. Add to that her down-to-earth personality, ever youthful spirit and appearance (despite her health issues), and you can't help but be charmed. In 2011, she attended the special 100th Birthday Tribute to Lucille Ball, held at the Hollywood Museum. When asked how she remains so down-to-earth, Harper replied, "We're all just people! We're all the same inside. We all have the same needs."

In 1982, Larry Brody cowrote Valerie's NBC TV-movie titled *Farrell for the People*, which was slated as a backdoor pilot for a new series. "Everyone associated with the project was fantastic," Brody recalls. "It was the most talented group I'd ever worked with," including Harper, who he says, "was and is absolutely a doll . . . a mensch, filled with energy and idealism and big, big, big ideas . . . a wonderful person."

Harper's humanity and presence in Hollywood commenced with her career as a dancer with the corps de ballet at Radio City Hall. She eventually gravitated toward acting with diverse performances ranging from industrial shows to regional theater to Chicago's famous Second City comedy troupe. In time, she was appearing on Broadway in shows like "Dear Liar," the Tony Award–winning "Story Theatre," "Something Different," and more.

Her appeal as an actress and a person stems from her unaffected demeanor and sense of humor. She was born Jewish but raised a Catholic and is a native of Suffern, New York ("I was born to suffer," she once joked—if now, in perspective, uncomfortably so). As such, Harper developed a dynamic personality with a dual heritage that served her life and career well; it was a double dose of life experience that she brought to Rhoda, a character she was clearly born to play.

According to *Mary Tyler Moore Show* writer Treva Silverman, when producers James L. Brooks and Allan Burns created the character of Rhoda as best friend to Moore's Mary Richards, "they set up a perfect balance between the superego and the id." Richards represented the "*I don't know if we should* polite Midwestern values," while Harper's Rhoda imbued the "Jewish from New York" straightforward sensibility of "Come on! Come on!" It was "a great marriage" of iconic TV characters, Silverman concludes.

However, as journalist Peggy Herz assessed back in 1975, the Rhoda character had changed a great deal from her early days on *The Mary Tyler Moore Show* to when she was given her own series. Mary Richards had been just as svelte and elegant as she had always been. But Rhoda went through a metamorphosis. In the early years of the *Moore Show*, she was always struggling with her weight. She was mostly seen in blue jeans and big, oversized frumpy shirts. As Herz pointed out, "She could laugh at her lack of dates—and you'd believe her."

As time went on, the Rhoda persona had changed because Valerie Harper was not the same person as when she initially played the character. She trimmed down and became more confident. Rhoda wasn't as dowdy or insecure, which was certainly the case by the time she received her own sitcom. As Harper told Herz, "I think Rhoda is an important show because viewers see a woman at home and at work. Rhoda doesn't pour coffee for men all day. She worked in publishing briefly. And she just doesn't have a job. She has a career—and she has a husband. So many TV shows still have numerous men and one woman—the woman interest. That's like having 'the butler.' . . . I like to see women shown as full human beings."

As she mused in *Renew Magazine* in the summer of 2013, "People still ask, 'Hey—how's Mary? How's Brenda? How's Carlton, the Doorman?'" all of whom were Rhoda's costarring characters at various times on the *Mary Tyler Moore* and *Rhoda* sitcoms. Brenda was Rhoda's sister, as played by Julie Kavner (Marge Simpson on *The Simpsons*), and Carlton the Doorman never appeared onscreen, and was voiced by writer Lorenzo Music (who passed away in 2001).

When Rhoda wed the available and charismatic Joe Gerard (David Groh) in the fall of 1974—the opening of the *Rhoda* show's first season—52 million viewers tuned in, making it the highest-rated TV episode since Lucy gave birth to Little Ricky on *I Love Lucy* in 1953.

As she continued to explain to *Renew*, her objective was always: "Stay present to your success and to your life. Enjoy every moment. Be here now. . . . Whatever comes your way, you want to face it with grace, dignity, and courage. Whether it's hurt, anger, or grief, you have to work through it. You must press on."

Press on she did, even after she was voted off *Dancing* early in the competition. Around that time, she appeared on ABC's *Good Morning, America* saying, "When you have cancer and they say you have three months in January and it's October, you've gotta feel good about that. And the drugs I'm taking . . . are working right now. So we'll see what goes. And everyone should live like that, one day at a time." In all, she wanted her *Dancing* appearance to inspire those faced with adversity to never give up.

Harper, with the loyal support of her husband, producer Tony Cacciotti, has chosen acceptance and to remain optimistic. "That fear will overtake you unless you say, 'Okay, fear—I know you're there. But I also know I control you, not the other way around,'" she said.

Having defied the medical odds, the 74-year-old actress is seizing the opportunity to make a difference. November is Lung Cancer Awareness month, and Harper and writer/producer Marta Kauffman (*Friends*) are leading the charge to raise funds for research into finding a cure.

ICONIC FACTS

Birth Data: Born Valerie Kathryn Harper on August 22, 1939, in Suffern, New York.

Education: Attended Lincoln High School in Jersey City, New Jersey; graduated from Young Professionals School in New York.

Family: Parents, Iva and Howard Harper; married actor Richard Schaal (1964–1978); producer Tony Cacciotti (1987–present); one daughter, Cristina Cacciotti.

VALERIE HARPER (*RHODA*)

Most Memorable TV Role: Rhoda Morgenstern on *The Mary Tyler Moore Show* (CBS, 1970–1974); *Rhoda* (CBS, 1974–1978), for both of which she won a total of four Emmys.

Benchmarks: Played Valerie Hogan in the NBC series *Valerie*, which she left in 1987, due to a contract dispute. The show's title was changed to *Valerie's Family*, then *The Hogan Family* when it went on without her until 1991. She sued for breach of contract and won. She later starred in TV's *The City* (1990); TV-movies include *Farrell for the People* (NBC) and *Don't Go to Sleep* (ABC). She's also appeared in feature films like *Freebie and the Bean* (1974), *Chapter Two* (1979), *The Last Married Couple in America* (1980), among others; and portrayed Tallulah Bankhead in the live stage play "Looped" at the Pasadena Playhouse from June 27 to August 3, 2008, which also had a run on Broadway. As for recent roles, Valerie continues working in television with *Hot in Cleveland*, *The Simpsons,* and *Drop Dead Diva*. She is a strong supporter of civil rights.

Prime Quote: "I used to get some ego thing out of saying I wasn't a star, just an actress. Forget it. I'm a star. I wanted it. I worked for it. I got it."

A Living Legend.

44

Suzanne Somers

(Three's Company)

I knew what Chrissy Snow would and would not do. She'd never tell a lie. She'd never steal anybody's boyfriend. Everything was always absolutely honest with her. And I think that's what endeared her to the public.

—Suzanne Somers

After Farrah Fawcett hit the airwaves as Jill Munroe on ABC's *Charlie's Angels* in 1976, network television executives, including more than a few connected with ABC, began flooding the airwaves with blond bombshell characters on what became known as *jiggle shows*. Whereas Farrah returned glamour to Hollywood and the television drama in a way like no one had since the big-screen days of Marilyn Monroe, Suzanne Somers did the same for the blond icon persona in a small-screen sitcom by playing the ditzy Chrissy Snow on the network's superhit comedy *Three's Company*.

Alongside Somers, *Company* (which debuted as a midseason replacement series in January 1977) also featured Joyce DeWitt as Janet and John Ritter (late

of *The Waltons* and son of western film icon Tex Ritter) as Jack Tripper (which he did a lot!). All three performers took physical comedy to new heights, the likes of which had not been seen on TV since the heyday of *I Love Lucy*. In fact, Lucille Ball was a fan of *Company*, as well as *Laverne & Shirley*, ABC's other physical-comedy-geared hit—so much so that the red-headed comedy legend hosted a special about *Company*.

Whereas Penny Marshall and Cindy Williams's Laverne and Shirley characters had personalities that contributed to their physical comedic appeal, Somers had a more aesthetically pleasing "built"-in physical "jiggle" appeal that was accentuated by and surely somewhat reminiscent of her Monroe-like dumb blonde interpretation.

Whereas Farrah created the feathered-hair look, Somers tasseled her frosted locks with an ever-altering, multisided ponytail that only added to Chrissy's zany appeal. Braless and brainless, Somers's Chrissy was the central figure. As *Three's Company* continued, she became so popular that the series could have easily been retitled *Two's Company and Three's a Crowd*, the latter of which was not only used for a spin-off starring Ritter (once *Company* concluded), but also could have defined the somewhat tense relationship of the core cast behind the scenes.

Due to Somers's popularity, Ritter and DeWitt sided against the actress, whose demands for a salary increase and other perks (each encouraged by her manager husband Alan Hamel) put a wall up between the performers. The show's producers also weren't too happy with Somers. Before ultimately exiting the series for good (in the fourth season), Somers would literally "phone in" her lines from a studio set that was separate from the main set that housed Ritter and DeWitt. In time, her appearances on the show ended completely, and she would subsequently be replaced by Jennilee Harrison (as Chrissy's younger sister) and then Pricilla Barnes (a new roommate for Jack and Janet altogether).

Says Margaret Wendt: "I loved Suzanne Somers in *Three's Company*. I think she was fabulous, and I liked her in everything she did. But I think she made a huge mistake by demanding too much money to stay on the show."

While many in and outside the industry would assuredly agree with Wendt, Somers certainly never hurt for public or professional appearances, performances, or endorsements. She went on to star in two new sitcoms (the syndicated *She's the Sheriff* and ABC's Friday-night staple in the 1990s, *Step by Step*), and found astounding success as a health-fitness spokesperson for the Thighmaster and as an author.

In recent years, the actress has also documented just how . . . ahem . . . *satisfying* . . . her personal life has been with Hamel, claiming that they have an extremely healthy sex life (sometimes going the distance four times a day).

So, she must be doing something right!

ICONIC FACTS

Birth Data: Born Suzanne Marie Mahoney on October 16, 1946, in San Bruno, California.

Education: Attended Capuchino High School in San Bruno, and the San Francisco College for Women.

Family: Parents, Marion and Francis Mahoney; married Bruce Somers (1965–1968); Alan Hamel (1977–present); one son, Bruce Somers.

Most Memorable TV Role: Chrissy Snow on *Three's Company* (ABC, 1977–1981).

Benchmarks: She was the "Blonde in the T-Bird" in *American Graffiti* (1973); starred in the syndicated 1980s series *She's the Sheriff*; was Carol Lambert opposite Patrick Duffy in *Step By Step* (ABC, 1991–1998). In the 1980s, she found astounding success as the spokeswoman for Thighmaster, the exercise machine. She battled breast cancer, won, and went on to write several best-selling health-oriented memoirs and books. In 2012, she hosted *The Suzanne Show*, a talk show that covered health topics.

Prime Quotes: "I do good in the world—at least I try to. I speak on behalf of women, and I know I have made the lives of women happier as a result of teaching them what I have learned relative to true health, rather than disease care." * "Sometimes, when you are in the public eye, you just really need to just be part of the crowd, and look at other people rather than other people look at you." * "Forgiveness is a gift you give yourself."

A Living Legend.

Loni Anderson
(WKRP in Cincinnati)

> The theater is where I belonged; I simply wanted to be an actress my
> whole life.
>
> —Loni Anderson

There are not many actresses who filled out a sweater better than Loni Anderson as Jennifer Marlowe on *WKRP in Cincinnati*, which was originally broadcast on CBS from 1978 to 1982. In a very short period of time, it may have been a bit too obvious that Jennifer was built for sex. However, Anderson played against type and gave depth and texture to the character in several unexpected and remarkable ways.

In fact, it could be said that she changed the face—and body—of television females. Before her groundbreaking performance as Jennifer on *WKRP*, "beautiful blond bombshells" were considered a cliché. But she turned that concept on its head, if by turning heads in the process. As she once explained on two different occasions: "I started acting when I was 10, doing musical theater. I was a brunette at that time. I was always cast in all the exotic parts." And, "As a brunette, I had previously been this serious actress. Then I became a blonde and got to play a completely different, comic role."

In playing Jennifer (who, by the way, did have a middle name: Elizabeth), Loni delivered a smart, witty performance that introduced viewers to a new way of perceiving women on television. With Jennifer, Anderson proved that there are many other forms of beauty beyond the exterior; there is the beauty of intelligence; the beauty of humor; the beauty of loving kindness. She brought all of that, and more, to playing Jennifer, who in many ways was the heroine of *WKRP*. She'd always save the day; she'd never deliberately hurt anyone's feelings, and many times at the sacrifice of her own. As Jennifer, Loni gave women who just so happened to be beautiful, an added layer of elegance that gleamed from the inside.

ICONIC FACTS

Birth Data: Born Loni Kaye Anderson on August 5, 1945, in St. Paul, Minnesota.

Education: Attended Alexander Ramsey High School and University of Minnesota.

Family: Parents were model Maxine Hazel and Klydon Carol Anderson, an environmental chemist. She married Bruce Hasselberg (1964–1966, with whom she had one daughter, Diedra Hoffman); Ross Bickell (1973–1981); Burt Reynolds (1988–1993, with whom she adopted one son, Quinton Anderson Reynolds); Bob Flick (2008–present).

Most Memorable TV Role: Jennifer Marlowe on *WKRP in Cincinnati* (CBS, 1978–1982), for which she received two Emmy Award nominations.

Benchmarks: She won numerous beauty pageants as a teenager and worked as a schoolteacher to support herself and her first child through college. One early day as a teen, she and her mother were watching TV; an attractive actor came on the screen and her mother suggested that was the type of man her daughter should marry. That actor was Burt Reynolds, who became her third husband. Her father had emphysema, and both of her parents had chronic bronchitis and ultimately died of cancer. As such, she has dedicated much of her life to charity work in those areas, and in recent years, she became a spokesperson for the National Lung Health Education Program's campaign to increase awareness about chronic obstructive pulmonary disease. With regard to her entertainment career, she amassed an impressive body of work beyond *WKRP*—a career that became equally distinctive, everything from early smaller roles on shows like *Barnaby Jones*, to her stunning portrayal as the TV-movie lead in *The Jayne Mansfield Story*, to series work in programs like *Nurses*, *Partners in Crime* (which costarred fellow female TV icon Lynda Carter), *The Mullets*, and more.

Prime Quotes: "Look up the definition of rejection in the dictionary, get really comfortable with it, and then maybe you can go into acting." * "When I was fourteen, my measurements were 37D–20–32. Now I feel more in proportion at 36–24–36 instead of outrageous." * "I have an education degree from the University of Minnesota, and I was a teacher for about a minute." * "My memory of my mom is a wine glass in one hand and a cigarette in the other. She was a runway fashion model, and she was quite a glamorous woman."

A Living Legend.

Appendix

The Other Girls with Something Extra— A List of Honorable Mentions

There are countless additional female television actresses who portrayed charming and memorable teenage, twentysomething, or early thirtysomething characters over the decades, and while it has not been possible to profile each of them in depth, it is certainly feasible to at the very least include a list of honorable mentions. But before doing so, following are a few notes about this list.

In most cases, the dates referenced are those during which the actress appeared on her given series (and not the time frame when the show originally aired in full). Some child stars who did not make this Honorable Mention list were omitted because they did not mature into their teens or young womanhood while their particular series was airing. That said, here now is the list.

Prime-Time Superstar Honorable Mentions: Melissa Sue Anderson (*Little House on the Prairie* (1974–1981), Lucie Arnaz (*Here's Lucy*, CBS, 1968–1974), Catherine Bach (*The Dukes of Hazzard*, CBS, 1979–1985), Angela Cartwright (*Make Room for Daddy*, ABC, 1957–1964; *Lost in Space*, CBS, 1965–1968), Tina Cole (*My Three Sons*, CBS, 1967–1972), Kami Cotler (*The Waltons*, CBS, 1972–

1979), Anita Corsaut (*The Andy Griffith Show*, CBS, 1964–1968), Yvonne Craig (*Batman*, ABC, 1966–1969), Pam Dawber (*Mork & Mindy*, ABC, 1978–1982), Joyce DeWitt (*Three's Company*, ABC, 1977–1984), Susan Dey (*The Partridge Family*, ABC, 1970–1974), Sandy Duncan (*Funny Face*, CBS, 1971; *The Sandy Duncan Show*, CBS, 1972), Georgia Engle (*The Mary Tyler Moore Show*, CBS, 1970–1977), Gail Fisher (*Mannix*, CBS, 1967–1975), Lisa Gerritsen (*My World and Welcome To It*, NBC/CBS, 1969–1972; *The Mary Tyler Moore Show*, CBS, 1970–1975); *Phyllis*, CBS, 1975–1977), Theresa Graves (*Laugh-In*, NBC, 1969–1970; *Get Christie Love*, ABC, 1974–1975), Linda Gray (*Dallas*, CBS, 1978–1991), Shelley Hack (*Charlie's Angels*, ABC, 1979–1980), Lisa Hartman (*Tabitha*, ABC, 1977), Marilu Henner (*Taxi*, ABC/NBC 1978–1983), Connie Hines (*Mister Ed*, CBS, 1961–1965), Gunilla Hutton (*Petticoat Junction*, CBS, 1965–1966), Anne Jeffreys (*Topper*, ABC, 1953–1955), Julie Kavner (*Rhoda*, 1974–1978), Eartha Kitt (*Batman*, ABC, 1968–1969), Marta Kristen (*Lost in Space*, CBS, 1965–1968), Cheryl Ladd (*Charlie's Angels*, ABC, 1977–1981), Betty Lynn (*The Andy Griffith Show*, CBS, 1960–1968), Barbara Mandrell (*Barbara Mandrell and the Mandrell Sisters*, NBC, 1980–1982), Audrey Meadows (*The Honeymooners*, CBS, 1955–1956), Lee Meriwether (*Time Tunnel*, ABC, 1966–1967; *Barnaby Jones*, CBS, 1973–1980), Juliet Mills (*Nanny and the Professor*, ABC, 1970–1971), Erin Moran (*Happy Days*, ABC, 1974–1983), Denise Nichols (*Room 222*, ABC, 1969–1974), Kathy Nolan (*The Real McCoys*, ABC, 1957–1962), Judy Norton Taylor (*The Waltons*, CBS, 1972–1979), Susan Olsen (*The Brady Bunch*, ABC, 1969–1974), Melody Patterson (*F Troop*, ABC, 1965–1967), Dolly Parton (*Dolly*, syndicated, 1976; *Dolly*, ABC, 1987–1988), Bernadette Peters (*All's Fair*, CBS, 1976–1978), Mackenzie Phillips (*One Day at a Time*, CBS, 1975–1980), Maggie Pierce (*My Mother, The Car*, NBC, 1965–1966), Paula Prentiss (*He & She*, CBS, 1967–1970), Pat Priest (*The Munsters*, ABC, 1964–1966), Victoria Principal (*Dallas*, CBS,

1978–1991), Eve Plumb (*The Brady Bunch*, ABC, 1969–1974), Jeannine Riley (*Petticoat Junction*, CBS, 1963–1965), Tanya Roberts (*Charlie's Angels*, ABC, 1980–1981), Marion Ross (*Happy Days*, ABC, 1974–1984); Susan St. James (*McMillan & Wife*, NBC, 1971–1977), Julie Sommers (*The Governor and J.J.*, CBS, 1969–1972), Marcia Strassman (*Welcome Back, Kotter*, ABC, 1975–1979), Sally Struthers (*All in the Family*, CBS, 1971–1978), Loretta Swit (*M*A*S*H*, CBS, 1972–1983), Lauren Tewes (*The Love Boat*, ABC, 1977–1986), Charlene Tilton (*Dallas*, CBS, 1978–1991), Sigrid Valdis (*Hogan's Heroes*, CBS, 1965–1971), Tuesday Weld (*The Many Loves of Dobie Gillis*, CBS, 1959–1963), Pat Woodell (*Petticoat Junction*, CBS, 1963–1965).

Daytime Superstar Honorable Mentions: Deidre Hall (*Days of Our Lives*, NBC, 1976–2013), Genie Francis (*General Hospital*, ABC, 1977–2013), Susan Lucci (*All My Children*, ABC, 1970–2011), Lara Parker and Kathryn Leigh Scott (both of *Dark Shadows*, ABC, 1966–1971); Kristin Alfonso (*Days of Our Lives*, NBC, 1983–present).

Bibliography and Sources

BOOKS

Austin, John. *Hollywood's Babylon Women*. New York: S.P.I. Books, 1994.

Bloom, Ken, and Frank Vlastnik. *Sitcoms: The Greatest TV Comedies of All Time*. New York: Black Dog and Levanthal Publishers, 2007.

Duke, Patty, and Kenneth Turan. *Call Me Anna*. New York: Bantam Books, 1987.

Durkee, Cutler, ed. *Television Shows That Changed Our Lives: Great Moments and Guilty Pleasures*. New York: People Books/Time Home Entertainment, 2010.

Eden, Barbara, with Wendy Leigh. *Jeannie Out of the Bottle*. New York: Crown Archetype, 2011.

Frost, Tony, ed. *Farewell Magazine: Stars We Loved and Lost in 2009*. Periodic and Book Association of America/Distribution Services, 2009.

Garver, Kathy, with Geoffrey Mark. *The Family Affair Cookbook*. Albany, Georgia: BearManor Media, 2009.

Green, Joey. *Hi Bob! A Self-Help Guide to The Bob Newhart Show*. New York: St. Martin's Press, 1996.

Hamner, Earl, and Ralph Giffen. *Goodnight John-Boy: A Celebration of an American Family and the Values That Have Sustained Us through Good Times and Bad*. Naperville, IL: Cumberland House, 2002.

Herz, Peggy. *TV 74*. New York: Scholastic Book Services, 1973.

———. *TV Talk: Your Handy Guide to Faces and Places in TV-Land*. New York: Scholastic Book Services, 1975.

———. *TV Talk 2: Exploring TV Territory*. New York: Scholastic Book Services, 1976.

———. *TV Time 78*. New York: Scholastic Book Services, 1978.

———. *TV's Fabulous Faces*. New York: Scholastic Book Services, 1977.

———. *TV's Top Ten*. New York: Scholastic Book Services, 1976.

Javna, John. *Cult TV: A Viewer's Guide to the Shows America Can't Live Without*. New York: St. Martin's Press, 1985.

Jewell, Geri, with Ted Nichelson. *I'm Walking as Straight as I Can: Transcending Disability in Hollywood and Beyond*. Toronto, Ontario: ECW Press, 2011.

Jones, Gerard. *Honey, I'm Home*. New York: St. Martin's Press, 1992.

Manago, Jim, with Donna Manago. *Love Is the Reason for It All*. Albany, Georgia: BearManor Media, 2008.

McClay, Michael. *I Love Lucy: The Complete Picture History of the Most Popular TV Show Ever*. New York: Warner Books, 1995.

McDonough, Mary. *Lessons from the Mountain: What I Learned from Erin Walton*. New York: Kensington Publishing, 2011.

McNeil, Alex. *Total Television: A Comprehensive Guide to Programming from 1948 to the Present*, 2nd ed. New York: Penguin Books, 1984.

Meehan, Diana M. *Ladies of the Evening: Women Characters of Prime-Time Television*. Metuchen, NJ: Scarecrow Press, 1983.

Mitz, Rick. *The Great TV Sitcom Book*. New York: Richard Marek Publishers, 1980.

Newmar, Julie. *The Conscious Catwoman Explains Life on Earth*. Eleven Books, 2011.

Reuter, Donald F., and Anthony Turtu. *Gaborabilia: An Illustrated Celebration of the Fabulous, Legendary Gabor Sisters*. New York: Three Rivers Press, 2001.

Rios, Tere. *The Fifteenth Pelican: The Incredible Adventures of a Nun Who Discovers She Can Fly*. Garden City, NY: Doubleday and Company, 1965.

Shulman, Arthur, and Roger Yourman. *The Television Years*. New York: Popular Library Publishers, 1973.

Smith, Ronald L. *Sweethearts of '60s TV: Interviews and Photos of the Real Women behind TV's Most Memorable Female Characters*. New York: S.P.I. Books/Shapolsky Publishers, 1993.

Story, David. *America on the Rerun: TV Shows That Never Die*. New York: Citadel Press/ Carol Publishing Group, 1993.

Waldron, Vince. *Classic Sitcoms: A Celebration of the Best in Prime-Time Comedy*. New York: Macmillan Publishing Company, 1987.

PERIODICALS

Archerd, Army. "Army Archerd Calling . . ." *Movie Life Magazine,* January 1969.

Barnes, Mike. "*Dallas* Actor Larry Hagman Dies at 81." www.hollywoodreporter.com. Accessed November 23, 2012.

——. "*Happy Days* Writer-Producer Bob Brunner Dies at 78." *The Hollywood Reporter,* November 8, 2012.

Bego, Mark. "Cher Gets 'Closer to the Truth' with New Album." *Boulevard Magazine.* Holiday Edition, 2013.

Berg, Sandi. "Barbara Eden Shares Insights on Her Career, Keeping Fit and Aging." *Life After 50 Magazine,* March 26, 2012. Accessed November 13, 2013.

——. "Diahann Carroll: The Barrier-Breaking Beauty on Acting, Activism, and Aging." *Life After 50 Magazine,* August 3, 2011. Accessed February 18, 2014.

Carter, Jack. "The Stars of *Father Knows Best*: Where Are They Now?" *Globe Magazine,*
    February 18, 2013.

Curra, Jennifer. "Diahann Carroll Says, 'We're All Very Grateful.'" WebProNews.com.
    Accessed September 23, 2013.

Dasm Lina. "Heartache: For years *Hart to Hart*'s Stefanie Powers has put up with jibes
    about her lover William Holden's death . . . now she's setting the record straight."
    DailyMail.co.uk.com. Accessed December 21, 2013.

Day, Patrick Kevin. "Valerie Harper Has Brain Cancer." *Los Angeles Times,* March 7, 2013.

Erskine, Chris. "Lunching with One Legend at Another." *Los Angeles Times,* September 7,
    2013.

Franklin, Garth. "*Gidget* Gets Film & TV Reboots." Dark Horizons, May 2010.

Gelineau, Kristin. "James Earl Jones to Star in *Driving Miss Daisy*." Yahoo News! Accessed
    January 7, 2013.

Gil, Virginia. "Mary Tyler Moore Meets 'Sex' Meets 'Girls.'" www.DoYouRemember.com.
    Accessed September 26, 2013.

James, Susan Donaldson. "Meredith Baxter Alleges Ex-Husband David Birney Abused
    Her." ABCNew.com. Accessed January 18, 2014.

King, Susan. "A New Heyday." *Los Angeles Times*, January 6, 2012.

———. "Bill Persky, That Guy from *That Girl*." *Los Angeles Times*, January 2, 2013.

———. "Like Old Pals." *Los Angeles Times,* September 22, 2011.

Laurell, David. "Lindsay Wagner: The Perceptive Woman." *Life After 50 Magazine,*
    September 2013.

———. "Julie Newmar Explains Life on Earth." *Life After 50 Magazine,* March 2012.
    Accessed November 13, 2013.

Lieberman, Matthew. "Hollywood Take Note: Here's What TV Viewers Really Want."
    Hollywood Reporter, September 25, 2013.

Malcom, Andrew. "Sotomayor: Inspired by Perry Mason." *Los Angeles Times,* January 15,
    2013.

Manikar, Sheila. "Asner on *Mary Tyler Moore*, Broadway." Yahoo News! Accessed December 12, 2012.

Mann, Chris. "Re-imagined TV." *Los Angeles Times,* September 27, 2011.

McCaine, Florine. "Marlo Thomas: What She Had to Do to Become a Star." *TV Radio Show Magazine,* October 1967.

McNamara, Mary. "Modern Issues." *Los Angeles Times,* September 24, 2012.

Morrison, Patt. "Seriously Funny." *Los Angeles Times,* June 20, 2012.

Rogers, John. "Beav's Brother Tony Dow Now an Abstract Artist." Associated Press, September 22, 2012.

Rooney, David. "The 65th Primetime Emmy Awards: TV Review." *Hollywood Reporter,* September 23, 2013.

Stanton, Kate. "Trailblazer Diahann Carroll Presents with Kerry Washington at the Emmys, Compliments TV's Attractive Men." UPI.com, September 23, 2013.

Thomas, Marlo. "From Peanuts to Grinches to Elves—Time for Those Christmas Classics." www.huffingtonpost.com/marlo-thomas. Accessed December 7, 2012.

———. "Marlo and Sofia's Special Family Affair." www.huffingtonpost.com/marlo-thomas .com. Accessed November 19, 2012.

Valby, Karen. "Why Funny Gals Rule the World." *Entertainment Weekly,* October 7, 2011.

TV GUIDE

Gehman, Richard. "Women's Home Companion." *TV Guide,* July 31–August 6, 1965.

"Go Boutique." *TV Guide,* April 11–17, 1970.

"Good Morning Ladies." *TV Guide,* July 31–August 5, 1965.

Graff, Richard. "Dear Sir: You Cur . . ." *TV Guide,* April 11–17, 1970.

"It Was Typecasting." *TV Guide,* September 25–October 1, 1965.

"Julie Newmar in Bed in the Middle of Times Square." *TV Guide,* February 14–20, 1970.

MISCELLANEOUS SOURCES

"Bea Arthur." Woman's Hour, August 8, 2003. http://www.bbc.co.uk/radio4/
womanshour/2003_31_fri_03.shtml.

"*Family Ties* Star Meredith Baxter Marries Partner Nancy Locke." www.huffingtonpost.com.
Accessed December 9, 2013.

"Five Great TV Shows That Changed the World." Reader's Digest Online, www.rd.com.
February 2013. Accessed March 3, 2013.

"Home Style with Diana Rigg." *International Press Bulletin*. Special Limelight Edition, vol.
II, no. 3, 1968. Associated Newspapers Limited.

"Lindsay Wagner." The Biography Channel website, http://www.biography.com/people/
lindsay-wagner-585880. Accessed August 31, 2013.

"Lynda Carter." The Biography Channel website, http://www.biography.com/people/lynda
-carter-10073461. Accessed August 31, 2013.

"Marlo Thomas: Sometimes You Have to Make Your Parents Cry." *TV Radio Show
Magazine,* December 1966.

"Patty Duke." The Biography Channel website, http://www.biography.com/people/patty
-duke-9542536. Accessed August 31, 2013.

Ronnie Schell commentary. DVD documentary for *Good Morning, World*, 1967. S'More
Entertainment, 2005.

Shelley Fabares interview on *Good Morning, America*. ABC. January 1991.

"Spending Time with Sally Field." *TV Radio Show Magazine*, October 1967.

The Unofficial Isis Appreciation Page. http://www.angelfire.com/tv2/isis/home.html.
Accessed November 2, 2011.

Notes for Iconic Facts

Unless otherwise noted within the given chapter (or elsewhere within this backmatter), the main sources that were used for the opening quote, narrative, or Iconic Facts sections for each profile were websites like www.biography.com, www.wikipedia.org, and www.brainyquote.com, all of which were accessed in November and December 2013, and as outlined below. Additional material came from books, magazines, TV documentaries, and so forth, as mentioned in the bibliography.

PART 1: THE JILL OF ALL TRADES

Chapter 1: Sally Field (*Gidget / The Flying Nun*)

http://en.wikipedia.org/wiki/Sally_Field

http://www.imdb.com/name/nm0000398/bio?ref_=nm_ov_bio_sm

http://www.brainyquote.com/quotes/authors/s/sally_field.html#M5xHmh9 LQbI5x4q5.99

Chapter 2: Marlo Thomas (*That Girl*)

http://www.brainyquote.com/quotes/authors/m/marlo_thomas.html

http://en.wikipedia.org/wiki/Marlo_Thomas

http://www.imdb.com/name/nm0005486/bio?ref_=nm_ov_bio_sm

Chapter 3: Diahann Carroll (*Julia*)

http://en.wikipedia.org/wiki/Diahann_Carroll

http://www.imdb.com/name/nm0140792/bio?ref_=nm_ov_bio_sm

http://www.brainyquote.com/quotes/authors/d/diahann_carroll.html

http://www.diahanncarroll.net/biography.htm

Chapter 4: Goldie Hawn (*Laugh-In*)

http://en.wikipedia.org/wiki/Goldie_Hawn

http://www.brainyquote.com/quotes/authors/g/goldie_hawn.html#7Z6siId
M1FtwfR4F.99

http://www.searchquotes.com/quotes/author/Goldie_Hawn/

Chapter 5: Mary Tyler Moore (*The Dick Van Dyke Show* /
The Mary Tyler Moore Show)

http://www.imdb.com/name/nm0001546/bio?ref_=nm_ov_bio_sm

http://en.wikipedia.org/wiki/Mary_Tyler_Moore

Chapter 6: Cher (*The Sonny & Cher Comedy Hour*)

http://www.biography.com/people/cher-9246148

http://en.wikipedia.org/wiki/Cher

http://www.imdb.com/name/nm0000333/bio?ref_=nm_ov_bio_sm

http://en.wikipedia.org/wiki/The_Sonny_&_Cher_Comedy_Hour

Chapter 7: Marie Osmond (*The Donny & Marie Show*)

http://en.wikipedia.org/wiki/Marie_Osmond

http://www.brainyquote.com/quotes/authors/m/marie_osmond.html#J6EEolBk
TQxSQ8V8.99

http://www.imdb.com/name/nm0005288/bio?ref_=nm_ov_bio_sm

PART II: THE TEEN ANGELS

Chapter 8: Elinor Donahue (*Father Knows Best*)

http://www.imdb.com/name/nm0231942/bio?ref_=nm_ov_bio_sm

http://en.wikipedia.org/wiki/Elinor_Donahue

http://www.people.com/people/article/0,,20097226,00.html

Chapter 9: Shelley Fabares (*The Donna Reed Show*)

http://www.upi.com/topic/Shelley_Fabares/#ixzz2lVJTPdMB

http://www.imdb.com/name/nm0001193/bio?ref_=nm_ov_bio_sm

http://www.thoughtjoy.com/shelley-fabares

http://www.glamourgirlsofthesilverscreen.com/show/532/Shelley+Fabares/index
.html

http://www.youtube.com/watch?v=CjYQ1sNotqI

http://www.brainyquote.com/quotes/authors/s/shelley_fabares.html

Interview with Charles Gibson on *Good Morning, America*, August 18, 1994

Chapter 10: Patty Duke (*The Patty Duke Show*)

http://en.wikipedia.org/wiki/Patty_duke

http://www.imdb.com/name/nm0001157/bio?ref_=nm_ov_bio_sm

Chapter 11: The Lennon Sisters (*The Lawrence Welk Show*)

http://en.wikipedia.org/wiki/The_Lennon_Sisters

http://www.imdb.com/name/nm1293376/bio?ref_=nm_ov_bio_sm

http://raleightelegram.com/201308275900

Chapter 12: Kathy Garver (*Family Affair*)

http://www.imdb.com/name/nm0308744/bio?ref_=nm_ov_bio_sm

http://en.wikipedia.org/wiki/Kathy_Garver

Chapter 13: Maureen McCormick (*The Brady Bunch*)

http://en.wikipedia.org/wiki/Maureen_mccormick

http://www.imdb.com/name/nm0566572/

http://www.brainyquote.com/quotes/authors/m/maureen_mccormick
.html#QTWDPwz1AS8cJ83C.99

Chapter 14: Mary McDonough (*The Waltons*)

http://www.imdb.com/name/nm0568169/

Chapter 15: Melissa Gilbert (*Little House on the Prairie*)

http://www.imdb.com/name/nm0001271/bio?ref_=nm_ov_bio_sm

http://en.wikipedia.org/wiki/Melissa_Gilbert

http://www.biography.com/people/melissa-gilbert-9542501

http://www.brainyquote.com/quotes/authors/m/melissa_gilbert.html

Chapter 16: Valerie Bertinelli (*One Day at a Time*)

http://www.imdb.com/name/nm0000933/bio?ref_=nm_ov_bio_sm

http://www.biography.com/people/valerie-bertinelli-281955

http://www.dumb.com/actress-quotes/valerie-bertinelli-quotes/

Chapter 17: Kristy McNichol (*Family*)

http://www.brainyquote.com/quotes/authors/k/kristy_mcnichol.html#8z3sXKf
GBAXK7gL3.99

http://en.wikipedia.org/wiki/Kristy_McNichol

http://www.imdb.com/name/nm0001531/bio?ref_=nm_ov_bio_sm

http://www.people.com/people/article/0,,20080601,00.html

http://www.people.com/people/archive/article/0,,20072235,00.html

http://en.wikipedia.org/wiki/North_Hollywood_High_School

PART III: THE COUNTRY GIRLS

Chapter 18: Donna Douglas (*The Beverly Hillbillies*)

http://en.wikipedia.org/wiki/Donna_Douglas

http://www.imdb.com/name/nm0235031/bio?ref_=nm_ov_bio_sm

Chapter 19: Inger Stevens (*The Farmer's Daughter*)

http://www.classicimages.com/people/article_1e7f82c6-bac3-57e9-a1bb-2d301
aee1af7.html

http://en.wikipedia.org/wiki/Inger_Stevens

Chapter 20: Linda Kaye Henning, Lori Saunders, Meredith MacRae (*Petticoat Junction*)

Linda Kaye Henning

"Henning, Linda 1944– (Linda Kaye Henning, Linda Kaye)." Contemporary
Theatre, Film and Television. 2009. *Encyclopedia.com*. December 2, 2013.
http://en.wikipedia.org/wiki/Linda_Kaye_Henning

http://www.imdb.com/name/nm0377407/bio?ref_=nm_ov_bio_sm

http://www.boston.com/ae/tv/articles/2008/12/18/actress_recalls_her_days_in_petticoat/

Lori Saunders

http://www.imdb.com/name/nm0766883/bio?ref_=nm_ov_bio_sm

http://en.wikipedia.org/wiki/Lori_Saunders

Meredith MacRae

http://www.classictvbeauties.com/meredithmacrae.html

http://en.wikipedia.org/wiki/Meredith_McRae

http://www.imdb.com/name/nm0534297/bio?ref_=nm_ov_bio_sm

Chapter 21: Dawn Wells (*Gilligan's Island*)

http://www.imdb.com/name/nm0920171/bio?ref_=nm_ov_bio_sm

http://en.wikipedia.org/wiki/Dawn_Wells

http://www.starpulse.com/Actresses/Wells,_Dawn/

Chapter 22: Linda Evans (*The Big Valley*)

http://www.brainyquote.com/quotes/authors/l/linda_evans.html

http://www.brainyquote.com/quotes/authors/l/linda_evans.html#r6wFiuvCIIFfYw5V.99

http://www.imdb.com/name/nm0002067/bio?ref_=nm_ov_bio_sm

http://en.wikipedia.org/wiki/Linda_Evans

PART IV: THE SUPERSLEUTHS

Chapter 23: Barbara Feldon (*Get Smart*)

http://www.imdb.com/name/nm0271156/bio?ref_=nm_ov_bio_sm

http://en.wikipedia.org/wiki/Barbara_Feldon

Chapter 24: Anne Francis (*Honey West*)

http://en.wikipedia.org/wiki/Anne_Francis

http://www.imdb.com/name/nm0004282/bio?ref_=nm_ov_bio_sm

http://articles.latimes.com/2011/jan/03/local/la-me-anne-francis-20110103

http://www.nytimes.com/2011/01/04/arts/04francis.html

http://www.hitfix.com/articles/forbidden-planet-honey-west-actress-anne
-francis-dies-at-80#Aiqg5MfyUQT96MSi.99

Chapter 25: Barbara Bain (*Mission: Impossible*)

http://en.wikipedia.org/wiki/Barbara_Bain

http://www.imdb.com/name/nm0000828/bio?ref_=nm_ov_bio_sm

http://www.nerdist.com/2012/12/should-you-choose-to-accept-mission
-impossibles-barbara-bain/

http://www.craveonline.com/lifestyle/interviews/200573-an-interview-with
-actress-barbara-bain

http://www.nbcbayarea.com/entertainment/entertainment-news/Original
-Mission-Impossible-Bombshell-Barbara-Bain-Remains-Explosive-182839021
.html

Chapter 26: Stefanie Powers (*The Girl from U.N.C.L.E.*)

http://en.wikipedia.org/wiki/Stefanie_Powers

http://www.imdb.com/name/nm0694619/bio?ref_=nm_ov_bio_sm

http://www.nj.com/entertainment/index.ssf/2011/09/stefanie_powers_interview_girl.html

http://www.broadwayworld.com/boston/article/bww-interview-stage-and-screen-star-stefanie-powers-draws-on-personal-experience-for-looped-20130502-page2

http://articles.latimes.com/2010/nov/03/entertainment/la-et-classic-hollywood-20101103

http://www.dailymail.co.uk/femail/article-1362659/Heartache-Hart-To-Harts-Stefanie-Powers-setting-record-straight.html#ixzz208FoGvWw

Chapter 27: Diana Rigg (*The Avengers*)

http://www.imdb.com/name/nm0001671/bio?ref_=nm_ov_bio_sm

http://en.wikipedia.org/wiki/Diana_Rigg

http://www.brainyquote.com/quotes/authors/d/diana_rigg.html#jAXiBkOg20slSMHS.99

Chapter 28: Peggy Lipton (*The Mod Squad*)

http://www.imdb.com/name/nm0005152/bio?ref_=nm_ov_bio_sm

http://en.wikipedia.org/wiki/Peggy_Lipton

http://reocities.com/Paris/theatre/8630/peggylipton.html

Chapter 29: Farrah Fawcett, Kate Jackson, and Jaclyn Smith (*Charlie's Angels*)

Farrah Fawcett

http://www.imdb.com/name/nm0000396/bio?ref_=nm_ov_bio_sm

http://en.wikipedia.org/wiki/Farrah_Fawcett

http://www.brainyquote.com/quotes/authors/f/farrah_fawcett.html

http://www.top10-best.com/f/top_10_best_farrah_fawcett_quotes.html

Kate Jackson

http://www.imdb.com/name/nm0000462/bio?ref_=nm_ov_bio_sm

http://en.wikipedia.org/wiki/Kate_Jackson

http://www.brainyquote.com/quotes/authors/k/kate_jackson.html

Jaclyn Smith

http://en.wikipedia.org/wiki/Jaclyn_Smith

http://www.imdb.com/name/nm0000646/bio?ref_=nm_ov_bio_sm

http://www.brainyquote.com/quotes/authors/j/jaclyn_smith.html

PART V: THE WONDER WOMEN

Chapter 30: Elizabeth Montgomery (*Bewitched*)

http://en.wikipedia.org/wiki/Elizabeth_Montgomery

http://www.imdb.com/name/nm0000548/bio?ref_=nm_ov_bio_sm

Chapter 31: Barbara Eden (*I Dream of Jeannie*)

http://www.imdb.com/name/nm0001174/bio?ref_=nm_ov_bio_sm

http://en.wikipedia.org/wiki/Barbara_Eden

Chapter 32: Julie Newmar (*My Living Doll / Batman*)

http://www.imdb.com/name/nm0628325/bio?ref_=nm_ov_bio_sm

http://en.wikipedia.org/wiki/Julie_Newmar

Chapter 33: Nichelle Nichols (*Star Trek*)

http://www.imdb.com/name/nm0629667/bio?ref_=nm_ov_bio_sm

http://en.wikipedia.org/wiki/Nichelle_Nichols

Chapter 34: Lindsay Wagner (*The Bionic Woman*)

http://en.wikipedia.org/wiki/Lindsay_Wagner

http://www.imdb.com/name/nm0905993/bio?ref_=nm_ov_bio_sm

http://retroality.tv/RetroHotLindsayWagner.html

Chapter 35: Lynda Carter (*Wonder Woman*)

http://www.imdb.com/name/nm0004812/bio?ref_=nm_ov_bio_sm

http://en.wikipedia.org/wiki/Lynda_Carter

PART VI: THE LIBERATED SOULS

Chapter 36: Gale Storm (*My Little Margie*)

http://en.wikipedia.org/wiki/Gale_Storm

http://southernaristocracy.org/2012/10/12/gale-weathered-the-storm/

http://www.imdb.com/name/nm0832561/bio

Chapter 37: Barbara Hale (*Perry Mason*)

http://en.wikipedia.org/wiki/Barbara_Hale

http://www.imdb.com/name/nm0354853/bio?ref_=nm_ov_bio_sm

http://www.whosdatedwho.com/tpx_4283/barbara-hale/quotes

http://www.barbarahale.com/barbarahale_biography.htm

Chapter 38: Tina Louise (*Gilligan's Island*)

http://en.wikipedia.org/wiki/Tina_Louise

http://www.imdb.com/name/nm0001481/bio?ref_=nm_ov_bio_sm

Chapter 39: Karen Valentine (*Room 222*)

http://www.imdb.com/name/nm0884259/bio?ref_=nm_ov_bio_sm

http://en.wikipedia.org/wiki/Karen_valentine

http://www.nj.com/entertainment/index.ssf/2013/10/karen_valentine_room_222
.html

Chapter 40: Adrienne Barbeau (*Maude*)

http://en.wikipedia.org/wiki/Adrienne_Barbeau

http://www.imdb.com/name/nm0000105/bio?ref_=nm_ov_bio_sm

http://www.brainyquote.com/quotes/authors/a/adrienne_barbeau.html#5
FOW0GjB3V4mGBO5.99

Chapter 41: Meredith Baxter (*Bridget Loves Bernie*)

http://en.wikipedia.org/wiki/Meredith_Baxter

http://www.imdb.com/name/nm0000880/bio?ref_=nm_ov_bio_sm

http://www.brainyquote.com/quotes/quotes/m/meredithba507462.html#Hx
KEC6BclbKwqAj0.99

http://www.biography.com/print/profile/meredith-baxter-9542147

Chapter 42: Suzanne Pleshette (*The Bob Newhart Show*)

http://www.imdb.com/name/nm0687189/bio?ref_=nm_ov_bio_sm

http://en.wikipedia.org/wiki/Suzanne_Pleshette

Chapter 43: Valerie Harper (*Rhoda*)

http://www.imdb.com/name/nm0001320/bio?ref_=nm_ov_bio_sm

http://en.wikipedia.org/wiki/Valerie_Harper

Chapter 44: Suzanne Somers (*Three's Company*)

http://www.imdb.com/name/nm0001755/bio?ref_=nm_ov_bio_sm

http://en.wikipedia.org/wiki/Suzanne_Somers

http://emmytvlegends.org/interviews/people/suzanne-somers

http://www.imdb.com/name/nm0001755/bio?ref_=nm_ov_bio_sm

Chapter 45: Loni Anderson (*WKRP in Cincinnati*)

http://www.imdb.com/name/nm0000756/bio?ref_=nm_ov_bio_sm

http://en.wikipedia.org/wiki/Loni_Anderson

http://www.brainyquote.com/quotes/authors/l/loni_anderson.html#QkjUh AvbQEFf58uz.99

Acknowledgments

The completion of any book or major creative project is always the combined result of several talented individuals, and *Glamour, Gidgets, and the Girl Next Door* is no exception.

First and foremost, my heartfelt gratitude to those who granted exclusive interviews and observations for this book, including top female TV icons like Adrienne Barbeau, Barbara Bain, Elinor Donahue, Donna Douglas, Kathy Garver, Barbara Hale, Mary McDonough, and Nichelle Nichols; top male TV icons such as Tony Dow and Billy Gray; as well as the children of other top TV icons, including Peter Ackerman (son of Elinor Donahue and producer Harry Ackerman) and Mary Owen (daughter of Donna Reed and producer Tony Owen).

I would also like to thank television writing legends Sam Bobrick, Larry Brody, Ron Clark, Fred Freeman, Arnie Kogen, Bill Persky, and Treva Silverman for their astounding and genius contributions to this book; along with the insight provided by entertainment historians and archivists Pat McFadden, Rob Ray, Steve Randisi, and Stu Shostak; writers Tamara Anne Fowler, Dan Holm, and Virginia Reeser;

producers Les Perkins (www.lesismoreproductions.com), Dan Weaver, and Margaret Wendt; and journalist and syndicated broadcaster Matthew Worley.

Although they did not offer new commentary directly for this book, appreciation is extended to Barbara Eden, Diahann Carroll, Florence Henderson, Julie Newmar, and Lindsay Wagner, whose previously published insight appears courtesy of David Laurell, editor in chief of *Life After 50 Magazine*, without whom this book would be less of a publication. Gratitude is also expressed to actor Ronnie Schell for the insight he provided into Goldie Hawn (via the documentary on the DVD release of *Good Morning, World*) and author/journalist Peggy Herz, whose publications about television in the 1970s provided key insight into a number of female TV stars, such as Lynda Carter, Melissa Gilbert, Marie Osmond, and others.

Further appreciation is extended to those who contributed to or were responsible for the conceptualization, production, and presentation of this book: my publisher Rick Rinehart, who approached me with his pristine idea and vision, and the entire team at Taylor Publishing, including Kalen Landow and Sam Caggiula in marketing, editorial assistant Karie Simpson, and production editor Alden Perkins.

Those who further enhanced the quality of this publication in countless ways include top-notch research and entertainment historian Mary Holm, writer/historians Ken Gehrig and Bob Miller, classic TV historian Jeffrey D. Dalrymple, publicist Harlan Boll, and entertainment representative Gilbert Bell, all of whom coordinated a great deal of the new celebrity interviews. The book's especially stunning packaging would not have been possible without the photographic and aesthetic expertise, counsel, and guidance provided by entertainment archivist Fred Westbrook.

ACKNOWLEDGMENTS

A particularly special acknowledgment of gratitude is extended to my agent and manager Melissa McComas, whose genius business acumen and creative insight is second to none.

I would also like to thank my dear friends Rudy Anderson, Catherine Burnett, Linda Burton, Dottie Clark, Matthew Cook, Giovanna Curatello, Kathy and Larry Finucane, Roger Hyman, Jeff and Monica Lindgren, Marty McClintock, Maria Pellegrino, Marypat and Joseph Pena, Steve Reeser, John, Lou, and Peter Tomassetti, and Carol Zazzaro, for their assistance in a variety of ways.

In closing, I would very much like to acknowledge my family for all the love and support they have offered through the years, including my sister Pam, brother-in-law Sam, and nephew Sammy Mastrosimone; my cousins David and Eva Easton Leaf, and Marie Burgos and her son Nicholas; among countless more cousins, aunts, and uncles, living and in Heaven; and particularly and especially my beautiful parents, Frances Mary Turri and Herbert Pompeii, otherwise known to the Universe as St. Frances of Turri and St. Pompeii.

Nothing, of course, would be possible without the great Mother and Father of us all, otherwise known as Love = God. As such, I say:

"Dear Abba Father of Lights, King of Kindness, Prince of Peace, Divine Blessed Mother of the Mighty Heart and Queen of the Angels; thank You for leading me to Love, for allowing Love to lead me in all of my ways, for all of my days, as I cling myself to Thee, to Thine to Thy Love . . . now and forever. Amen."

About the Author

Herbie J Pilato is the author of several media tie-in books, including *The Essential Elizabeth Montgomery*, *Twitch Upon a Star*, *Retro Active Television*, *NBC & ME*, *Life Story—The Book of Life Goes On*, *The Bionic Book*, *The Kung Fu Book of Wisdom*, *The Kung Fu Book of Caine*, *The Bewitched Book,* and *Bewitched Forever*.

Pilato has worked as a producer, consultant, and commentator for various television networks, including the TV Guide Channel, Bravo, SyFy, TLC, A&E, E!, and film studios such as Sony, Warner Bros., and Universal, appearing in the process on hundreds of radio and television news shows and magazines, including *Entertainment Tonight*.

As an actor, he's appeared on TV shows like *The Bold and the Beautiful*, *General Hospital*, *The Golden Girls*, and *Highway to Heaven*. He's also directed live stage productions of "A Phoenix Too Frequent," "Birdbath," and "Little Shop of Horrors."

Pilato is also the founder and executive director of the Classic TV Preservation Society (a nonprofit organization that seeks to close the gap between popular culture and education); presides over Television, Ink. (a TV, film, and literary production company in Burbank, California, where he resides); has several television shows and feature films in development; frequently contributes to Jack Myers's www.MediaBizBloggers.com and Larry Brody's www.TVWriter.net; and is writing and recording songs for his first music CD.

COMING OF
AGE IN THE
OTHER AMERICA